What they're saying about...

The Power and Promise of Pathways

"Aligning education pathways with careers will be easier for those who read Hans Meeder's book -- broad in scope, and yet practical in application. Take advantage of his long experience helping students down the pathway from classroom to better jobs."

>Ned McCulloch, JD, Global Issue Manager,
>Skill Development and Education, IBM

"In this important work of preparing students for college, career and life, none of us have the luxury of failing our youth. Hans has drawn on his experience and relationships to provide an incredibly comprehensive and yet easy to navigate guide to help individuals, foundations, districts and employers engage in this complex work. This book is for everyone interested in supporting education. "

>Cheryl Carrier, Executive Director
>Ford Next Generation Learning

"For those interested in building career pathways systems at the community level to help young people acquire the academic, technical, and professional skills needed to get launched in our increasingly complex and challenging labor market, Hans Meeder has produced an eminently readable and comprehensive guidebook and resource. Highly recommended!"

>Bob Schwartz, Senior Research Fellow
>Harvard Graduate School of Education,
>co-author of Pathways to Prosperity and
>co-founder of the Pathways to Prosperity Network

"This book is a great resource for schools and districts implementing the academy model. Hans has pulled together the research and best practices from all across the country to serve as a guide for this important and difficult work."

>Dr. Jay Steele, School Improvement Consultant
>Former Chief Academic Officer, Metro Nashville Public Schools

"In The Power and Promise of Pathways, Hans Meeder has written the definitive piece on the need for educational pathways that prepare all young people for life and work. It's a combination essay, opinion piece, and toolkit, and includes insightful observations on education policy and context based on Hans' many years' of experience. The section on creating a Career Development System alone is worth its weight in gold. This is a go-to resource for policy leaders, educators, employers, community leaders, and anyone who is interested in helping provide smoother transitions to adult life and careers for our kids."
Betsy Brand, Executive Director,
American Youth Policy Forum

"This is a remarkably comprehensive guide designed for those who want to build a high-quality pathway system in their school, college and/or community in order to better prepare students for career success. Meeder is the ideal author for such a guide. Because he's worked intimately to help communities and schools build pathway systems, Meeder understands the challenges you're likely to face and offers sage advice on how to overcome them. And because he's also worked at the national level, he brings a deep understanding of the evolution of the pathways movement. This book is must reading for anyone disturbed by our current failure to prepare many of our youth for economic independence."
William C. Symonds, Director of the Global
Pathways Institute at Arizona State University
Primary author of Pathways to Prosperity

"As an assistant superintendent, I am constantly looking for ways to engage students in their education. Developing pathways has been instrumental in helping students make connections between their education and their future. This insightful book provides the energizing motivation and the practical framework to bring about lasting change in schools."
Dr. Lorraine Sakoian, Assistant Superintendent,
Twin Valley School District, Elverson, Pennsylvania

About the National Center for College and Career Transitions

The National Center for College and Career Transitions, or NC3T, has a twofold mission: "Every Learner with a Dream and a Plan, and Every Community with a Capable, Ready Workforce." The organization works to connect schools, postsecondary institutions, and employers in order to introduce students to the array of options available to them, and to help them prepare for the types of opportunities for which they are best suited.

NC3T provides planning, coaching, technical assistance and tools to help community-based leadership teams plan and implement their college-career pathway systems. For more information, visit www.NC3T.com.

Published by

This book is intended to be the starting point, not the end point, for your work on Pathways. To continue learning and to join the conversation, visit the following website for additional resources and regular updates from the author:

www.pathwayssherpa.com

Table of Contents

Appendices

Preface

A few years ago, my wife and I set out on a beautiful Saturday morning to get outdoors and enjoy some hiking and time together. We ventured to a state park that is not far from our home. Near the parking area, we found a shed that offered maps of the park and the paths that had been laid out within it. The map that was in the box was quite crude and had been photocopied multiple times, making it relatively illegible. Nonetheless we found the nearest trailhead, tried to orient ourselves on the map, and began our hike. After 15 minutes, we came to a fork in the trail and discovered that the map was not only illegible, it may have been incorrectly drawn or not drawn to scale. We made a turn, hoping that we were heading in the right direction, but weren't really sure because markings on the trail itself were almost nonexistent. We continued walking, following the trail, but with every turn losing the general sense of direction as to where our parking space was, and not knowing how we would get back to our starting point without just reversing course.

This was not a life-threatening situation at all, but it still raised the level of unease and uncertainty in my mind. I felt a little more responsibility for the situation since, of the two of us, I'm the one who has the better sense of direction. So what was meant to be a vigorous but enjoyable walk became more of a stress-inducing experience.

While a crude analogy, this is the difficult and perplexing experience of most young people trying to navigate the world of careers today. Among a world of options in America's highly mobile, inter-connected, and advanced economy, including thousands of occupations, thousands of postsecondary education and training providers, and millions of employers, they must choose a career path for themselves. They must find a way to become economically self-sufficient, and hopefully find a measure of happiness and well-being along the way.

This difficulty that youth and young adults are having – making successful transitions into college and careers – presents more than a personal challenge. On the aggregate, these clunky, difficult transitions add up to a workforce that is out of kilter and that isn't working as well as it could, for both employers, workers, and job creators.

In the coming pages, we will explore innovative and proven strategies that can help more and more youths and adults find pathways to success, and also chart a better pathway for the nation's schools and colleges. We will explore both the promise and the power of pathways.

Part I

Why Pathways Matter

Chapter One

Discovering Pathways

America's Long Winter of our Discontent

America is troubled, and Americans are worried. We see it every day on cable news and Twitter feeds, and feel the unease surrounding us like a cloud of thick smoke. Here is what we know.

◊ Families in our rural communities are struggling with and losing to an epidemic of addiction and overdoses of pain-killing opioids and heroin.[1]

◊ Our inner-cities are filled with joblessness, drug and alcohol addiction, multi-generational dependence on government assistance, absent fathers and over-stressed mothers, and gang-led violence that attracts and leads to the death and disability of thousands of young men and women.

◊ We hear stories about growing income inequality and wages that are stagnant or falling, while the wealthiest class accumulates more and more of our nation's wealth. [2]

◊ Millions of young men from middle class and working class families play video games for hours on end and hold low-end jobs, but aren't interested in attending college or developing a real career.[3]

◊ Two million high school graduates head off to college each fall, but after six years, fewer than half of them have completed an education program. Hundreds of thousands of dropouts struggling with crushing debt, and even those who do graduate, must pay off an average of $29,000 during their early working years.[4] Further, while the U.S. once had the highest postsecondary attainment rate among all industrialized countries, now the attainment rate among young Americans has fallen far behind many other countries.[5]

◊ While our national unemployment rate has fallen to less than 5 percent, the real rate of unemployment and underemployment is about 15 percent; this rings true because we all know people who are marginally employed or have pulled out of the productive workforce entirely.[6]

◊ Millions of baby-boomers approach the end of their working lives with no savings or assets, and the financial naiveté of our population contributed to a massive housing bubble, the Great Recession, and slews of personal bankruptcies.[7]

◊   Our politics in Washington are characterized by extreme polarization,
amplifying other concerns like fighting terrorism, violence by and against
police, and worry and consternation about the role of government. One
extreme wants national government to solve all our personal and social
problems; another extreme blames all our social and personal problems
on the national government.

What is the Underlying Source of Our Discontent?

Taken one by one, these issues may seem random and disconnected. There
are hundreds of books, essays, and research studies that address each of these
individually, all of which are available through Amazon or your local newsfeed.
But I believe there is a connection among them.

It has to do with jobs – good jobs and meaningful careers.

To have happy lives, people must do something meaningful, and that means
productive work of some type. Let's not confuse "work" with "employment"
(or a job) right now. When I say work, I am talking about the need to feel
they are making a contribution to their families, their communities, and their
nation. Parenting is work. Caring for an ailing grandparent is work. Not all
work is paid employment, but often it is. In our work, we need to feel a sense of
personal satisfaction with a job well done, and that we have addressed a human
need. Not everyone has to have a traditional job, but everyone needs to have
meaningful work.

But still, many people need a job – that is, paid employment. They need cash
to buy things and pay for services and other needs.

The Gallup Organization has confirmed this human need through its "World
Poll." In surveying millions of people around the world, Gallup has determined
that the number one desire of people, consistent across all cultures and
continents, is what Gallup calls "a good job." This means a job that offers 30
or more hours per week, consistent employment, and getting paid enough to
cover your expenses. It's a pretty simple expectation, isn't it?

The reality however, is that only about 43 percent of the jobs in the U.S.
qualify as "good jobs" and even fewer are "great jobs," meaning a job where
you find inherent meaning and value in the work. Great jobs are our ultimate
aspiration, but most people are willing to settle for a good job as a starting
point.

I need to digress briefly. For some readers, this last statement that most
people want a good job may have actually raised your eyebrows. In your
experience, you may have observed people and communities that have

completely lost a connection to work because the community is dominated by multi-generational joblessness and government dependence. In some of these pockets of America, the notion of the imperative of work is a lost value. Some people see work as optional, and certainly not worth pursuing if it would endanger a loss of government assistance. I believe that part of this is misguided government policy, but also, at a cultural level, we have degraded the value of low-skilled and entry-level work, only honoring professional skilled work. At all class levels, many Americans have lost an understanding of the inherent dignity of work and the need to do work, any work, for a sense of self-respect and pride in a job done with excellence. This is a massive cultural challenge that we need to face up to. Although I cannot give it the fullest treatment in this book, we should keep this dynamic in mind. All of the efforts that we recommend in building a Pathways System have to do with honoring the dignity of all work (from the landscaper to the land developer) and instilling the value of excellence and pride in one's work.

Secondly, Gallup also discovered that worldwide, out of a total population exceeding 7 billion people, about 3 billion people want and need a good job to take care of themselves and their families. But they also note that there are currently only about 1.2 billion good jobs in existence, resulting in a global shortfall of 1.8 billion good jobs.

When people aren't personally fulfilled, taking care of their families through meaningful work, they are much more susceptible to danger. They are susceptible to addictions that mask their sense of pain and longing – alcohol, drugs, pornography, unhealthy eating leading to obesity, even "safe" addictions like video gaming and TV binging. Others try to fill the void by attaching to religious extremism and the violence expounded through those movements.

When Our Summer Turned to Winter

In some ways, the post-war 20th century from 1945 to the early 1970s, (even with its social inequities and the Cold War threat) was a period of general prosperity and calm. But since the 1970s and the initial global economic war with Japan and Germany, the world has changed dramatically and the American juggernaut of high employment and high pay for medium-skills manufacturing jobs has evaporated.

Trade, transportation, and technology (the Three Ts) have created a global market for goods, services, and jobs. Thomas Friedman, in his provocative book, "The World is Flat," explained how multiple trends converged – the fall of the Berlin Wall, opening up Eastern Europe and China to the global markets, new international trade supported by cheaper transportation, outsourcing of manufacturing to Mexico and east Asian countries, and offshoring of knowledge-based jobs through digitization – and have fueled the growth of a global economy and a global workforce that is more tightly interconnected and ruthlessly competitive than ever before.

Globalization has been very good for many parts of the world, raising standards of living and health for millions, and beginning to open up political systems. But for America, the Three Ts have changed our labor market rapidly and dramatically, and it continues to evolve faster than we can understand or mentally process. Towns and cities that were hubs of large-scale manufacturing have hollowed out – many of those who are unemployed leave, and those who are left don't have successful ways to fend for themselves. The elderly live off Social Security payments, and many others are lured into declaring permanent disability to receive some sort of income support.

In addition to the external challenges of globalization, our immigration system has dramatically changed the demographics of our nation. On the positive side, many immigrants come to the U.S. with an advanced education, they highly value education, and they have passed along these values to their children. These immigrants have made tremendous contributions to innovation and economic growth. But conversely, a large group of immigrants have entered our borders (some without legal means) in a survival mode, trying to simply make a better life for their families through low-skilled labor. While low-skilled work is typical for a first-generation immigrant, too many immigrants do not have experience with educational success, do not understand the American system of K-12 and higher education, and are not fully equipped to pass along the values of education and economic advancement to their children. This doesn't mean they can't or won't be partners in education, but this responsibility now falls on our schools and social organizations, and our schools in particular are faced with significant challenges in dealing with these massive demographic changes.

Now, as difficult as all this feels in the moment, if we put a historical lens on it, this is not the first time America has experienced this level of difficult change. From my reading of history, we are experiencing a level of social and economic upheaval that is quite similar to what was experienced during the Industrial Revolution, following our Civil War, when the U.S. emerged as a world economic power. The big difference however, is that the Industrial Revolution generated millions of low and medium-skilled jobs. Now, the current digital/robotics economic revolution is generating a lot of medium and high-skilled jobs that pay a decent wage. We have a severe mismatch between the good jobs available and the workers who have the skills and knowledge, and live in the right locales, to access those jobs.

The Changing Nature of Work and Education

During much of America's history, high school students were categorized as either "college-bound" or "career-bound." Students were sorted by their perceived aptitudes and for an industrial system in which most jobs did not require postsecondary education. The skills associated with career readiness were thought to be fundamentally different from those required for college success. Employers looked for job-specific skills coupled with general trainability and work ethic. Vocational programs, which hearken back to the early 20th century, trained individuals for skilled work in the trades, for business work, for agriculture, and for the domestic arts. Colleges trained future professionals in academic knowledge, especially in the disciplines of math, science, and the liberal arts.

These two tracks largely reflected the demands of education and the workforce with a wide disparity between professional and management jobs and a preponderance of jobs that required no more than on-the-job training.

As recently as 1973, workers with postsecondary education held only 28 percent of jobs; by comparison, they held 59 percent of jobs in 2010 and will hold 65 percent of jobs in 2020.[8]

As this shift in the workforce was happening, a third education option for employment preparation began to appear, sitting between workforce entry immediately after high school and the four-year college degree. These are jobs that require some sort of education and training beyond high school, but not actually requiring a bachelor's or advanced degree.

According to analysis by the Georgetown University Center for Education and the Workforce (CEW), the United States is more educated than ever, and the percentage of jobs requiring post-secondary education and training beyond high school is steadily increasing. CEW estimates there will be approximately 55 million job openings in the economy through 2020:

◊ 35 percent of the job openings will require at least a bachelor's degree;

◊ 30 percent of the job openings will require some college or an associate's degree; and

◊ 36 percent of the job openings will not require education beyond high school.[9]

While it is simplest to think about "tracks," this mental picture really isn't accurate. The "some college" category covers a wide mix of education and training experiences – apprenticeship programs, short-term skills certifications, and associate degrees.

Instead of three "tracks," we might better think of a skills and training continuum. Frankly, there are some jobs that lead to a skilled career (the energy industry is one example), in which a worker can get a decent job right after high school and then acquire on-the-job training and formalized education to advance up through the organization. Other occupations are highly regulated and the individual must engage in a formalized education and training program, and then pass a state licensing exam. Nursing is a prime exam of a state-regulated field like this.

With this evolution of the modern American workforce, the old mental model of "college bound" and "job bound" is now a relic of the 1960s and 1970s. It should be firmly and finally thrown into the dustbin of economic history.

The Twin Skill Gaps

Throughout the Great Recession and its aftermath, there were 9 to 10 million chronically unemployed workers, but at the same time, employers were decrying a "skills gap." There were about 3.5 million jobs that were chronically unfilled – for jobs such as machinists, welders, drivers, health care workers, sales professionals, and math and science teachers. The so-called skills gap was the gap between the skills that employers needed to fill their open positions and the actual, available workforce. This skills gap was exacerbated by jobs that were re-engineered, using increasing amounts of technology and automation. Some workers couldn't adapt to the changes in the workforce, and not enough younger workers were being attracted into those middle skill jobs.[10]

But a different kind of skills gap showed up among college graduates. In this case, many college graduates were unemployed or underemployed for long stretches of time after receiving their college diploma, taking jobs that didn't

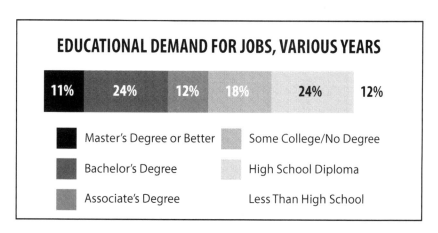

EDUCATIONAL DEMAND FOR JOBS, VARIOUS YEARS

| 11% | 24% | 12% | 18% | 24% | 12% |

Master's Degree or Better   Some College/No Degree

Bachelor's Degree   High School Diploma

Associate's Degree   Less Than High School

really require a four-year college degree. While they possessed the thinking, analytical or interpersonal skills typical of those with a college degree, many graduates didn't have the tangible, verifiable skills that employers needed.[11]

Are the Robots Coming to Steal Our Jobs?

Exacerbating the skills gap is the fact that automation technology is rapidly changing the nature of many jobs. What were once lower-skilled jobs now require a higher level of skills in operating, programming, and troubleshooting machines and software programs. No longer is it adequate to "work with your hands." Most jobs require the worker to work with their "hands and their head."

In their provocative book, "Race Against the Machine," Harvard economists Eric Brynjolfsson and Andrew McAfee have taken on a closely related issue.[5] Is the development of robotics, automation, and other "artificial intelligence" materially different from other technological revolutions in the past? They observe that in the past, disruptive technologies (steam engines, mass production, electricity, automobiles, air flight, computers) upended certain occupations, but ultimately created economic growth, so humans could find more productive work in other venues.

With the evolution of the modern American workforce, the old mental model of "college bound" and "Job bound" is now a relic of the 1960s and 1970s. It should be firmly and finally thrown into the dustbin of economic history.

But with today's rapidly emerging automation, robotics, and, one day, artificial intelligence, technology is becoming smarter and more capable of doing things that previously only a human being could do. The authors wonder if this means society won't ultimately need as many human beings to do the basic work that is needed in an advanced economy. We could have a very advanced, high-tech world that is very productive, but with many people sitting on the sidelines.

For example, as noted in "Race Against the Machine," in 2004 Harvard economists Frank Levy and Richard Murnane said that driving an automobile was so complex, with so much processing of information and making judgments, that driving would likely remain a human responsibility. But in 2010, just six years later, Google announced it was developing and testing the driverless automobile. As of the writing of this book in 2016, companies in the U.S. were beginning to pilot test driverless taxis in Pittsburgh, and full implementation of such taxis was already happening in Singapore. It could well be that in the near future a large number of jobs associated with driving and delivery will be at risk because of these technologies.

Another massive shift is the emergence of high-level computing, close to what technologists have envisioned as "artificial intelligence." The IBM computing system Watson is harnessing enormous processing power and complicated algorithms that make sense of text and human speech, to almost instantaneously analyze, rate, and make predictive answers based on tens of thousands of documents and data sources.

Watson is being used to assist doctors in making cancer treatment decisions based on instantaneous access to worldwide clinical tests and results. Computer research tools are dramatically reducing the number of young lawyers needed to conduct research which, along with internet-based legal services, is causing a dramatic reduction in entry-level jobs in the legal profession and a subsequent retreat from 2nd and 3rd tier law schools.

So, how many jobs for humans will disappear? The research is still mixed. Despite the potential to eliminate millions of human jobs, it doesn't appear this is yet happening on a widespread scale. Humans still have "it," even when a computer can conduct search and processing tasks almost instantaneously.

In what makes eminent sense, Brynjolfsson and McAfee vouch for the mindset of "racing WITH the machine." This approach acknowledges the benefits of technology in making our work less mundane and repetitive by outsourcing those tasks to the machine. To race with the machine, the knowledge worker of the coming decades must become truly technology literate and know how to harness and guide technology, not just for gaming and socializing, but to accomplish meaningful work.

If this becomes the reality of skilled, good-paying jobs in the American economy, we must make changes to engage the minds of our students, fast!

University-for-All Hits a Wall

To summarize what we've explored thus far, we understand that our world has changed drastically since the 1970s through the forces of trade, transportation and technology. The angst brought on by these many changes in our global economy and the resulting pressures on the U.S. workforce have been exacerbated because the education solutions we have pursued as a nation – higher standards, testing, charter schools -- just don't seem to be working well enough. Parent by parent, family by family, we know how difficult it is for our youth – even our college-educated youth – to find their paths to personal success. Since we have not discovered a credible strategy for improving education that leads to a more engaged, effective workforce, our national sense of unease continues. But fortunately, this unease is opening the way to re-thinking some long-held assumptions.

In the mid 20th century, most American high schools promoted a comprehensive approach that prepared youth either for college, for skilled vocations, or for low-skilled employment (called "Life Adjustment Education.")[13] Beginning in 1983 with the call to action of the "A Nation at Risk" report, calling for higher course-taking standards, the need for high expectations and undoing the paternalism, racism, and sexism of the past morphed into a simple message – college for all. Not everyone actually went to college or finished college, but the message was clear. High expectations means that every student should plan to attend college, and if they fall by the wayside, so be it. But college – the four-year bachelor's degree variety – was the gold standard by which individuals and schools were judged.

We understand that our world has changed drastically since the 1970s. The angst brought on by these many changes have been exacerbated because the education solutions we have pursued as a nation just don't seem to be working well enough. This unease is opening the way to re-thinking some long-held assumptions.

In 2011, an important report from Harvard University – "Pathways to Prosperity" – brought a new focus to a systemic problem that the "university-for-all" message was masking.[14] By emphasizing one preferred university-for-all pathway, schools are actually inadvertently disengaging many students from learning and building many other very effective pathways – pathways to underemployment, unemployment, career frustration, and under-utilization of human talent. We explore these outcomes extensively in Chapter 2.

"Pathways to Prosperity" called for a different approach – multiple pathways.

> *"We fail these young people not because we are indifferent, but because we have focused too exclusively on a few narrow pathways to success. It is time to widen our lens and to build a more finely articulated pathways system-one that is richly diversified to align with the needs and interests of today's young people and better designed to meet the needs of a 21st century economy."* [15]

Do Pathways Mean a Return to Low Expectations?

For many decades, large swaths of youth in America were held to very low expectations, based in large part on their race, ethnicity, social standing, or gender. So education reform advocates began promoting the notion of high expectations for all. But there is a huge difference between setting high expectations for children and assuming that the highest personal aspiration for every student is for them to pursue a four-year college education.

As a country, we need to hold each person up to the highest possible individual expectation, helping every student develop strong learning skills. But we should not apply a one size-fits-all expectation that every student learn exactly the same way or pursue the same educational goal.

As a country, we need to hold each person up to the highest possible expectation, helping every student develop strong learning skills. But we should not apply a one-size-fits-all expectation that every student must learn exactly the same way or pursue the same educational goal. Instead, the pathways approach offers a variety of educational options, or Pathways Programs, linked to career development, and strong connections to employer and community organizations. All of this creates compelling relevance to school for the student, which is much more likely to engage the student's aptitudes and interests, and lead to a better career fit with a greater chance for economic success and social mobility.

Discovering Pathways as a Credible Solution

The term "pathways" seems to be everywhere in today's parlance. It's almost as ubiquitous a term as STEM (science, technology, engineering, and math) or Common Core when people are discussing education. Why is this?

The current fascination with pathways has roots that go back several decades to the first career academies created in Philadelphia in 1969.[16] In some ways, the underlying debates between academic and vocational preparation go back even further, to the dawning years of public education when there was a continuous tug and pull between academic education and practical, or vocational, education.

But the term "pathways" is still relatively new, and interest in them and the sense of their importance has grown exponentially in the years following the 2007-2009 Great Recession, as concerns over the viability of the U.S. workforce have become fierce.

This call to action builds on the work of numerous organizations, schools, and educational movements that have been toiling for decades in the shadow of the university-for-all monolith, waiting for the cracks in its foundation to become apparent.

Pathways for All

In this book, we talk about Pathways-for-All as a way to engage all youth in deeper learning and propel them forward into meaningful pathways of study and training. For those in need, it can help to break the strong gravitational pull of family and community poverty.

The theory of action is this: by developing a student's career interests, by engaging them in Pathways Programs to deeply explore career interests, and by providing meaningful, real-life connections to employers and community-based learning experiences, we help students become more internally motivated and directed. This internal motivation is what is missing from American education today. Education is something we do TO children, rather than something we do WITH them.

Only by rekindling internal motivation, hope, and ambition can our youth and young adults learn deeply and make successful transitions into postsecondary education and training, and into skilled, in-demand careers.

Pathways will help more American students enter and complete postsecondary education and training, navigate the complexities of a career, and create a better match between the skills of individuals and opportunities for economic

What is a career pathway?

There is now a federally-legislated definition for career pathway, and individuals often attribute slightly different meanings when using the term in discussion. We explain these in more detail in Chapter 3. But for the purpose of this book, we will be using the following definition of a Pathways Program.

A Pathways Program is a program of inter-connected academic and elective classes revolving around a career or subject theme. It is integrated with experiential learning and close connections between secondary and postsecondary education, training, and apprenticeship. The program is designed to support the development of Career and Life Readiness for the learner, so that the individual can successfully enter and advance in a career path.

and personal success. Pathways will be good for students and their families, as well as lead to sustainable economic growth and greater social mobility.

Even utilizing a "pathways-for-all" approach, there are a wide variety of creative ways to implement the pathways model. In this book, I present a six-component Pathways System Framework™, but the framework is flexible and adaptable to local needs. It provides needed structure for your work in pathways, but it allows adaptation to local needs and constraints so that the approach you develop can achieve maximum impact.

The Pathways System is not a panacea for our education and workforce ills. Implementing a pathways model requires hard work and an attention to effective implementation of the model. But the Pathways System model does build upon and incorporate all that is right with current efforts at improving schools – better standards and active teaching and learning – and brings them into a unifying Pathways System Framework™ made up of its interconnected components.

The Pathways System Framework™ fills in the critical missing elements – an understanding of career options, developing a holistic approach to Career and Life Readiness, and stronger connections to employers and the community. Through employer and community connections, the pathways model builds social capital for youth and young adults, and also helps develop a meaningful connection between exploring careers and choosing among postsecondary education and training options.

No matter how well developed the pathways model becomes, and how effective it is in reaching and energizing students, there will always be a struggle and a fight to reach more students and touch them more deeply.

For many readers who are considering the pathways model, as attractive as the destination sounds, it seems like it will be a long journey ahead. That's OK. As the Chinese philosopher Lao Tzu said, "A journey of a thousand miles **begins with a single step.**"

That's all we're asking for today – a step. Read on, and let's take that step.

Bringing the Components Together Into a Framework

A framework, a term derived from the words "frame" and "work," means a structure in which pieces are fitted together so they support and enhance one another. In education, a framework is a way to structure and connect multiple initiatives so they complement and support one another, creating the environment for synergy to happen. That is why we have developed the

Pathways System Framework™, a structure that supports the development and implementation of sustainable career and STEM Pathways Systems.

The Pathways System Framework™ builds upon current education reforms including standards-aligned curriculum and assessments, literacy and technology across the curriculum, and the use of research-proven instructional practices such as project-based learning. The framework focuses on six broad components that all work together in synergy to develop learners who are Career and Life Ready.

A brief description of the Pathways System Framework™ components follows. A more detailed description of each framework component is found in Chapter 4.

◊ **Career and Life Readiness.** Partners define the mix of applied knowledge, technical skills, employability skills, and other competencies that prepare individuals for success in postsecondary education, the skilled workplace, and personal life.

◊ **Career Development.** Learners gain the knowledge and skills to make informed choices about careers and related education and training.

◊ **Pathways Programs.** Pathways programs at the secondary and postsecondary levels are aligned with workforce demands, and are structured to help develop academic, technical, and employability skills.

◊ **Employer and Community Engagement.** Employers and community partners help students experience the workplace and build positive relationships with employer mentors.

◊ **Dynamic Teaching and Learning.** Research-based educational practices engage learners in rigorous and active learning, and educators continue to grow in their skills and knowledge.

◊ **Cross-Sector Partnerships.** Partnerships among K-12 education, postsecondary education, workforce systems, and other entities create sustained collaboration to develop the local Pathways System.

The Pathways Pledge and Actions

The Pathways System Framework™ is a very useful organizational tool, but it runs the risk of coming off as too mechanistic, whereas education is actually a very human, relational enterprise. The changes we need in our schools and communities cannot be fulfilled simply by a system; these changes must be carried out by people. That is why I believe that the leaders of your pathways movement need to make a personal pledge to the youth and young adults in your community, and to each other. What follows is a human version of the pathways model, articulated in a set of "we will" pledge statements.

To chart their path to career and life success, our youth and young adults need critical knowledge, skills and experiences to make well-informed decisions about their future education and careers, and to successfully navigate through the challenges of work, family, community, and citizenship. To help them successfully launch:

◊ We will recapture the essential purpose of education to prepare individuals for success (not just teaching subjects). We will work to ensure that every learner, both youths and young adults, develops the knowledge, skills, and attitudes necessary for career and life success.

◊ We will ensure that every youth and young adult participates in meaningful career development to help them find a good personal fit between their skills, knowledge and passion and quality career opportunities.

◊ We will build a variety of engaging and relevant Pathways Programs so youth and young adults can explore their career interests and participate in secondary and postsecondary education, training and apprenticeships that support their career aspirations.

◊ We will strive to make every class and school experience engaging and meaningful by utilizing dynamic teaching and learning strategies.

◊ We will engage a large percentage of employers and community organizations with our Pathways Programs in schools and colleges, so learners can get a meaningful understanding of the expectations of the workplace.

◊ We will develop strong and sustainable collaborations between key community partners, including schools, colleges, employers, community organizations, and workforce systems.

The Call to Leadership

I agree with Jim Clifton's assessment of the need for local leadership in his important book, "The Coming Jobs War."[17] He asserts that "strong leadership teams are already in place within cities," and that they have to align all their local forces to double the level of entrepreneurial energy.

He also warns, "Don't allow your local constituencies to look to Washington," meaning: Don't look for federal government funding and policies to save the day when it comes to job creation. I would also flip the argument– "Don't allow your local constituencies to blame all your local problems on Washington."

Conservatives have been waiting for someone to finally slash and burn up the "welfare state" and get the government off our backs. Liberals are looking for Washington to finally get serious about ending poverty through massive housing programs, job training, and universal health care.

America has an amazing wealth of creativity, energy, and goodwill among its people, its schools and colleges, its businesses, and its social, religious and cultural institutions. We have a deep tradition of local people rolling up their sleeves, taking responsibility, and getting to the work at hand.

Let's get serious about this. Help is not coming from Washington. I worked in Washington for 15 years, and things have only gotten worse since I left.

But the good news is, America has an amazing wealth of creativity, energy, and goodwill among its people, its schools and colleges, its businesses, and its social, religious, and cultural institutions. We have a deep tradition of local people rolling up their sleeves, taking responsibility, and getting to the work at hand.

The only way forward is for local leaders to emerge and make change happen.

Even with today's existing government programs and levels of funding, they're not really holding us back from doing what we need to do, nor is the funding too small to do what is needed. We have the motivated and caring local leaders we need. What has been missing is a credible strategy for developing the Career and Life Readiness of our youth and young adults, and developing the next generation of talented entrepreneurs and job creators.

For too long, education is something we have tried to DO TO a student, rather than engaging and unleashing their natural God-given talents and aspirations. We have unwisely advised every youth that the answer to success is "go to college" instead of a more humane message, "discover your strengths, develop your strengths, understand the world's needs, and find a way to apply your strengths to the world's needs."

This book offers a strategy – the Pathways System approach – that is credible. It builds on valuable, well-tested innovations that have been bubbling up through our education system since the 1970s. It integrates the best of these reforms and adds the biggest missing ingredient, the heart of the student.

For too long, education has been something we have tried to do TO students, rather than engaging and unleashing their natural, God-given talents and aspirations. We have unwisely advised every youth that the answer to success is "go to college" instead of a more humane message, "discover your strengths, develop your strengths, understand the world's needs, and find a way to apply your strengths to the world's needs."

William Butler Yeats observed, *"Education is not the filling of a pail, it is the lighting of a fire."*

It is time to start lighting the fire of ambition and aspiration in our children, youth, and young adults. As we fan those flames, our young people will be more receptive to the knowledge, skills, and attitudes that we, as adults, have learned really make a different in career and life success.

Your Perspective on Pathways

The purpose of this book is to foster and inform local leadership. I want to help you discover the essential knowledge that will empower you to lead a pathways initiative in your community, school, or college. Whatever your perspective, I think you will find something of value in the pages ahead.

Perhaps you are a school superintendent or high school principal who is frustrated by the slow pace of improvement in your schools.

You might be a concerned employer who feels that, even among recent college graduates, the individuals you are hiring just don't seem to have a grounding in real-world business, work ethic, or "the basics."

Maybe you're a parent of a teen and you worry about how your child is going to make good decisions that make the most out of your college investment.

Perhaps you know too many young adults who went to college and earned some credits, but got distracted because they never really had a game plan. Now, they're still not thriving. At best, they're surviving.

Regardless of what lens you are looking through, it is a fair question – is there a better way to connect what students learn today to what they will need for future success? Can we develop more motivated students, who learn more deeply and gain practical experiences at the same time?

What about Adult Learners and Adult Career Pathways Systems?

The concepts in this book about developing a pathways system are very transferable to colleges, adult education programs, and workforce systems that are serving adult learners, particularly under-employed individuals who are trying to find meaningful, family-sustaining careers.

But to be clear, this book is specifically written with a perspective about implementing a pathways model within the K-12 environment. This requires strong cross-sector connections to employers, workforce systems, and postsecondary education, of course, but in this book, I don't provide a lot of specific input regarding how those systems should independently advance their own version of the pathways agenda.

Other resources, professional development and coaching available from the National Center for College and Career Transitions more directly address the role of colleges, adult education providers, and workforce development systems. (www.NC3T. com)

Yes. But in order to reach this level of stronger motivation and deeper engagement, first we need to face some hard facts about education and our changing workforce.

Where is the STEM in Pathways?

STEM (an acronym for Science, Technology, Engineering and Mathematics) is a high-visibility education reform movement, moving parallel and intersecting continually with the pathways movement.

Some STEM advocates focus on after-school and summer activities to get youth interested in and excited about STEM careers such as engineering, information technology, and health science. This approach relates to the pathways component concerning Career Development. Other educators use STEM more as an adjective to describe a means of teaching – one that uses investigative and problem solving techniques – what we refer to as "active learning" in this book. This focus on instruction correlates with the pathways component for Dynamic Teaching and Learning.

Other advocates refer to STEM more for one of the specific sub-disciplines or for career-connected programs. In this usage, many Pathways Programs are very STEM-intensive, like information technology, engineering, and biomedical research. But STEM is not relegated to just careers requiring bachelor's and advanced degrees. According to the Brookings Institution, only about 5 percent of U.S. jobs fall within the college-preparatory narrow definition of STEM, but using a broader definition, including careers that have a technology, math, science, or engineering emphasis (but not all four), about 20 percent of jobs could be considered STEM jobs, and a large percentage of these are so-called "middle-skill" jobs. This means they are jobs that require strong competence in one or more of the STEM disciplines, but do not necessarily require a bachelor's degree.[18] I prefer to think of these as "STEM-infused" jobs – and they include a wide variety of careers like automotive technology, economics, financial planning, carpentry, construction, architecture, and therapeutic health services.

This is the only section in this book in which I explicitly refer to STEM education, although a previous book I authored, "The STEM Leader Guide," focuses entirely on how to implement STEM school-based programs.[19] But rest assured, any school that adopts a pathways approach will also be embracing multiple forms of STEM education, both in encouraging students to get excited about STEM through career development activities using an inquiry-based and project-based active learning approach, and helping youth actually explore real STEM-intensive and STEM-infused career options.

My Journey

Before we go further, I would like to explain how this book came to be.

My personal journey with pathways began in a somewhat happenstance fashion. My early career in public policy and working on Capitol Hill led me to education, with work at both the U.S. Department of Education and the U.S. House of Representatives Committee on Education and the Workforce. In 1997, I left Capitol Hill and led some small-scale education consulting projects, after which I was recruited as Executive Director of the 21st-century Workforce Commission, a federal commission charged with exploring how to fill the high demand for information technology jobs without relying only on H-1B immigration visas. The solutions our commission identified were mostly aimed at the K-12 education system, helping schools expand career development and career pathways to develop a larger overall pool of talented, motivated youth, from which a larger pool of information technology workers could emerge.

Following this work, I found my way to the National Alliance of Business, which also promoted education/business partnerships and career-related initiatives. Then my personal career path led me back to the U.S. Department of Education with an appointment as Deputy Assistant Secretary for Education from 2001 to 2005, in the office that managed funding for both career technical education and adult basic education. I also took a leadership role in exploring how high schools could be re-imagined and connected more effectively to pathways programs at community colleges.

Upon my departure from the DoE in 2005, I linked up with the Ford Motor Company Fund and its work around project-based learning and career academies, and had an opportunity to learn the school improvement protocols of the Southern Regional Education Board's High Schools That Work initiative. On behalf of Ford, I conducted several site visits and wrote case studies of career academy focused communities, and led numerous other site visits and studies through consulting projects. Over these years, I wrestled with the evidence and became more and more strongly convinced that the career academy approach and related efforts like Linked Learning were providing compelling results. I decided to begin working solely in the education consulting field and create a new organization (with my co-founder Brett Pawlowski) that could help advance this agenda. Thus, the National Center for College and Career Transitions was born, and we developed our work to spread the word on the urgency for pathways and to build the capacity of local leaders to develop and implement pathways systems.

To make the pathways work accessible to the typical high school and community, we spent about six months reviewing in detail the different high school redesign models and criteria of organizations like High Schools That Work, Ford Next Generation Learning, Linked Learning (ConnectEd California) and the Career Academy Standards of Practice utilized by the National Career Academy Coalition.

All of this good work contributed to the NC3T model, the Pathways System Framework™, which we have been using with a variety of schools and community settings ever since. The past several years have essentially been a research and development phase to develop a well-organized and replicable pathways model that is also flexible enough to be adopted in a wide variety of urban, suburban and rural school settings.

From all the knowledge I have gained from others (see the acknowledgements at the end of this book), and through the many experiences and knowledge I have gained in my eclectic career, I felt that the field would benefit from a book that is aimed at both the community leader and the school leader, and speak in practical terms about how to move forward with the pathways agenda. Further, I saw benefit in not only dealing with pathways-specific content, but also folding in an understanding of other disciplines and strands of thought – career development, project-based learning, organizational leadership, branding and marketing, and the diffusion of innovations. Thus, the work you have in front of you is essentially the learning and musings of the last 15 years of my professional career.

What's ahead?

Now that we've introduced you to the power and promise of pathways, the remainder of the book will help you discover all the essential knowledge that will empower you to lead a pathways initiative in your school, your college, and your community. Chapter by chapter, we will review the essential components of a Pathways System, using straightforward, clear, and action-oriented terminology. Here is what you can expect.

Chapter 2: The Urgency for Pathways

In this chapter, we make the case for pathways, and give you the details you need to share with others. You will learn about both the visible evidence of the need for a pathways model: employer difficulty in filling critical skilled jobs, the low attainment of postsecondary degrees among young Americans, and the preponderance of young adults who are under-skilled or over-credentialed. We also examine the underlying root causes – too little career-mindedness and career development, too few employer-school connections, course-based high schools that offer little relevance to the present or the future, a vague university-for-all culture in schools and society, and low-engagement classrooms.

Chapter 3: The Power of Pathways
This chapter is meant for the friendly skeptics, those who will consider the pathways model, but only if there is credible evidence that this approach will work. We share the most pertinent findings from a wealth of rigorous research.

Chapter 4: Pathway Essentials
In this chapter, we'll share all the key definitions of pathways and the Pathways System Framework™, and also reviews the most commonly asked questions about Pathways.

Chapter 5: Career and Life Readiness
Chapter 5 addresses the big question - is education about teaching coursework or is it really about preparing individuals to succeed in life? Of course I believe it's about people – preparing them for success in college (postsecondary education and training), careers, and life. This chapter provides a holistic definition about what that means, and provides guidance for how pathway partners can create a shared definition of Career and Life Readiness and work together to develop it in their learners and workers.

Part II. How to Design a Pathway Program and Pathways System
In Part 2, we go from building foundational knowledge to a very practical hands-on, let's-get-to-work approach.

Chapter 6. Designing the Pathway Program
Chapter 6 provides an in-depth explanation of the 12 elements of a high quality Pathway Program, and a detailed walk-through about how a school, career technology center, or college can go about developing a new program or study or modernizing its existing programs accordingly.

Chapter 7. Designing the Pathways System
This chapter expands beyond a focus on an individual Pathway Program to looking at all the components of a Pathways System – cross-sector partnerships, career development, a portfolio of Pathway Programs, dynamic teaching and learning; and employer and community engagement. Each section of the chapter describes a component, provides questions for reflection, and provides Action Steps related to that component.

Chapter 8. Exploring and Planning for Careers
This chapter provides an explanation of the key elements of a robust career development system, and the key strategies that can be utilized across the K-12 and adult education spectrum.

Chapter 9: Leading Through Change
Leadership is a critical factor in any organizational change, especially in creating a Pathways System. Chapter 9 explores proven concepts of personal leadership, like Daniel Goleman's work on emotional intelligence and John Kotter's 8 steps for leading change.

Chapter 10. Communicating About the Power and Promise of Pathways
Brand strategy expert Pam Daly guest authors this chapter based on her experience with prominent education initiatives like the Academies of Nashville, for which she helped develop brand strategy to support their education reforms. You will learn the basics of creating a brand and an aligned communications plan.

Chapter 11. Policy Agenda for Pathways Systems
Local change requires the alignment of practice, policy, and funding to support pathways efforts. Further, state-based policy and funding can either impede or support the development of strong local Pathways Systems. This chapter explains how states can create a coherent system of policy and support for local pathways initiatives, drawing from exemplars across the nation.

Chapter 12. Advancing the Pathways Movement
This culminating chapter envisions the future of the pathways movement and forecasts how positive change can take hold in every school system, college, and community across the nation. This call to action explains how leaders at the local, state, and national levels can play a constructive role in achieving this vision.

Profiles of Promising Practices
Throughout the book, profiles of exemplary Pathways Programs, Pathways Systems, and engaged employer and community partners are presented. These profiles provide real-life examples of how the Pathways System framework™ is already being accomplished.

Chapter Two

The Urgency of Pathways

Section 1. Understanding the Urgency for Change

Any type of change process involves some risk of failure and the potential loss of familiar roles and processes. Not surprisingly, to get enough buy-in to implement change, you will need to make a credible case of two things to your colleagues and stakeholders.

First, the status quo is not tolerable. Second, there are strong potential benefits that outweigh the difficulty of changing the status quo.

You and your fellow change agents will need to make a compelling case that change is imperative. Using data and stories, you will need to be clear about the problems that are driving the need for a pathways-systems approach. That's why in this chapter, we're going to focus on the urgency for change by looking at two types of issues, the Visible Challenges and the Root Causes.

You will also need to make a credible case for the potential benefits of change. In what ways are your students and the community at large likely to benefit, and what kind of evidence can you present to that effect? In Chapter 3, I lay out the evidence in favor of a Pathways System approach.

Visible Challenges. These are the observable problems that we "see," but they are really symptoms of deeper, underlying systemic problems. For example, in a business setting, a visible challenge might be low profits, low stock prices, and low sales figures.

Root Problems. These are less obvious, but they are at the root of what is contributing to the visible problems. In a business setting, poor sales figures could be attributed to multiple factors such as poorly designed products that aren't visually attractive or intuitive to users, or untrained sales people who don't know the product, among other factors. Finding these root problems is called "root-cause analysis" because you are going below the surface to the "root". Root-cause analysis is not an exact science, and often the only way to really know the true root cause is to begin tweaking the variables and observe for any changes in results associated with the visible problems.

Why is it so important to distinguish between the two types of problems, the visible challenges and the root causes? If you don't get to the actual root of the problem, you may tend to select a somewhat superficial change strategy that looks good in the short term, but doesn't actually address the real problem. You could exert some significant effort and yet see very little real change in results. Lack of results can breed cynicism and resistance to future change efforts, with a "we tried that before and it didn't work" reaction.

Section 2. What We See: The Visible Challenges

There are seven visible challenges we should consider when thinking about the future of American opportunity and prosperity. In this section, we review the evidence suggesting these trends.

The Visible Challenges are:

1. The Skills Gap: Too Few Skilled Workers and Slow Growth

2. The Entrepreneurship Gap

3. Shrinking Workforce Participation

4. Youth Not Working and Not Going to School

5. Youth Not Completing Postsecondary Education

6. Slipping Competitiveness of the U.S. Workforce

7. Economic Setbacks Facing Young Adults

Challenge 1. The Skills Gap: Too Few Skilled Workers and Slow Growth

Since the 1970s, the American economy and workforce has experienced a radical shift brought on by the dual pressures of technology innovation and globalization. These forces have shifted many moderate- to low-skilled jobs, first to lower cost regions of the U.S. and then to other nations, while the remaining mix of U.S.-based jobs shifted to a need for much higher levels of education, training, and underlying skills. The U.S. workforce has not kept pace with the shifting demands, thus there is a skills gap – that gap between millions of skilled jobs that can't be filled easily, and millions of potential workers, even some with postsecondary education, but without the specific skills needed to fill these jobs.

More Than 5 Million Unfilled Jobs: Employers Can't Fill Many Skilled Positions

In March 2016, the monthly Jobs Openings report from the U.S. Department of Labor indicated that there were 5.8 million job openings, a record since this report was first issued in 2000.[1]

According to DHI hiring, in March 2016, employers on average took 28 days to fill a job opening, just under the longest time of 28.4 days recorded in August 2015. This was more than three days longer than in 2007, before the financial crisis. Average vacancies were even worse in high-skilled professions: 47.7 days in health services, 42.6 days in financial services, 30.6 days in technology, and nearly 32.4 days in manufacturing.[2]

This difficultly in hiring skilled workers has been intensifying for some time. In a 2014 survey conducted by CareerBuilder, more than half of the U.S. employers surveyed said they had open positions for which they could not find a qualified applicant. Eighty-one percent of employers said it was at least somewhat difficult to fill job vacancies because of a "skills gap," defined as "the gap between the skills applicants possess and the skills required for employer's jobs."[3]

Finally, the Manpower Group, in its 2015 Talent Shortage report, says that in the U.S., 32 percent of employers reported difficulties filling jobs in 2015. This is down somewhat from 40 percent in 2014.[4]

According to the Manpower Group, the top 10 jobs that U.S. employers reported having trouble filling in 2015 were:

◊ Skilled trade workers

◊ Drivers

◊ Teachers

◊ Sales representatives

◊ Administrative professionals

◊ Management/executives

◊ Nurses

◊ Technicians

◊ Accounting and finance staff

◊ Engineers[5]

Skills Gap Impacts Companies Negatively

A survey conducted by CareerBuilder found that 60 percent of employers are concerned about the costs associated with delays in filling open positions. One in four said they have experienced lost revenues as a result of unfilled positions, and they also report lower productivity, reduced work quality, and a rise in voluntary employee turnover.[6]

Here are the consequences that employers report, attributed to the skills gap:

◊ Lower morale due to employees shouldering heavier workloads – 41 percent

◊ Work does not get done – 40 percent

◊ Delays in delivery times – 34 percent

◊ Declines in customer service – 30 percent

◊ Lower quality of work due to employees being overworked – 30 percent

◊ Employees are less motivated – 29 percent

◊ Loss in revenue – 25 percent

◊ Employees making more mistakes, resulting in lower quality of work – 25 percent

◊ Higher turnover because employees are overworked – 22 percent[7]

Negative Impact of Skills Gap

Respondents to the Manpower Talent Shortage survey indicated the following ways that talent shortages affect their businesses:

◊ Reduced ability to serve clients – 43 percent

◊ Reduced competitiveness/productivity - 41 percent

◊ Increased employee turnover – 32 percent

◊ Higher compensation costs – 32 percent

◊ Lower employee engagement/morale - 32 percent

◊ Reduced innovation and creativity - 22 percent[8]

Challenge 2. The Entrepreneurship Gap

Slow Down in Business Start-ups

America has a business start-up problem. According to a World Bank report for the Center for American Progress, the rates of individuals in the U.S. starting businesses grew significantly in the 1970s, 80s and 90s. At the beginning of this period, about 3 percent of Americans started a new business every year and by the end of the 90s, that number was up to 5 percent. But since the early 2000s, the percentage of new business start-ups has stagnated and even fallen. If previous trends had continued, we would now have 1 million more entrepreneurs than we actually do in the United States. [9]

Starting a business seems to be getting harder or riskier. Now, the average person starting a business is older than in the past (47 years vs. 41 years), has more college education (67 percent vs. 60 percent), and needs more capital, often derived from personal savings.

Analysis by the Kaufman Foundation also indicates that immigrants now account for 20.6 percent of all business owners in the U.S., up from just 10.9 percent in the 1997 index. This current level is the largest share of immigrant entrepreneurship in our history. In fact, in 2014, immigrants were 24.7 percent more likely than native-born citizens to own businesses.[10] While having a large number of businesses created by immigrants is a positive development, nevertheless it raises concern that native-born Americans are not doing so at the same rate.

What are the causes of these slow-downs and shifts in entrepreneurship? Have native-born citizens lost their aspiration or understanding of the benefits of starting a business? Have the stories of mega-start-ups like Microsoft, Apple, Facebook, and Google made the more typical start-up seem out of reach? Is there some sort of shift in U.S. culture away from risk-taking and toward safe and secure job prospects?

Or are there structural barriers to entrepreneurship, real or perceived? For example, does the effect of student loan debt, which currently averages almost $29,000 per person, play a role?[11] In a fall 2015 open forum, Gallup Education Director Brandon Busteed said that some of the delay in business start-ups among younger workers is attributed to increased levels of student loan debt.[12]

Challenge 3. Shrinking Workforce Participation

Discouraged and Disabled Workers Pulling Out of the Workforce

In 2007, 66 percent of Americans had a job or were actively seeking work. As of September 2016, that number is at 62.8 percent — almost the lowest level since 1977.[13] Each year, more working-age Americans are withdrawing from the workforce. They are moving from the position of making an economic contribution to becoming a neutral force – and in some cases becoming a recipient of various government benefits such as food stamps, subsidized health insurance, disability payments, and housing assistance.

While some adults pulling out of the workforce are parents who choose to raise their children full-time, and some are truly retiring, an increasingly large number are "discouraged workers" – those who looked for work after being laid off and ultimately joined the ranks of the long-term unemployed.

This signals two disturbing trends:

◊   The societal stigma of not working is fading, and millions of Americans have some level of comfort with not working at all and receiving governmental benefits;

◊ For many, finding meaningful employment that pays a decent income has become so difficult that choosing not to work has become a viable lifestyle.

Challenge 4. Youth Not Working and Not Going to School

There are 5.5 Million Disconnected Youth and Young Adults

Disconnected youths are defined as individuals between the ages of 16 and 24 who are not working or in school. In 2015, approximately 5.5 million youths, or one in seven, fit this category. To put this in perspective, the total population of disconnected youth in the U.S. is about the same as the population of Minnesota.[14]

Youth disconnection rates for blacks (21.6 percent), Native Americans (27.8 percent), and Hispanics (16.3 percent) are significantly higher than for Whites (11.3 percent) and Asian Americans (7.9 percent). [15]

The Cost of Disconnected Youth

It is difficult to ascertain the full social and economic costs attributed to disconnected youth, but a conservative estimate for four direct costs – incarceration, Medicaid, public assistance payments, and Supplemental Security Income payments – shows a direct one-year cost to taxpayers of $26.8 billion.[16]

> *In 2015, approximately 5.5 million youths, or one in seven young adults in the U.S., were disconnected – meaning they weren't working and they weren't in school or college. To put this in perspective, the total population of disconnected youth in the U.S. is about the same as the total population of Minnesota.*

Many disconnected youths face several challenges in connecting to education or the workforce, thereby preventing successful transitions to adulthood. They often are disconnected from their families and do not belong to a strong social network. In addition, disconnected youth tend to have lower levels of educational attainment and are more likely to live in poverty than connected youths. In 2007, approximately 47 percent of all disconnected youth were poor, compared to 15 percent of connected youths.[17] They also are more likely to be involved in the criminal justice system. For example, an MDRC report on disconnected youth indicates that "one in 10 young male high school dropouts — and one in four young Black male dropouts — is either in jail or juvenile detention at any point in time."[18]

The personal outcomes for individual disconnected youth are no doubt troubling as they struggle to successfully transition to adulthood with solid education credentials and secure employment. But the concern does not rest with only the youths themselves. When lost earnings, lower economic growth, and lower tax revenues are considered in addition to government spending for these individuals, the substantial fiscal burden disconnected youth place on their communities is extensive. It is estimated that over the course of a 20-year-old disconnected youth's lifetime, the taxpayer burden for that individual is $235,680. The social burden is an estimated $704,020. (These lump sum amounts are expressed in 2011 dollar values.)[19]

Challenge 5. Youth Not Completing Postsecondary Education

Postsecondary education and training are vitally important to success in today's high-skilled economy, but despite decades of increased enrollment in postsecondary education, too few students are actually completing their chosen postsecondary education program. Only 41 percent of young adults complete postsecondary education.

College Enrollments and Low Degree Attainment

Throughout the 20th century – particularly after creation of the post-World War II GI Bill and the federal student aid programs in the 1960s – college enrollments grew rapidly. The percentage of recent high school graduates who immediately enrolled in college peaked at 70 percent in 2009 and has since slipped to 66 percent in 2013. For students from higher income families, about 80 percent of high school graduates enrolled in college immediately after high school.[20]

Recent data indicate that about 55 percent of students who enroll in a four-year college complete their degree at that institution within six years. Further, among those enrolled at two-year degree colleges, fewer than 30 percent complete a degree or certification within three years.[21]

Among young American adults, only four in ten completed at least a two-year college degree. Almost 60 percent of young adults had NOT earned a two-year or four-year college degree.

This low level of postsecondary enrollment and completion seems surprising given the strong university-for-all message that had been communicated during their school years. These young people started school at about age six between 1984 and 1993, during the early drive of reform measures to raise academic graduation rates and promote the use of education standards. They would have graduated from high school between 1996 and 2005, when about 65 to 68 percent of recent high school graduates were entering college.[22]

To sum up the implications of this data: The combination of two factors, a large number of students who do not enroll in college at all, and the low rate of completion among those who do enroll, leads to a very surprising and disturbing end result. As recently as 2012, only 41 percent of young Americans age 25 to 34 had completed at least a two-year college degree, meaning that 59 percent had not earned either a two- or four-year degree.[23] It is apparent that the widespread university-for-all message is not having its desired impact.

Challenge 6. Slipping Competitiveness of the U.S. Workforce

U.S. Slips in Level of Higher Education Attainment

The U.S. has fallen to 10th in the world's share of adults 25 to 34 years old with postsecondary education degrees. In past decades, the U.S. workforce held the highest percentages of degrees among its workforce.

The U.S. rate trails global leaders South Korea, Canada, and Japan and is in the middle of the pack among other developed nations. This reflects two big changes: the major expansions of college attendance in Asia and Europe and the continuing emphasis on four-year degrees in the U.S. while other nations focus far more on one- and two-year professional credentials.[24]

While U.S. Millennials may be the most educated in American history, they lag behind their international peers, not just in degree completion but also in actual skills attainment. The problem is not that we are losing most low-skilled manufacturing jobs, but we are also at risk for being out-competed for the high skilled technical jobs.

U.S Adults Slipping in Attainment of Workforce Skills

According to international studies of workforce skills, U.S. adults don't stack up well against their counterparts in the developed world. The Program for the International Assessment of Adult Competencies, PIACC, examined 16- to 65-year-olds for a set of skills deemed to be important for success in the working world. Unlike school-based surveys, this assessment was designed as a household study.

The report found that U.S. adults' literacy, numeracy, and problem-solving skills were below international averages. The study also showed deep skills disparities within the United States, corresponding to factors such as income, education, and health.[25]

Only 12 percent of U.S. adults (aged 16-65) scored at the highest level of proficiency in literacy, compared with 22 percent in Finland and 23 percent in Japan. In every age group except for Americans aged 55 to 65, the U.S. approximated or lagged behind the international average.[26]

U.S. Millennials Lag Behind Their International Counterparts
The Education Testing Service conducted a deeper analysis of the PIACC, looking closely at Millennials – youth and adults born after 1980 – who at the time of this writing are age 16 through 35 years.[27]

While U.S. Millennials may be the most educated in American history, they lag behind their international peers, not just in degree completion but also in actual skills attainment.

In literacy, U.S. Millennials scored in the bottom third among the 22 participating countries that took the PIAAC. U.S. adults born after 1980 scored below Millennials in 15 countries, and scored in the same range as four other countries. Only Spain and Italy had significantly lower scores.

In numeracy, U.S. Millennials ranked last, along with Italy and Spain.

In problem solving in technology-rich environments (PS-TRE), U.S. Millennials also ranked last, along with the Slovak Republic, Ireland, and Poland.

The youngest segment of the U.S. Millennial cohort (16- to 24-year-olds), who could be in the country's labor force for the next 50 years, ranked last in numeracy along with Italy and among the bottom countries in PS-TRE. In literacy, they only scored higher than their peers in Italy and Spain.

The gap in scores (139 points) between U.S. Millennials at the 90th and 10th percentiles was higher than the gap of 14 of the participating countries and was not significantly different from the gap in the remaining eight countries. This signals a relatively high degree of inequality among U.S. young adults.[28]

Americans have clung to the idea that these findings are not accurate because other countries exclude all their struggling students and adults from these international assessments, but this belief is not founded in reality. All the countries that participate in this survey agree to very high standards of program design, so it is impossible that large gaps of lower performing adults are left out of the survey.

These results are difficult to hear, but they are important. American young adults at all levels of performance and income are falling behind their peers from other countries with moderately to highly developed economies. The problem is not only that we are losing most low-skilled manufacturing jobs, but we are also at risk for being out-competed for the high skilled technical jobs.

Challenge 7. Economic Setbacks Facing Young Adults

70 Percent of College Students, Plus Those Who Drop Out, Carry Student Loan Debt

Seven in 10 seniors (69 percent) who graduated from public and nonprofit colleges in 2014 had student loan debt, with an average of $28,950 per borrower. This was a 2 percent increase from the average debt held by 2013 public and nonprofit graduates. [29]

As the recession of 2008-09 proceeded, college enrollment spiked as individuals sought to increase their existing skills or develop new ones. At the same time, state budgets were imploding. As college leaders faced increased enrollments and falling subsidies, they raised tuition rates accordingly. Students, feeling the pressure of getting more education and training, swallowed hard and paid the increased tuition, often taking on an uncomfortable amount of debt.

> *Seven in 10 (69 percent) college graduates in 2014 had student loan debt, with an average of almost $29,000 per borrower. This was a two percent increase from the average debt of 2013 public and nonprofit graduates.*

Yes, college is an excellent investment, if the student finishes, enters his or her profession of choice, and then can afford to pay off the investment. But for students who drop out, the loan they have taken on is no longer an investment. Rather, it is a cost, and because they have to start repaying the loan very soon after dropping out, it can become a millstone, pulling them down toward economic devastation. About 21 percent of borrowers who did not complete any degree or certificate and were no longer enrolled in college reported being behind on payments, according to a survey released in May 2015 by the Federal Reserve Board. [30]

Delayed Emerging Adulthood

Between 2008 and 2011, the proportion of young adults living in their parents' home increased, according to a report from the U.S. Census Bureau. The percentage of men age 25 to 34 rose from 14 percent in 2005 to 19 percent in 2011, and for women, from 8 percent to 10 percent. Similarly, 59 percent of men age 18 to 24 and 50 percent of women in that age group resided in their parents' home in 2011, up from 53 percent and 46 percent, respectively, in 2005. "The increase in 25 to 34 year olds living in their parents' home began before the recent recession, and has continued beyond it," said the report's author, Rose Kreider." [31]

Section 3. What We Don't See – The Root Causes

There are eight underlying root causes that contribute to the visible problems we have identified:

1. Many Youths Don't Experience Impactful Career Development.
2. U.S. Culture is Dominated by "University-for-All" Message.
3. Most Schools Don't Embrace Employer Perspectives on Career Readiness.
4. Too Many Youth Are Disengaged From Learning.
5. Too Many Youth Have Weak Academic Skills and Lack College Readiness.
6. Too Many Students Still Drop Out of High School.
7. Very Few High School Graduates Have Well-Developed Career and Technical Knowledge.
8. Large Achievement Gaps Persist Linked to Family Income and Race.

Root Cause 1. Many Youth Don't Experience Impactful Career Development

Very Little Help from the High School

Research conducted by Michigan's Ferris State University concluded that the major influence over teen career goals was their parents and they perceived very little help coming from high school staff. [32] Teachers were identified as helping with career decisions by 25 percent of survey respondents and counselors by 21 percent, but more than half (51%) said that "no one" from the high school was helping with advice on career options to further the student's education. Specific findings included:

Who is primarily responsible for helping plan a career or job?

◊ One or both parents: 78 percent

◊ School personnel: 10 percent

◊ Other: 7 percent

◊ Undecided: 5 percent

Who in the high school has been helpful in advising on career options to further your education?

◊ No one: 51 percent

◊ Teacher: 24.8 percent

◊ Counselor: 21.1 percent

◊ Administrator: 1.1 percent

◊ Other: 2 percent

Similar findings come from a 2015 report issued by the nonprofit group YouthTruth, which specializes in learning about student and youth perceptions. Just 46 percent of youth responded affirmatively to the statement, "My school has helped me figure out which careers match my interest and abilities," and 49 percent affirmed that "my school has helped me understand the steps I need to take in order to have the career I want." [33]

According to the survey, students who receive support services for career development and college admissions generally rank them highly, assigning about 4 of 5 stars in terms of quality, although access to or utilization of these support services was very low. Among high school juniors, only 37 percent accessed support related to "Future Career Possibilities," and only 48 percent of seniors accessed these services.

Lack of Career Direction for College Planning

A survey administered by CareerBuilder in 2014 indicates that only 25 percent of job seekers reported receiving any "career pathing" exploration and advising services while they were in high school, while 23 percent of career seekers say they received "no guidance". Forty-one percent of job seekers said they wished they had received more career guidance. [34]

Over half of American high school aged youth (51 percent) said that "no one" from the high school was helping in advising them on career options to further their education.

An international survey report by McKinsey demonstrates that youth also don't know much about the job market when they make career and education decisions. Just 41 percent of American youth enrolling in postsecondary education reported having a good sense of job openings, wages, and graduation placement rates when making college course selections. [35]

Students Not Making Informed College Major Choices

According to research by ACT, Inc., what high school students think they want to study in college doesn't always match their identified interests and academic strengths. About one-third of the students who took the ACT college-entrance test indicated that they planned to major in a subject that, according to correlated information and results of their assessments, would not be a good fit for them. That mismatch can lead to switching majors, transferring schools, and higher college costs overall.[36]

Root Cause 2. U.S. Culture is Dominated by "University/College-for-All" Message

For decades, policy-makers have observed data indicating that individuals with a four-year or advanced degree earn much more, over a lifetime, than those with an associate degree, high school diploma, or less.

In general, according to data compiled by the College Board, annual earnings by degree are as follows:

◊ Less than a high school diploma: $25,100

◊ High School Diploma: $35,400

◊ Some College, No Degree: $40,400

◊ Associate Degree: $44,800

◊ Bachelor's Degree: $56,500

◊ Master's Degree: $70,000

◊ Doctoral Degree: $91,000

◊ Professional Degree: $102,200[37]

Based on the wide reporting of these data by school counselors and college recruiters, and on the natural urge to better the lives of our youth, it seems that the cultures of both the United States and its schools have evolved to the extent that obtaining a four-year college degree is seen as the ideal outcome of K-12 education, particularly for the more academically successful students. This ideal may be particularly strong among education reform and civil rights advocates, who recognize that the talents of many poor and minority students were not recognized or developed because of classism and racism, thus many deserving individuals who would have done well in college or university were denied access. Furthermore, almost all educators, policy-makers, and education reform advocates are themselves the product of earning a bachelor's degree or higher. Higher education has contributed to their personal success, so it may seem self-evident that the more people who can complete a four-year degree, the better.

However, the cultural touchstone of "college for all" doesn't actually match up to the current economic reality in the U.S.

The Center for Education and the Workforce estimates there will be approximately 55 million jobs openings in the economy through 2020:

◊ 35 percent will require at least a bachelor's degree.

◊ 30 percent will require some college or an associate's degree.

◊ 36 percent will not require education beyond high school.[38]

There is also evidence that the particular field of study, more than the time spent earning a degree, has a major impact on earnings. For example, high-demand fields in technology, health care, and the skilled trades can provide very attractive incomes.

◊ 31 percent of workers who hold an associate degree earn more than individuals with a bachelor's degree.

Clarity about High Expectations and "University/college-for-all"

In this book, I actively critique the notion of "college for all" or "university for all" that has taken hold of K-12 education since the 1980s. However, this is a tricky and sensitive subject.

I believe we must hold every student to the highest possible expectations and encourage them to reach as high as they can go. The data is clear that most family-sustaining wage careers require some sort of postsecondary education, training, and/or apprenticeship beyond high school. To succeed in any decent career, whether or not it requires postsecondary education, the individual needs a strong foundation of excellent reading, writing, mathematical, problem-solving, and interpersonal skills. This foundation is also indispensable for personal life success and civic engagement.

But since not every good career requires a four-year degree for entry, that should not be the default expectation for every student. Even very bright students may not find a university education is the best fit for their aptitudes and interests.

So while I strongly value the benefit of ongoing education and training, this book promotes a more personalized and career-based approach to helping youths make the decision about what kind of education and training they want and need after high school.

◊ 27 percent of workers with a license or certificate earn more than workers with only a bachelor's degree.

◊ 43 percent of workers with a license or certificate earn more than workers with only an associate degree.

Systemic misconceptions about earnings, the workforce, and the number of workers needed with bachelor's degrees may be subtly influencing postsecondary education decisions in a way that is not beneficial for every student.

Root Cause 3. Most Schools Don't Embrace Employer Perspectives on Career Readiness

College Students and Employers Differ Over Workplace Readiness

In 2015, Hart Research conducted research of upper-level college students and the employers that hire students. Sixty percent of employers believe that college graduates with either a two- or four-year degree need to have field-specific knowledge and skills along with a broad range of cross-cutting employability skills. [39]

In the same study, both employers and recent college graduates were asked to evaluate recently-hired employees regarding how well prepared they were in terms of important cross-cutting skills. Across the board, the recent graduates expressed a greater sense of confidence in their readiness than did their employers. [40] The following examples demonstrate the disconnect in perceptions between recent college graduates and employers:

Working with others in teams
◊ Student perception of readiness: 64 percent
◊ Employer perception of readiness: 37 percent

Critical/analytical thinking
◊ Student perception of readiness: 66 percent
◊ Employer perception of readiness: 26 percent

Being innovative/creative
◊ Student perception of readiness: 57 percent
◊ Employer perception of readiness: 25 percent

Locating, organizing, evaluating information
◊ Student perception of readiness: 64 percent
◊ Employer perception of readiness: 29 percent

Ethical judgment and decision-making
◊   Student perception of readiness: 62 percent
◊   Employer perception of readiness: 30 percent

Written communication
◊   Student perception of readiness: 65 percent
◊   Employer perception of readiness: 27 percent

Oral communication
◊   Student perception of readiness: 62 percent
◊   Employer perception of readiness: 28 percent

Based on the disparity between the sense of work readiness between employers and college students, we can conclude that college students (and perhaps their teachers) need a better sense of the reality waiting for them in the workplace. The link between the workplace and education is a challenge for many postsecondary education programs, as well as high schools.

College Students Are Not Receiving Career Readiness Support
The problem of career development is not just a secondary school problem. In a recent survey conducted for McGraw-Hill Education by Hanover Research, 1,000 college students were asked about their preparation for the workforce. Sixty-five percent of those who went on to college said that high school prepared them pretty well for college, but in terms of college preparing them for the workforce, they were underwhelmed and underserved. Only 20 percent of college students said they felt very well prepared for the workforce. [41]

Only 20 percent of college students said they felt very well prepared for the workforce.

Fifty-eight percent of students agreed that college should adequately prepare them for the workforce, but just 35 percent said that college was actually effective in preparing them for a job.

◊   About half (51 percent) of college students did not learn how to write a resume in college.

◊   More than half (56 percent) did not learn how to conduct themselves in a job interview.

◊   Almost six in ten (58 percent) did not learn how to network or search for a job.

College students know that career preparation should be an important component of their collegiate experience, but they are not getting enough right now. A significant majority of college students (67 percent) want more internships and professional experience, 61 percent want classes that are designed to build career skills, and 58 percent want more time to focus on career preparation. [42]

Root Cause 4. Too Many Youth Are Disengaged From Learning

Most high school students are disengaged, dreaming, or dabbling

Research by Dr. William Damon, University of Oregon and Stanford University, discovered that a majority of young people were struggling to make the leap into adulthood because they lacked a sense of purpose. Damon and his team conducted research by surveying 1,200 young people between the ages of 12 and 26 over a five-year period.[43] They grouped respondents into the following categories:

◊ 20 percent of students were termed "Purposeful," those who had found something meaningful to dedicate themselves to, who had sustained this interest over time, and who had expressed a clear sense of what they were trying to accomplish in the world.

◊ 30 percent were "Dabblers," youths who had tried a number of potentially purposeful pursuits but who had yet to find reason to commit to any of them.

◊ 25 percent were "Dreamers," those who could imagine themselves doing great things in the world but who had yet to do anything to pursue their ideas in a practical way.

◊ 25 percent were "Disengaged," young people who had neither a purpose in life nor an inclination to find one.

Students Report Being "Bored" (aka Disengaged)

In education research, there is not an agreed-upon definition of "boredom," but researchers believe the phenomenon represents some level of temporary disengagement from school, and it is important for schools to understand both the extent of students' boredom and the reasons why they are bored.

According to the High School Study of Student Engagement (HSSSE), nearly half of students (49 percent) are bored every day, and approximately one out of every six students (17 percent) is bored in every class.[44]

The HSSSE asked two direct questions about boredom:

◊ "Have you ever been bored in class in high school?" and,

◊ "If you have been bored in class, why?"

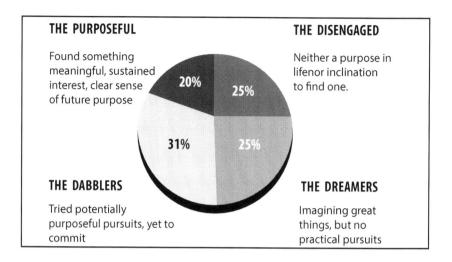

THE PURPOSEFUL

Found something meaningful, sustained interest, clear sense of future purpose

THE DISENGAGED

Neither a purpose in lifenor inclination to find one.

THE DABBLERS

Tried potentially purposeful pursuits, yet to commit

THE DREAMERS

Imagining great things, but no practical pursuits

Not surprisingly, almost all students (98 percent) say they were bored sometimes, and of these, the material being taught was the issue for more than four out of five.

◊ 81 percent of students said that a reason for their boredom was "material wasn't interesting."

◊ About two out of five (40 percent) claimed that the lack of relevance of the material caused their boredom.

◊ About one third (33 percent) were bored because "work wasn't challenging enough."

◊ About one fourth (26 percent) were bored because "the work was too difficult."

Instructional interaction played a role in students' boredom as well. More than one third of the respondents (35 percent) were bored due to "no interactions with teacher."

Root Cause 5. Too Many Youth Have Weak Academic Skills and Lack College Readiness

Millions of Youth Enter the Workforce with Very Low Academic Skills

According to the best data available, about 3.2 million youths are graduating from high school each year. The National Assessment of Education Progress, a national data sample, indicates that about 40 percent of high school seniors are reading at a "proficient" level, and about 32 percent can carry out mathematics at a proficient level. These trend lines are similar to what ACT and SAT scores indicate as meeting their "college ready" metrics.

To extrapolate, that means that of the 3.2 million graduates each year (excluding the 750,000 who drop out), only 1.28 million graduates are actually proficient in reading or math.

Using a more generous measure on the National Assessment of Educational Progress, "at or above basic," about 80 percent of seniors are proficient in reading, and about 65 percent are at a similar level in mathematics. This would mean that 2.56 million graduates can read at a functional level, and about 2.08 million graduates can do functional math.

Looking at the flip side of the equation, among high school graduates, 640,000 youths receive a high school diploma each year but cannot read at a functional level, and 1.12 million graduates cannot do math at a functional level.

Only about 40 percent of American high school graduates are academically ready to do college-level work, according to the SAT and ACT analyses.

To summarize, each year, 750,000 high school dropouts enter the potential workforce with very low functional academic skills, and another 1.1 million have a minimally functional, but not proficient, level specifically in reading and math.

Small Percentage of High School Seniors Are "College Ready"

In addition to flat academic scores, college entrance tests also signal trouble. According to data from the two national college testing organizations, College Board and ACT, almost 60 percent of the juniors and seniors who took the tests are not "college ready," meaning they likely would not do very well in freshman-level college courses.

In 2015, only 41.9 percent of students who took the SAT scored well enough to be considered "college ready," meaning their scores are correlated with those of students who did relatively well in freshman-level college courses. A significant majority of these test takers – 58 percent – did not score well enough to be considered "college ready." [45]

According to ACT's estimate, only about 40 percent of graduating high school students who took the ACT exam showed a "strong readiness" for college in most subject areas, and over 30 percent of the test takers did not meet any of the four college readiness benchmarks. [46]

The problem with these low levels of postsecondary readiness is that about 65 percent of current and future jobs require some level of postsecondary education, training, industry-based certifications, and college degrees, according to research from the Georgetown University Center for Education and Workforce. About 68 percent of recent high school graduates enroll in postsecondary education, but only about 40 percent are academically ready to do college-level work.

Disconnect Between High School Teachers and College Faculty Expectations for Readiness

A survey released by ACT found that 89 percent of high school teachers reported that their students were "well" or "very well" prepared for college level work in the subjects they taught. However, just 26 percent of college instructors said incoming students were "well" or "very well" prepared for entry-level courses. These findings were part of the 2012 ACT National Curriculum Survey results. To bridge the divide in expectations and understanding between high school and college instructors, ACT recommended greater collaboration between K-12 and postsecondary educators on curriculum and academic expectations.[47]

Root Cause 6. Too Many Students Still Drop Out of High School

Three-Quarters of a Million High School Dropouts Annually

Fortunately, the "on-time" high school graduation rate has risen to over 82 percent in recent years.[48] This is likely a reflection of increased efforts by schools to intervene with students likely to drop out, and it may reflect the fact that there are fewer and fewer decent jobs available for individuals with less than a high school diploma. The last time the graduation rate was as high as it is now was during the recession years of the late 1970s.

Even with an improved on-time graduation rate, there is still an annual loss of about 750,000 youth who leave high school without earning a high school diploma.

However, even with an improved on-time graduation rate, there is still an annual loss of about 750,000 youth who leave high school each year without earning a diploma.[49] These dropouts are the least likely to succeed in the workplace, and they offer little in the way of tangible skills to a potential employer.

The Ultimate Disengagement – Dropping Out

When asked in the High School Study of Student Engagement (HSSSE) about dropping out of school, one out of five students (21 percent) who took the survey had considered dropping out at some point during high school. Seven percent of the respondents had considered dropping out many times. Among the reasons students think about dropping out are: [50]

◊   I didn't like the school (50 percent)

◊   I didn't see the value of the work I was being asked to do (42 percent)

◊   I didn't like the teachers (39 percent)

◊   The work was too difficult (35 percent)

◊   The work was too easy (13 percent)

In the report "Silent Epidemic," researchers surveyed recent high school dropouts to understand their reasons for quitting school. Nearly half (47 percent) said a major reason for dropping out was that their classes were not interesting, reporting that they were bored and disengaged from high school. Even for students with relatively high GPAs, this was a common complaint. Nearly 7 in 10 respondents (69 percent) said they were not motivated or inspired to work hard. In fact, most dropouts were students who could have, and believed they could have, succeeded in school.[51]

Nearly 7 in 10 youths who dropped out of high school (69 percent) said they were not motivated or inspired to work hard. In fact, most dropouts were students who could have, and believed they could have, succeeded in school.

Root Cause 7. Very Few High School Graduates Have Well-Developed Career and Technical Knowledge

According to the National Center for Education Statistics, about 20 percent of high school students take a concentrated course of study (three or more courses) in career and technical education. A large percentage takes at least one CTE course in high school, which can mean a computer applications course or an entry-level course in another CTE field. Far fewer students earn at least two credits in an occupational area, and just 19.1 percent earn three or more CTE credits. [52] The occupational areas are ranked in order below:

Percentage of public high school graduates who earned at least 3.0 credits in the occupational area, 2009	
All graduates	19.1%
Ag/Natural resources	2.6%
Business	2.4%
Health sciences	2.6%
Consumer and culinary services	2.4%
Communications and design	2.2%
Repair and transportation	2.1%
Manufacturing	1.3%
Construction and architecture	1.1%
Computer and information sciences	1.0%
Engineering technologies	0.9%
Marketing	0.9%
Public services	0.6%
Source: U.S. Department of Education, Institute of Education Sciences, National Center for Education Statistics, High School Transcript Study (HSTS), 2009.	

So among the annual 3.2 million high school graduates each year, only about 608,000 of them have any type of marketable career-related skills.

Root Cause 8. Large Achievement Gaps Persist Linked to Family Income and Race

U.S. Schools Are Becoming Increasingly Diverse

In fall 2014, for this first time, the overall number of Latino, African American, and Asian students in U.S. K-12 classrooms surpassed the number of non-Hispanic Whites. The collective number of non-Whites was an estimated 50.3 percent, and was driven largely by the growth of the Latino population and the decline of the White population. To a lesser degree, there has been a steady rise in the number of Asian Americans, but the African American percentage of the population has been flat.[53]

By 2019-20, 45 percent of public high school graduates in the U.S. will be non-White. This is up by more than 7 percent over the class of 2009 and is driven by a rapid increase in the number of Hispanic students completing high school.

There will also be an overall decline in the number of graduates. After a 15-year increase, the number of graduates topped out at 3.4 million in 2010-11 but is expected to decline and stabilize at about 3.2 or 3.3 million. [54]

In 2001, Hispanics, African Americans, Asians, and other minorities accounted for 50.4 percent of births, 49.7 percent of all children under five, and slightly more than half of the 4 million children under 1 year old.[55]

In 2044, the U.S. population will become "majority minority," according to recent updates of population projections by the U.S. Census Bureau. At that time, it is estimated that Whites will make up 49.7 percent of the population compared with 25 percent for Hispanics, 12.7 percent for Blacks, 7.9 percent for Asians, and 3.7 percent for multiracial persons.[56] This trend line is based on projections that the White population will grow and then begin to slightly shrink due to deaths and lower replacement birth rates, and there will be higher growth rates of minorities and multiracial groups due to a combination of birth rates and continued immigration.

Achievement Gaps Closely Track Economic and Racial Disparities
While not new, academic achievement gaps related to income and race continue at significant levels.

According to the 2013 National Assessment of Educational Progress, the average scale score for math among 8th grade students was 284. Higher income students averaged a score of 297, but the average scale score for low-income students was 27 points lower at 270. For White students, the score was 293 and for Asian students, it was 306, but African Americans scored at 263, Latinos at 271, and American Indians/Alaska Natives at 270.[57]

Gaps for reading levels were also similarly large. For reading, the 2013 NAEP score for Grade 8 was 266. Higher income students scored an average of 278, and low-income students scored at 254, a gap of 24 points. For White students,

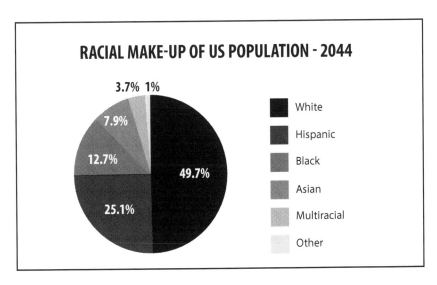

RACIAL MAKE-UP OF US POPULATION - 2044

3.7% 1%
7.9%
12.7%
49.7%
25.1%

- White
- Hispanic
- Black
- Asian
- Multiracial
- Other

the score was 275 and for Asian students, it was 279. African Americans scored at 250, Latinos at 255, and American Indians at 252.[58]

The modest good news is that the gaps are shrinking. Low-income students grew in math (+12) and reading (+8) from 2003 to 2013, a faster rate of growth than the national average for math (+7) and reading (+5). Growth in math scores for African Americans (+11) and Latinos (+13) also exceeded the national average growth rate, although for American Indians the growth rate did not change. For reading, African Americans (+6) and Latinos (+11) exceeded the national growth rate of (+5). [59]

The big challenge, however, is that most American youth do not come close to performing at a proficient level for math (299) or reading (281). On average, students fall short of proficiency by 14 points for math and 15 points for reading, respectively, and just 36 percent of students are performing at the proficient and advanced levels for both reading and math. Thus, 64 percent of 8th graders remain in the basic and below basic levels of math and reading performance. This means they are poorly prepared for either college-level work or performance in the skilled work environment. [60]

Not only did youth from other countries on average outperform U.S. students, data also indicates that wealth and poverty have a bigger impact on student performance in the U.S. than in many other countries.

A huge amount of work remains to be done, both to raise overall student achievement and to close achievement gaps more quickly. Daria Hall, director of K-12 policy development at the Education Trust, an educational advocacy and research organization, explained, "While we have seen some gap-closing over the past decade, nationally the gaps are not closing fast enough, and the impact is devastating to our nation's most vulnerable students. We must – and can – do better for students of color and low-income students."[61]

Poverty Has a Greater Effect on Achievement than In Other Nations

According to the Program for International Study Assessment (PISA), not only did other countries out-perform U.S. students, data also indicates that wealth and poverty have a bigger impact on student performance in the U.S. than in many other countries. [62]

The results of the test, given to 15-year-olds in 57 countries, including 5,611 U.S. students, show that an estimated 18 percent of the variation in Americans' science scores were related to students' socioeconomic circumstances. The U.S. poverty impact rate – 18 percent – was significantly higher than the average level of impact – about 14 percent – among other industrialized countries. The rate was more than twice as high as that of several of the highest performing countries in science, such as Finland and Canada, where the poverty impact rate was about 8 percent.

Section 4. Implications in Thinking about Pathways

In this chapter, we identified seven visible challenges and eight root causes.

The Visible Challenges are:

1. The Skills Gap: Too Few Skilled and Credentialed Workers

2. The Entrepreneurship Gap

3. Shrinking Workforce Participation

4. Youth Not Working and Not Going to School

5. Youth Not Completing Postsecondary Education

6. Slipping Competitiveness of the U.S. Workforce

7. Economic Set-Backs Facing Young Adults

The Root Causes are:

1. Many Youth Don't Experience Impactful Career Development

2. U.S. Culture Is Dominated by "University-for-All" Message

3. Most Schools Don't Embrace Employer Perspectives on Career Readiness

4. Too Many Youth Are Disengaged From Learning

5. Too Many Youth Have Weak Academic Skills and Lack College Readiness

6. Too Many Students Still Drop Out of High School

7. Very Few High School Graduates Have Well-Developed Career and Technical Knowledge

8. Large Achievement Gaps Persist Linked to Family Income and Race

All the data presented in this chapter supports a simple message: The status quo is not acceptable; we must engage students more effectively. The answer lies in career relevance.

How to Use the Urgency Data

Once you understand data that identifies visible challenges, what do you do with it? In Chapter 7, we review the stages in building a Pathways System initiative, and the first phase is "Explore." Later, in Chapter 9, you can review the research on Leading Change that also provides the conceptual basis for why we need to build a sense of urgency. During the Explore Phase, you will be sharing the urgency data from this chapter and making the case that real change is needed. You can also share the evidence from the next chapter, about why the Pathways model holds promise. This means it may take a number of meetings, emails, phone calls, and informal conversations to share information in a way that helps build a sense of urgency for change.

Teachers have learned that "discovery" is generally a better way to teach than simply delivering a lecture. This means that when someone discovers information for himself or herself, they internalize and remember it, and they can share it with others. So, perhaps you gather your prospective partners over a cup of coffee and look at information you have collected that challenges their assumptions or that confirms their concerns. Maybe you also ask them to present information that would build the case for change.

Structure your discussions with questions such as these:

◊ What do you think about this finding?

◊ Is this result good enough for now? What about for the long-term? What would be a satisfactory result, realizing that perfection is not a realistic possibility?

◊ What will happen for youth and our community if nothing changes?

◊ If we could find effective solutions, would this problem be worth addressing?

In the next chapter, we'll provide additional knowledge to utilize with your friends and colleagues during the Explore Phase. You'll learn about the evidence for the pathways model and strategies related to pathways.

The Academies of Nashville

Quick Look

In one of the nation's most visible and well-known Pathways System initiatives, the Academies of Nashville initiative in Tennessee involves all twelve of Metro Nashville Public Schools' large high schools organized as small learning communities/academies with supportive Pathway Programs, providing students with increased personalized attention and providing teachers with valuable collaboration time to continually improve curriculum and instruction and build meaningful relationships with students.

Program Details[63]

Metro Nashville Public Schools (MNPS) serve over 84,000 students in Davidson County, Tennessee, making it the nation's 41st largest school district in 2014-2015. The students of MNPS are diverse, and many face challenges typically associated with a large, urban area: poverty, limited English language proficiency, and special learning needs.[64]

In 2008, the MNPS secured federal funding to help eight high schools begin implementing small learning communities (SLC) that included career-themed academies, advisory programs, and freshman academies. In 2012, district leadership required the four remaining zoned high schools to begin transitioning to a small learning community/academy model. As of 2016, all twelve of MNPS' large high schools are organized as small learning communities, providing students with increased personalized attention and providing teachers with valuable collaboration time to continually improve curriculum and instruction and build meaningful relationships with students. In alignment with the SLC approach, MNPS has also implemented career-themed academies, now branded as the Academies of Nashville, to engage students in learning that is rigorous and highly relevant, preparing them for college-level academic work through the context of career interests.

Freshman Academies and Open Enrollment

Each school also operates a freshman academy within the larger high school and providing targeted supports such as the advisory program; freshman academies quickly led to greater attendance and engagement and decreased discipline problems among ninth grade students. Today, most of the district's freshman academies are divided into three or four student teams, each with their own name, identity, Instructional Team, and designated guidance counselor. During grade nine, students learn about the career academies offered within their high school and select the one they wish to pursue beginning in grade ten. Beginning with the 2015-16 school year, the student awareness and planning has moved to the eighth grade, with students enrolling in an academy in grade nine.

The district also has created an open-enrollment policy, where students are allowed to enroll in an academy outside of their zoned high school if there is space available. The school district has worked out an arrangement with the city's public transportation system to allow for bus passes provided at no cost to students enrolled in an academy outside of their zoned school.

Community and Business Engagement

A critical component of the Academies of Nashville is the extensive and systematic utilization of community and business partnerships.

One of the key initiatives, led by the Chamber of Commerce and the PENCIL Foundation, are efforts to form industry councils (now called partnership councils) organized around five broad career clusters representing the high schools' career academies. These councils work to develop and maintain ongoing relationships between businesses and schools and allow all schools to have equal access to support. The partnership councils are Arts, Media and Communications; Business, Marketing and IT; Engineering, Manufacturing and Industrial Technology; Health and Public Services; and Hospitality and Tourism. According to the Academies of Nashville 2013-2014 Annual Report, 278 businesses actively partner with the academies.[65]

Academy Coaches and Ambassadors

Each MNPS high school includes a trained academy coach who holds several important responsibilities. For example, the academy coach serves as the key point of contact for business, community, and postsecondary engagement and coordinates the implementation of advisory boards for the academies within the building. The academy coach also engages with students by training them to act as tour guides for study visits. These students are known as "academy ambassadors."

Career Development K-12

MNPS follows a comprehensive Career Development strategy in all schools across the district. All students in MNPS experience career development appropriate to their age and grade level. By the end of the elementary tier, students participate in career fairs, goal-setting, basic skill readiness, college/trade school visits, college-going vocabulary, critical thinking, life and social skills, and study/organizational skills. By the end of middle school, students engage in interest inventories, college night, financial and college planning, beginning a 10-year Career and Education Plan, job shadowing, mock job interviews, and resume building. At the high school level, in addition to the student's participation in academy classes, there are four experiential learning activities for every student: during the freshman year, students participate in a city-wide Career fair; during the sophomore year, students participate in a meaningful job shadow/workplace visit; during the junior year, students visit at least one college campus; and, during the senior year, students prepare a capstone project, which involves an internship experience or project mentorship.

Results

In a high-poverty school district, the Academies of Nashville has yielded positive initial outcomes, such as increased graduation rates starting at 58 percent and reaching 81.6 percent by 2015; increased daily attendance rates; increased English I proficiency from 48.6 to 63.7 percent over six years; increased Algebra I proficiency from 28.7 percent to 56.4 percent over six years; increased ACT test-taking test-performance; increased number of early college credits and industry certificates earned by students; increased enrollment in postsecondary education; and increased participation in career-related clubs and workplace experiences.[66]

The Academies of Nashville has gained national recognition and was visited by President Obama in January 2014. When requests for school visits became overwhelming, MNPS leaders began working in close partnership with the Nashville Ford NGL Hub (managed through Alignment Nashville) to organize annual fall and spring study visits. During these visits, participants experience guided high school tours, highly focused and informative breakout sessions, and keynote presentations from school and business leaders. To date, over 2,500 visitors from around the world have joined these well-organized and well-attended events.[67]

#

Chapter Three

The Power of Pathways - What the Research Indicates

"In God We Trust; all others must bring data." If you're like me, you maintain a healthy skepticism about any claim. That's why, before we get into the intimate details of what a Pathway System is, I want to share the evidence behind components of the Pathways System Framework™. We've already determined from the urgency data in Chapter 2 that maintaining the status quo isn't a viable option. But is there enough evidence to justify moving forward with a Pathways-focused reform agenda? I'll let you make that decision, but I believe the evidence for this is as strong as or stronger than for any other educational approach. But what you may observe is that the Pathways-focused approach actually incorporates the best of discreet educational innovations and incorporates them into a systems approach to gain synergy among the individual components. In this case, the end is greater than the sum of the parts.

Of course, if you're already convinced that we need a pathways-focused reform agenda, you can come back to the data later when you need it, and jump ahead to Chapter 4, where we begin to unpack the components of the pathways approach.

But for now, let's see if there really is compelling evidence for pursuing a Pathways System.

Section 1. Outcomes for Integrated Pathways Systems

A strong college-career pathway program places a focus on six priorities:

◊ Defining and developing Career and Life Readiness;

◊ Engaging all students in career development;

◊ Offering learners engaging and relevant Pathway Programs;

◊ Connecting students with employers and community-based learning experiences;

◊ Creating engaging and connected learning across the curriculum; and,

◊ Linking programs and services across secondary, postsecondary, and workforce systems.

The research basis for integrated Pathways Systems is strong and getting stronger with each new research study. In this section, we share findings from research on Pathways Systems that pull all of these core components together. In short, Pathways Systems have been shown to achieve the following outcomes:

1. Pathways Initiatives Help Improve Academic Achievement

2. Pathways Initiatives Help Increase Rigorous Academic Course Taking

3. Pathways Initiatives Help Improve High School Graduation Rates

4. Pathways Initiatives Help Develop Career Readiness Skills

5. Pathways Initiatives Help Increase Long-term Earnings

1. Pathways Initiatives Help Improve Academic Achievement

Career academies are a very structured version of the Career Pathways model. In most cases, a career academy has one just Pathway Program represented, but in some places, such as the Academies of Nashville, an academy might be a school-within-a-school and include several inter-related Pathway Programs.

The California Partnership Academies are structured so one program exists within each academy. CPA is an approach that offers a high school curriculum that combines academic and technical classes with real world applications. The academies work with local business and industry partners to offer student internships, field trips, and other work-based opportunities that connect the real world to classroom learning. At least half of an academy's incoming class

In 2005, the graduation rate in Metro Nashville Public Schools was about 62 percent; in 2015, after full-scale implementation of the Academies of Nashville model, the graduation rate was 81.6 percent.

of students must be considered "at-risk" by meeting three of four criteria: a disadvantaged economic status, irregular attendance, low motivation, or low achievement levels.[1]

In March 2007, a study conducted collaboratively by Connect-ED California Center for College and Career and the Career Academy Support Network at the University of California at Berkeley found that students in California's Partnership Academies were more likely to pass the California high school exit exam as sophomores and more likely to graduate from high school.[2]

When comparing more than 12,000 sophomores from 287 academies with more than 460,000 sophomores across California, the academy students enrolled in the California Partnership Academies passed the tests at higher rates than did the general state population. On the English language arts test, 84 percent of academy students passed, compared with 76 percent of students statewide. On the mathematics exam, 80 percent of academy students passed, compared with 74 percent statewide.[3]

The Mountain Home High Academies in Mountain Home, Arkansas uses a Small Learning Community/Academies approach for its entire grades 10-12 campus (see the profile later in the book). Since implementing the model, it has seen significant academic achievement improvements. The school's ACT score average is consistently higher than the national average. In 2011-12, MHHS students averaged 22 on the ACT test, compared to the statewide average of 20 and the national average of 21. Student proficiency on state exams has increased 20 percentage points in literacy and 58 percentage points in Algebra I.[4]

2. Pathways Initiatives Help Increase Rigorous Academic Course Taking

The California Partnership Academies students were much more likely to complete the 15 academic courses, or "a-g requirements," needed to be eligible for admission to California's public colleges and universities. The study found that 50 percent of graduating seniors in academies had completed the a-g requirements, compared with 35 percent of graduates statewide.[5]

3. Pathways Initiatives Help Improve High School Graduation Rates

Based on the same 2007 study conducted by ConnectED California and other partners, we know that graduation rates were better for those attending California Partnership Academies, with 96 percent of academy seniors graduating compared with only 87 percent of high school seniors statewide. This research also indicated that Hispanic/Latino and Black academy students, respectively, graduated at rates 12 and 15 percentage points higher than their counterparts in the general student population. White and Asian academy students also graduated at higher rates than their counterparts in the general student population, but these differences were smaller.[6]

In 2005, the graduation rate in Metro Nashville Public Schools was 55 percent. In 2015, after full-scale implementation of the Academies of Nashville model, the graduation rate was 81.6 percent.[7]

For more information about the Academies of Nashville, see the Promising Practice Profile.

4. Pathways Initiatives Help Develop Career Readiness Skills

The Linked Learning Alliance 2014 survey of 11th grade students indicates that students participating in a Pathway Program of Study were:

◊ 23 percentage points more likely than comparison students to report that high school prepares them for working with people in professional settings and for working in groups to achieve a shared goal

◊ 20 percentage points more likely than comparison students to report improved presentation skills

◊ 14 percentage points more likely than comparison students to report improved ability to conduct online searches to answer a question

◊ 12 percentage points more likely than comparison students to report growth in their belief that they could reach their goals with enough effort[8]

5. Pathways Initiatives Help Increase Long-term Earnings

The career academy model has a strong component of employer involvement, and the long-term economic effect for career academy graduates is profound. According to a long-term study conducted by the research organization MDRC, academy group members earned 11 percent more (about $2,100) per year than non-academy students.[9] The benefit to young men of color is particularly strong. Young black men who participate in a career academy earn 17 percent more after ten years than their peers who did not participate in an academy. Researchers hypothesize that giving these young men an early programmatic connection to the world of work and helping them develop social connections to business people allowed these career academy graduates, many of whom also went on to postsecondary education, to make a more successful transition to the world of work, and thus accelerated their earning capability.[10]

The MDRC study also indicates that academy students are 33 percent less likely to drop out of high school than their peers who attend traditional schools. In another study, data show that participation in a career academy can raise academic achievement in high school (as measured by GPA), decrease the need for postsecondary remediation in English, and increase the likelihood of at-risk students graduating from a university.[11]

Section 2. Outcomes for Pathways-Related Strategies

The Pathways System model works to a high level when its various components are aligned and working in tandem, creating additional synergies. Still, even when not part of a fully integrated Pathways System, individual components of the pathways model have demonstrated positive outcomes. Here is a summary of these research conclusions, followed by more detailed descriptions of the research findings.

1. Career Development

◊ Career Development Helps Students Make Better College Choices

◊ Career Development Leads to Better Postsecondary Achievement

◊ Career Development Helps Students Make More Intentional Choices

◊ Career Courses Help Improve Academic Achievement

2. Career and Technical Education

◊ CTE Strengthens Student Achievement

◊ CTE Credentials Boost Earnings

◊ CTE Course-taking Reduces High School Dropout Rates

◊ Career Technical Student Organizations Enhance Student Engagement

◊ CTE Students Develop Workplace-relevant Competencies

◊ Arkansas CTE Improves Achievement and Graduation Outcomes

◊ Massachusetts CTE Elevates Achievement

3. Employer and Community Engagement

◊ Employer Engagement Enhances the Student Learning Experience

◊ Employer Engagement Improves Student Motivation for School Achievement

◊ Employer Engagement Helps Students Makes Better Career Decisions

4. Structured Student Supports

◊　High School Support Strategies Help Prevent and Reduce Student Dropouts

◊　High School Supports (AVID) Strengthen College Retention and Persistence

◊　College Support Improves College Retention and Completion

5. Structured Programming

◊　Early College Drives Postsecondary Enrollment and Completion

◊　Guided Pathways in Community Colleges Strengthen Student Retention and Completion

6. Dynamic Teaching and Learning

◊　Active Learning Strategies Help Improve Student Achievement

◊　Integrated Math-in-CTE Strengthens CTE Student Math Skills

◊　Integrated Literacy-in-CTE Strengthens CTE Student Literacy Skills

◊　Postsecondary Integration of Academic and CTE Content Promotes Student Success

◊　Postsecondary Accelerated Developmental Education Student Success

I. Career Development

Given the fast-changing nature of our economy and workforce, career development is a more important aspect of our education system than ever before. A well-planned career development program encourages students to identify personal aptitudes and interests, explore career options through multiple methods, and make informed postsecondary education and training decisions. In the K-12 system, these efforts begin early, intensify in the middle school years, and become even more focused during high school. Furthermore, the parents or guardians of students are actively engaged in the process.

Career Development Helps Students Make Better College Choices

Exploring and planning for career choices can offer far-reaching personal and economic benefits. The 2007 study Job Congruence, Academic Achievement, and Earnings[12] determined that high school and college academic preparation is not the foremost predictor for an individual's future salary attainment and earning potential. After looking at nearly 100,000 graduates from approximately 300 colleges, researchers found that those who were both academically prepared and worked within their stated career field of interest consistently earned a higher wage than their peers working in careers of less or no interest to them, even when education levels were equal. This was attributed to the idea that when individuals enjoy their career, they naturally perform better and thus earn more money. The study also found that the amount of satisfaction between an individual's stated career interest and their career ambitions increased.

After looking at nearly 100,000 college graduates from approximately 300 colleges, researchers found that those who were academically prepared and worked within their stated career field of interest consistently earned a higher wage than their peers working in careers of less or no interest to them – even when education levels were equal.

Career Development Leads to Better Postsecondary Achievement

The Interest-Major Congruence and College Success Relation: A Longitudinal Study[13] by Tracey and Robbins found that career interest is directly linked to postsecondary school performance. After surveying more than 80,000 students enrolled in 87 colleges, researchers determined that students majoring within their stated career field of interest had better grade point averages, retention rates, and graduation rates than students majoring in a field of less or no interest to them.

Career Development Helps Students Make More Intentional Choices

Students do seem to benefit, both vocationally and academically, from participation in career courses. In particular, they seem to increase their knowledge of careers and their ability to make career-related decisions.[14] Based on longitudinal data and career theory, researchers determined that "effective education-career planning systems in middle schools help students become intentional in their educational and career development." Longitudinal national research data show that the choices middle school students make – and particularly academic choices – have a strong bearing on their educational and career development for decades to come."[15]

2. Career Technical Education

Not every pathway involves a Career and Technical Education (CTE) program, but many do. Thus, a high quality Pathways System must be built on the foundation of high quality CTE programs. Given the wide range of CTE delivery models across states, there is a good deal of variability in CTE student performance from one state to the next. But there is strong evidence that CTE, when developed and delivered through a high-quality program, can have a very positive impact on student performance and on future earnings potential. The investment in CTE also pays a dividend to each community that invests in developing the skills of its youth and adult learners who become productive, skilled workers and business owners.

CTE Strengthens Student Achievement

Research documents the positive impact of CTE in improving student academic achievement. The Southern Regional Education Board (SREB) found that in schools with highly integrated and rigorous academic and CTE programs, students demonstrate higher achievement in reading, mathematics, and science than do students in schools with less integrated programs.[16] An academic study engaging middle school students in a year-long career course revealed that students who participated in a career planning course did better academically than their peers who did not.[17]

SREB discovered that, in schools with highly integrated and rigorous academic and CTE programs, students demonstrate higher achievement in reading, mathematics, and science than do students in schools with less integrated programs.

CTE Credentials Boost Earnings

On the whole, individuals with bachelor's and more advanced degrees earn more annually and over their lifetime than individuals with shorter duration degrees. However, there is considerable variability in earnings depending on the market demand for particular skills and credentials. Thus, in many cases, individuals who have finished a certification or two-year degree program can earn more than someone with a longer-term education degree.

For example, research from the Georgetown University Center on Education and the Workforce indicates that:

◊   43 percent of young workers with licenses and certificates earn more than those with an associate degree

◊   27 percent of young workers with licenses and certificates earn more than those with a bachelor's degree

◊   31 percent of young workers with associate degrees earn more than those with a bachelor's degree[18]

CTE Course-taking Reduces High School Dropout Rates

A ratio of one CTE class for every two academic classes minimizes the risk of students dropping out of high school. For example, in a typical 24-credit high school experience, if a student took 13 core academic credits, 6.5 CTE credits, and 4.5 other elective credits, he or she would be more likely to stay in school than a student who took fewer CTE credits.[19]

Career Technical Student Organizations Enhance Student Engagement

Many CTE programs are offered in conjunction with a Career Technical Student Organization (CTSO), which offers students the opportunity to participate in leadership, community service, skills competitions, and skill development. Research from the National CTE Research Center discovered that the more students participate in CTSO activities, the higher their academic motivation, academic engagement, grades, career self-efficacy, and college aspirations.[20]

CTE students also performed better than non-CTE students on the ACT WorkKeys assessment for skills related to "reading for information"; reading for information is an important workplace competency that includes literacy skills such as ability to read and comprehend memos, letters, policies and bulletins.

CTE Students Develop Workplace-relevant Competencies

CTE students were more likely than their non-CTE counterparts to report that they had developed problem-solving, project completion, research, math, college application, work-related, communication, time management and critical thinking skills during high school. CTE students also performed better on the ACT WorkKeys assessment for skills related to reading for information, which is an important workplace competency that includes literacy skills such as the ability to read and comprehend memos, letters, policies and bulletins.[21]

Arkansas CTE Elevates Achievement and Graduation Outcomes

A 2016 report released by the Fordham Foundation explores the impact of CTE. The report, entitled Career and Technical Education in High School: Does It Improve Student Outcomes?, draws upon connected secondary, postsecondary, and workforce data from Arkansas that clearly demonstrates positive outcomes for students enrolled in a sequence of three or more CTE courses during high school.[22]

Among the key findings cited are:

◊ Students with greater exposure to CTE are more likely to graduate from high school, enroll in a two-year college, be employed, and earn higher wages.

◊ CTE is not a path away from college. Students taking more CTE classes are just as likely to pursue a four-year degree as their peers.

◊ Students who focus their CTE coursework are more likely to graduate high school by 21 percentage points compared to otherwise similar students, and they see a positive impact on other outcomes as well.

◊ CTE provides the greatest boost to the kids who need it most—boys— and students from low-income families.[23]

Massachusetts CTE Elevates Achievement

In Massachusetts, there are 27,000 students enrolled in the Commonwealth's 32 regional Vocational Technical Education (VTE) schools. Unlike many states that utilize a part-day regional CTE center model, the Massachusetts schools offer full-day education, covering both academics and career skills. Each VTE school is considered its own district, with a school committee, superintendent, and the ability to create its own curriculum and instructional policies and methods. Approximately half of the students' instructional time is spent in "shop," the applied learning of career skills. Because students attend the entire day, the schools are able to construct a much more integrated and connected approach to blending academics and VTE skill instruction. Because of this intensive approach to enhancing academic skills instruction, Massachusetts VTE students have seen significant increases in achievement during the past decade.[24]

In Massachusetts, even through there is an over-representation of students with disabilities at the regional vocational-technical education schools (24 percent at the VTE schools vs. 17 percent in general high schools), special-education students in the VTE schools are counted among those with the highest graduation rates in the state.

◊ The pass rate on the state standardized English test (MCAS) is approximately 96 percent, which exceeds the net normal average of 94 percent.

◊   The math MCAS pass rate for VTE students is approximately 92 percent, compared to 91 percent for the general student population.

◊   The achievement gap between vocational and comprehensive high schools closed by 27 percent over a six-year period in Massachusetts, even with the over-representation of students with disabilities.

◊   More than 50 percent of VTE graduates pursue post-secondary education.

◊   VTE annualized dropout rates are significantly lower than state averages, 1.8 percent versus 3.8 percent.

◊   Even though there is an over-representation of students with disabilities at the VTE schools (24 percent vs. 17 percent in general high schools), special education students are among those with the highest graduation rates.

◊   The graduation rate of special needs students in VTE schools is almost 20 percent higher than the state average for special needs students, 82 percent vs. 62.8 percent.[25]

3. Employer and Community Engagement

While employer engagement in education seems like a "nice to have," it doesn't appear to always be a "must have." Engaging employers and community partners involves a great deal of outreach and ongoing logistics. Without a clear win-win-win (students-educators-employers), it will be difficult to sustain.

In 2010, the UK-based Institute for Education Business Excellence compiled a summary of research on the ways in which students benefit from working with employers.[26] Evidence of the following impacts was identified:

The majority of high school students said that mentoring has affected their wish to do well at school. 75 percent said that mentoring had a lot of impact on their motivation for general subjects.

Employer Engagement Enhances the Student Learning Experience

Employer engagement typically makes learning more enjoyable and interesting for young people. In 2008, the Institute for Education Business Excellence administered a survey of young people who had recently completed a work placement experience which showed that 49 percent found it "very enjoyable" with a further 31 percent calling their experience "mostly enjoyable."[27] A 2010 survey by the consulting/research firm

KPMG of 151 primary and secondary school leaders indicated that 75 percent of respondents agreed or strongly agreed that the involvement of employers in pupil learning specifically has a positive impact on student attainment.[28]

Employer Engagement Improves Student Motivation for School Achievement

Professor Andrew Miller's from the University of Warwick conducted an in-depth investigation of the impact of business mentoring. He discovered that "the majority of students said that mentoring has affected their wish to do well at school. Three quarters of these said that mentoring has had a lot of impact on their motivation in GCSE (the UK designation for General Certificate of Secondary Education) subjects." In addition, the best engagements of employers have significantly enhanced pupil learning and enthusiasm for the subject of study.[29]

Employer Engagement Helps Students Makes Better Career Decisions

The Institute for Education Business Excellence also identified a series of studies indicating that those young people who have had the greatest chance to interact with employers at school are better positioned to make informed and confident choices about future careers. Evidence suggests that there is an important link between employer engagement in education and ultimate social mobility.[30]

4. Structured Student Supports

Support Strategies Help Prevent and Reduce Student Dropouts

The National Dropout Prevention Center/Network has identified effective strategies for dropout prevention, most of which are incorporated into a robust Pathways System.[31] These Pathways System strategies are the following:

◊ Active learning

◊ After-school opportunities

◊ Career and technology education

◊ Family engagement

◊ Individualized instruction

◊ Mentoring/tutoring

◊ Safe learning environments

◊ School-community collaboration

◊ Service-learning

High School Supports (AVID) Strengthen College Retention and Persistence

New research suggests that the college readiness system known as AVID, Advancement Via Individual Determination, may be effective in preparing underserved students to succeed in college.[32] The National Student Clearinghouse found that high school graduates from 2010 and 2011 who participated in the AVID program persisted through their freshman and sophomore years of college at a higher rate than their peers who were not in the program. Eighty-seven percent of the AVID students enrolled in the second year of college, compared with just 77 percent overall.

40.1 percent of the program group receiving intensive college support services (the ASAP program) earned a degree after three years compared with 21.8 percent of a control group. Early indicators showed increased enrollments and increased credit accumulation by the ASAP students over the control group students.

College Support Improves College Retention and Completion

The Accelerated Study in Associate Programs (ASAP), initially implemented by the City University of New York, provides a very structured set of student supports and definitive program organization to strengthen student retention and completion. The ASAP program features the following components:

◊ Full-time enrollment

◊ Early enrollment in developmental courses

◊ Quick graduation

◊ ASAP seminar

◊ Block-scheduled classes

◊ Comprehensive advisement

◊ Tutoring

◊ Career services

◊ Tuition waiver

◊ Free MetroCards

◊ Free textbooks[33]

According to an evaluation by the research organization MDRC, ASAP demonstrated the "biggest increase in graduation – by far – MDRC has found." Findings included the fact that 40.1 percent of the program group receiving ASAP services earned a degree after three years compared with 21.8 percent of a control group. Early indicators showed increased enrollments and credit accumulation by the ASAP students over the control group.[34]

Similar findings have come from the services developed and implemented through the Northeast Ohio Council on Higher Education, a coalition that strives to increase educational opportunity and attainment leading to postsecondary credentials and employment for all Northeast Ohio citizens. For postsecondary students, colleges in the coalition stressed the need for students to take 15 credits per semester in order to complete a four-year degree on time, and provided a variety of other in-school supports and counseling services. The results were particularly strong in Akron, where the number of degree holders increased by more than 20 percent, from 10,500 in 2010 to 12,260 in 2013.[35]

5. Structured Programming

Early College Drives Postsecondary Enrollments and Completion

The Early College High School model is built on a close partnership between K-12 and a partner institution of higher education, usually a community college. Students take a very structured set of courses, most of which count dually for both high school and college credits, and often, courses are taken on the college campus. In some cases, the program is co-located on a college campus. The structured courses allow many students to earn a two-year college credential shortly after graduation from high school, or to earn both a high school diploma and college degree concurrently.

Rigorous research on the impact of the Early College High School model shows that these schools can be much more effective for students than a typical high school in terms of college enrollment and attainment of a college

In a rigorous study of early college high schools, 81 percent of early college students enrolled in college (compared with 72 percent of other similar students). During the study period, 25 percent of the early college students were able to earn a college degree (mostly associate degrees), as compared with only 5 percent of the comparison students.

degree.[36] In a rigorous, but small-scale study of early college high schools, 81 percent of those students enrolled in college, compared with 72 percent of students in traditional high schools. During the study period, 25 percent of the early college students were able to earn a college degree (mostly associate degrees), as compared with only 5 percent of the comparison students.[37]

Guided Pathways in Community Colleges Strengthen Student Retention and Completion

Given the extremely low rate of completion in American colleges and universities, leaders in postsecondary education have been working to implement a variety of interventions to strengthen student retention and shorten the time to program completion. Since about 2010, a growing number of colleges offering both four-year and two-year degrees are implementing an approach called "Guided Pathways." Summarized by the Community College Research Center (CCRC), the guided pathways model builds upon and synthesizes a number of stand-alone interventions to enhance on-time completion, and the approach differs significantly from a typical community self-service "cafeteria" model, in which students choose from an abundance of disconnected courses, programs, and support services and have little support and guidance as they navigate toward a degree.[38]

CCRC has identified four components of the guided pathways model, as described below:

1. Academic Program Structure
◊ Programs are fully mapped out and aligned with further education and career advancement.
◊ Critical courses and other milestones are clearly identified in program maps.
◊ Student learning outcomes are specified across programs.
◊ Predictable schedules are set based on analysis of courses students need to progress on their plans.
◊ High school and other feeder curricula are designed to prepare students to enter college programs in particular fields.

2. New Student Intake
◊ Academic plans, based on program maps, are required.
◊ Students are required to enter exploratory majors and choose specific programs on a specified timeline.
◊ Assessment is used to diagnose areas in which students need support.
◊ Instruction in foundation skills is integrated into and contextualized with critical program courses.

3. Instruction

◊ Faculty collaborate to define and assess learning outcomes for entire programs.

◊ Faculty are trained and supported to assess program learning outcomes and use results to improve instruction.

◊ Supporting motivation and metacognition is an explicit instructional goal across programs.

4. Progress Monitoring and Support

◊ Student progress on academic plans is closely monitored, with frequent feedback.

◊ Students can see how far they have come and what they need to do to complete programs.

◊ Early warning systems identify students at risk of failing critical courses and initiate timely interventions.

◊ Advisors work closely with program faculty, with a clear division of labor for monitoring student progress.

As indicated in an implementation case study on the work of guided pathways at Miami-Dade College (MDC) System, institutional researchers believe that the guided pathways reform contributed to a 13 percent increase in the rate at which recent high school graduates enrolled directly at MDC in the 2013 fall term compared to the previous year. They also discovered that, for students who met with an advisor and developed a personal academic plan, retention was 8 percentage points higher than retention for incoming students who did not meet with an advisor.[39]

At Florida State University, the guided pathways model contributed to an increase in year-to-year retention rates for first-time-in-college freshman from 86 percent to 92 percent between 2000 and 2009. The four-year graduation rate increased from 44 to 61 percent, and the percentage of students graduating with excess credits dropped from 30 to 5 percent.

For college students that participated in a "guided pathways" initiative, there was a 13 percent increase in the rate at which recent high school graduates enrolled directly at Miami Dade College in the 2013 fall term compared to the previous year.

At Guttman Community College, a new institution in New York City that is fully utilizing the guided pathways model, its inaugural class of 2014 had a two-year graduation rate of 28 percent, and the college reported it was on track to meet its three-year goal of graduating 35 percent of its students. This completion rate contrasts favorably with the 13 percent median three-year graduation rate for community colleges in large cities.

6. Dynamic Teaching and Learning

Active Learning Strategies Help Improve Student Learning

Active learning is an umbrella phrase that captures project-based, inquiry-based, and problem-based learning and encompasses techniques that activate curiosity and engage the student more directly in framing the problem and finding the solution. There is a clear body of evidence that demonstrates that active learning techniques produce better results for students engaged in STEM-related courses.

According to his 2004 study "Does Active Learning Work? A Review of the Research," Michael Prince of Bucknell University cites more than 15 studies that discuss the benefits of problem-based learning. These studies suggest that students involved in problem-based learning develop more positive student attitudes did their traditionally taught academic peers. They also gain improved knowledge retention over traditional instruction and attain a deeper approach to learning.[40]

A research synthesis published by the National Academy of Sciences in 2014 evaluated 225 studies in published and unpublished literature comparing a traditional lecture style of classroom delivery with an environment in which instructors utilized some version of active learning techniques.[41] To test the efficiency or the efficacy of constructivist versus exposition-centered course designs, the researchers focused on the design of class sessions as opposed to laboratories, homework assignments, and other exercises. Specifically, they compared the results of experiments and documented student performance in courses with at least some active learning versus traditional lecturing. The active learning interventions varied widely in intensity and implementation and included approaches as diverse as occasional group problem-solving, worksheets or tutorials completed during class, use of a personal response systems with or without peer instruction, and studio or workshop course designs.

The take-away summary from National Academies says, "The studies analyzed here document that active learning leads to increases in examination performance that would raise average grades by a half a letter, and that failure rates under traditional lecturing increase by 55 percent over the rates observed under active learning." So if you have two classes of 100 students each, one featuring active learning and one featuring lecture only, you might see 20 of the active learning students fail vs. 31 of the lecture-only students, attributed solely to the teaching model.[42]

Academic and Technical Skill Integration

Dating back to the 1980s, federal funding for career and technical education[43] has highlighted the importance of holding students to rigorous academic standards and integrating those expectations into CTE coursework. Since the late 1990s, federal accountability systems have required CTE programs to report student acquisition of reading and mathematics competencies.

To investigate the question of whether integrating CTE and academic skills was truly effective, beginning in 2005, the National Research Center for CTE conducted a rigorous review of several models for integrating math and literacy in career technical education. The experimental studies discovered that these approaches make a clearly identified positive impact on student learning.

Integrated Math-in-CTE Strengthens CTE Student Math Skills

The Math-in-CTE research study tested the model of curriculum integration to improve CTE students' understanding of mathematical principles.[44] In this study, CTE teachers from agriculture, auto technology, business/marketing, health, and information technology programs were each paired with a math teacher from his or her region. Over the course of the school year, the teams met for 10 days to learn the process of math and CTE integration. Teachers identified the math content that was embedded in the CTE curriculum through a curriculum mapping process. Then they developed math-enhanced lessons that brought out the embedded content and helped clarify how this math matched up with concepts that were taught in the traditional classroom. During the school year, the CTE teacher scheduled and taught each of the math-enhanced lessons, with a total of 136 CTE teachers and over 3,000 students taking part in the study.

After one year of exposure to CTE classes that had enhanced math included, students performed significantly better on two tests, the TerraNova and AccuPlacer, than students in general CTE classes.

After one year of exposure to the math-enhanced lessons, the students in the experimental classrooms performed significantly better on two tests, the TerraNova and AccuPlacer. On the TerraNova test, the average experimental class scored at the 71st percentile of the average control group class, while on the AccuPlacer test, the average experimental group scored at the 67th percentile of its counterpart. Both findings represented statistically significant differences between students who received instruction based on the Math-in-CTE model, compared to those students who received the regular CTE curriculum. Following the research phase, the National Research Center began to provide extensive professional development on the process model to a number of states and school districts.

Integrated Literacy-in-CTE Strengthens CTE Student Literacy Skills

A related study carried out by the National Research Center for CTE is "Authentic Literacy Applications In CTE: Helping All Students Learn." This study sought to determine the impact of literacy strategies on the reading comprehension, vocabulary development, and motivation to read for students enrolled in CTE courses. The study took place in both pilot and full phases using a randomized group trial design. During the half-year pilot, researchers refined and tested reading models and instructional strategies to improve reading comprehension of all CTE students, even those who struggled with reading for content knowledge and solving problems.[45]

This project tested two adolescent literacy models, both of which train CTE teachers in the use of literacy comprehension strategies for use in CTE classrooms, although the models themselves are not limited in application to CTE. The MAX Teaching approach (an acronym for Motivation, Acquisition, and eXtension) is a framework of classroom learning activities that uses systematic reading, and writing before, during, and after reading. The MAX model also includes two additional components, operative learning and skills acquisition. This approach considers four components: motivation, strategies, literacy across the curriculum, and organizational support. A third approach test was called the CTE Reading Framework, although it was used in the pilot test but not in the full study. These refined strategies were then tested in a full-year study.[46]

Findings included the following:

◊   CTE students often favored hands-on learning and showed opposition to reading, while many CTE teachers lacked tools to successfully implement literacy.

◊   Student resistance to reading decreased when they understood the purpose of completing the reading or were more actively engaged with the assignment.

◊   By combining reading with an activity, the students were able to be more interactive. In doing so, they gained a deeper understanding of the highly technical terminology that is prevalent in CTE texts.

◊   Using reading strategies can help students develop the disciplinary literacy skills needed in their field. By supplementing readings with activities, teachers saw an improvement in grades and in the quality of students' work.

◊ CTE classrooms require students to read highly technical and diverse texts that can often be daunting to struggling readers. By implementing literacy strategies, these texts can become manageable for students. Teachers understood the positive outcome of using strategies and appreciated the structure the strategies provided.[47]

Postsecondary Integration of Academic and CTE Content Promotes Student Success

At the postsecondary level, usually when low-skilled adults want to enroll in a career-related Pathway Program, they often have to first take and pass a range of basic math and reading "developmental education" (or remedial) courses. For these students, the front-loaded academic skills courses add time and expense, and create a deterrent toward program completion. One data source indicated that less than 25 percent of students referred to developmental education completed a community college program within eight years, whereas 40 percent of non-developmental education students completed a program in that time frame.[48]

Washington State's Integrated Basic Education and Skills Training (I-BEST) program has become a national model for helping students who test into the lowest levels of development education earn a job-related credential. The program, which is offered at 34 state schools, is particularly effective for adult basic education students and English language learners. I-BEST students' curriculum combines basic skills education (math, English language, and writing) with college-credit, career-training courses.[49]

The program pairs two instructors in the classroom – one to teach professional/technical or academic content and the other to teach basic skills in reading, math, writing, or English language, enabling students to move through school and into jobs faster. As students progress through the program, they learn basic skills in real world scenarios offered by the college and career part of the curriculum.

For adult learning students who experienced an integrated basic skills and technical skills training program, they were more likely to earn a job-related credential, accumulate slightly more college credits, and stay with their program, and demonstrated stronger math achievement among students enrolled in developmental education

Research indicates that I-BEST students:

◊ Are more likely to earn a job-related credential than similar students not enrolled in the program

◊ Accumulate slightly more college credits than comparison students

◊ Are more likely to be retained in the program than comparison students

◊ Demonstrate stronger math achievement among students enrolled in developmental education[50]

Postsecondary Accelerated Developmental Education Increases Student Success

Other community colleges are also offering students developmental education courses at a faster pace by allowing them to take accelerated courses. At the Community College of Denver (CCD), for example, students in the FastStart program take two semesters of developmental education in one semester. The program, which covers math, reading, and English, provides students with extra support, such as a required weekly study group.

Nearly 40 percent of all students enrolled in CCD are in at least one developmental education course. With this new program, early data is showing that students in FastStart have greater academic success than developmental education students who are not in the program. For example, students in the intermediate developmental math course improved their passing scores from 33 percent to 72 percent.[51]

Social-Emotional Learning Leads To Cognitive Gains

According to CASEL, the Collaborative for Academic, Social and Emotional Learning, "Social and emotional learning (SEL) is the process through which children and adults acquire and effectively apply the knowledge, attitudes, and skills necessary to understand and manage emotions, set and achieve positive goals, feel and show empathy for others, establish and maintain positive relationships, and make responsible decisions."[52]

CASEL sponsored a four-year review of studies of school-based programs designed to foster children's social and emotional skills. In reviewing 700 studies on a broad range of school-based programs, the researchers selected 207 studies that met their quality criteria. According to the research review, by taking time out of the curriculum to teach students to manage their emotions and practice empathy, caring, and cooperation, their academic achievement could also improve.[53] The review also found that the SEL programs did, in fact, work in strengthening the social-emotional capacity of students. After the lessons, the students in the experimental groups were better behaved, more positive, and less anxious than their control group peers.[54]

Students participating in social-emotional learning programs also improved their cognitive learning, as measured by their grades and test scores. As a group, the students scored 11 percentage points higher than the comparison group students on a measure known as the "improvement index."

The analysis also showed that the positive effects persisted six months or more after the students took part in the programs, although to a lesser degree. The SEL lessons were even more effective when teachers, rather than the program developers or researchers, provided them. It would appear that SEL knowledge and content benefits from the ongoing relationship the students have with the teacher, and perhaps the teacher's ability to reinforce the concepts in everyday applications.

In the same way that all students benefit from some degree of explicit literacy skill instruction, all students would likely benefit from the explicit instruction in social-emotional skills. This way, all students develop a shared vocabulary and tools for self-management and relational skills. Even in middle class communities, large numbers of children are dealing with varying levels of personal and family stress, as well as negative pressure from other students. But for students living in concentrated poverty, where there are multiple risk factors, disruptions, and stress facing them every day, social-emotional learning would appear to be a non-negotiable, given the evidence that it positively impacts both social and cognitive outcomes.

Researchers discovered that, when providing supports for social-emotional learning, students were better behaved, more positive, and less anxious than the control group peers. These students also had improved their cognitive learning, as measured by their grades and test scores.

* * *

As is clear from this chapter, there is compelling evidence for both the comprehensive Pathways System model and for targeted strategies that can be incorporated into the Pathways Model.

In the next chapter, we'll go deeper as to what are the important factors in a high quality Pathway Program and learn more about the six components of Pathways Systems. I also answer a number of frequently asked questions that you are likely to also encounter as your garner attention for the Pathways approach.

P-TECH

Quick Look

P-Tech, Pathways to Technology Early College High School, is a new school model that provides a highly focused school experience, including a grades 9-14 curriculum leading to a concurrent high school diploma and postsecondary credential, free-to-student postsecondary tuition, and extensive employer mentoring and business involvement.

Program Details

P-Tech has engendered a tremendous amount of recognition and immediate replication since the 2011 opening of the original P-Tech in Crown Heights, Brooklyn, with the partnership of the New York City department of Education, the New York City College of Technology, the City University of New York, and IBM.[55] IBM's head of corporate social responsibility, Stanley Litow, previously served as the city's deputy schools chancellor, and was a major force in the design of P-Tech.

The school shares some features of a typical early college high school, in that the campus is co-located with a college setting, and the curriculum is designed to be seamless between the secondary level and the postsecondary level. But the P-TECH approach adds some intensive additional features.

First, the design of the model is very straightforward in its expectations— the 9th grade student is actively enrolling in a 5- to 6-year sequence of courses that will result in an associate degree as well as a high school degree. P-TECH is not a 4 + 2 program, meaning a high school program with the option of two more years of college. The curriculum is designed as a fully integrated 6-year pathway.

Second, business involvement is extensive in all aspects of the design. IBM engineers and technologists have been at the table from the start, helping design the Pathways, ensuring that the current thinking about workplace needs, skills, and business processes are embedded into the curriculum.

But business involvement also involves the company making a firm commitment that its employees will serve as mentors to students, so that every student has a business mentor from the first day of the program. The mentors work with students on academic support as well as career and life goal setting.

IBM (the original P-TECH business partner) makes a guarantee for the sites with which it partners, that successful graduates will be at the head of the line when it comes to reviewing them as potential job applicants. The commitment doesn't go so far as to guarantee an actual job, but it does give the students a good sense they will get a very fair shot. Building close relationships with professionals at the company will certainly position the graduates well in the job search phase.

Third, the program is offered at no cost to the student. Most dual enrollment programs and some early college programs do incur some transcription fees, as well as the cost of books, but this program does not.

Replication

The first school officially accepted its first cohort of students in September 2011. Given IBM's worldwide scale, replication of the model was built into the early design process. A how-to guide was quickly developed to assist with the development of other P-Tech schools, and IBM announced its intent to help replicate the model within New York as well as multiple other states and locations. A new P-TECH 9-14 School Model Playbook website provides extensive details about the model and replication opportunities.[56]

In 2013, Governor Andrew Cuomo came on board, directing that funds from the New York State Education Department be allocated to run a grant competition, to spread the model across the state. The first round of grants set aside funds for each of the state's economic development regions and was awarded in 2013; they were intended to be funded through 2020. Since then two more rounds of P-Tech awards have been made in New York alone.

And with the influence of IBM and other corporate partners, the model has now replicated to 40 schools in the U.S., with 70 industry partners, and is projected to grow to 60+ schools by 2016. The program is managed through the Aspen Institute.[57]

# # #

Chapter Four

Pathway Essentials

Section 1. Is There Education Reform Overload?

In the previous chapter, we reviewed a number of pathways-related initiatives and the positive evidence supporting their use. Most of these stand-alone interventions have emerged from four strands of research and practice in recent decades.

First, the *Education Reform Movement* covered a broad spectrum of efforts aimed at creating high expectations, more innovation, and greater accountability for results. To some degree, the modern movement of education reform was instigated by the *Nation at Risk* report in 1983.[1] Education reforms that emerged over the decades following this call to action included:

◊ State Standards and Model National Standards

◊ Teacher Evaluation Linked to Student Achievement

◊ Themed Charter Schools

◊ Career Academies (aka College and Career Academies)

◊ Linked Learning

◊ Early College High Schools

◊ Small High Schools

◊ Pathway Programs

◊ Tech Prep

Second, beginning about 1999, the *Career Clusters Movement* emerged out of traditional vocational education to encourage a broader approach to career development for all youth and to allow for more diversity of career-related pathways.[2]

Third, circa 2009, the *College Completion Movement* arrived to address the completion problem: many, many individuals began postsecondary education but wouldn't complete their education due to a number of factors. Both the Lumina Foundation and the U.S. Department of Education were key actors in moving this movement forward.[3] One practical outgrowth of the urgency raised through the College Completion movement was called "Guided Pathways," an attempt to make community college programs more coherent and give more active career and programmatic guidance to incoming students, particularly those who wanted to move quickly into the workforce.[4]

One of the most pernicious problems facing education is what we call "initiative overload" and the resulting "initiative fatigue."

In 2011, the *Collective Impact Movement* gained stature as a way to sustain innovation and collaboration among the many education and workforce training partners and social services agencies that worked within a community, helping them create more synergies and collective impact.[5]

Too much reform?

Each of the four education movements mentioned in the previous section offers tangible benefits for the youth and adult learners whom they impact, but they lack coherence.

One of the most pernicious problems facing education leaders is what we call "initiative overload" and the resulting "initiative fatigue." In this case, education leaders and policy-makers are simultaneously working on vastly different agendas. Here are some common examples:

◊ A new Pathway Program relating to a high-demand career like advanced manufacturing, engineering, or bio-medical science is launched.

◊ A requirement for career development and personal academic and career plans comes down from the school board or state board of education.

◊ Administrators create new professional development for teachers around project-based learning.

◊ The school board mandates a "one laptop per learner" district-wide initiative.

◊ New state academic curriculum requirements for reading and mathematics suggest better applications of learning, some of which indirectly relate to the needs and demands of the workplace.

◊ A few entrepreneurial teachers decide to incorporate community-based learning projects into their Pathway Program.

◊ The superintendent decides that an employer engagement strategy is

RANDOM ACTS OF IMPROVEMENT

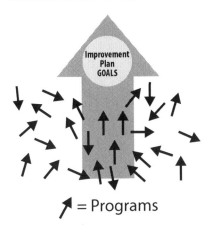

= Programs

needed, and urges some of the existing programs to actively recruit employer Advisory Committees.

◊ A local employer/industry committee wants to recruit students into their field of work, so they invite schools to send students on work-place tours.

◊ A community-service organization wants to help students, so they launch an initiative to help students learn interviewing skills, or they send volunteers into the schools to talk to students about the importance of rigorous course-taking to be truly ready for college and the workplace.

You might call these called "Random Acts of Improvement." Each initiative, on its own, is meaningful and well-intended, but it doesn't really connect to the other initiatives in the school or district. These programs end up competing with one another for attention and resources, instead of complementing another.

Sometimes we argue that American education needs more reform, but perhaps it actually needs less because few reforms are well-connected to each other. One could argue that we are "loving education to death" by smothering it with good intentions. Worse yet is what happens to these initiatives over time. Most of them die out prematurely because the next "big thing" takes away all the water and light that is needed for growth.

Suffice it to say, while these many initiatives are well-intended, they are not achieving a critical mass for the learners they are intended to help. The Pathways System can make the difference.

Section 2. The Pathways System Framework™

In a Pathways System, the unifying goal of all partners is to develop Career and Life Ready Learners, individuals who possess a mix of knowledge, learning skills, problem-solving and creativity, interpersonal skills, executive skills, career navigation skills, and civic engagement understanding that prepare them for success in postsecondary education, the skilled workplace, and citizenship.

For the purpose of building a Pathways System, the two basic terms of reference are a **Pathways System** and **Pathway Program** (used interchangeably with "Career Pathway." In this chapter, we start by revisiting the components of a Pathways System. We will also discuss the varied meanings people may bring to the broad term Career Pathway and provide a more specific, operational definition of a Pathway Program. We will also identify 12 elements that make up a robust Pathway Program.

Readers may occasionally hear other related terms such as Career Clusters, Career Fields, Career Technical Education (CTE), Career Technical Education Programs of Study, "Rigorous" Programs of Study, and Career Pathways, as defined in federal legislation. All of these interplay with Pathway Programs and Pathway Systems, so if they plan on going deep with this work, they will need to become familiar with what they mean. I have provided short explanations and website links for each of these terms in Appendix 1: Terms Related to Careers and Career Technical Education.

As noted earlier, a Career Pathway is a Pathway Program, whether it is offered to a youth or adult learner. At its heart, it is a sequence of courses developed around a theme. While the classroom instruction aspect of a Pathway Program is important, this is not enough. The learner also needs to experience effective career development, experiential learning (aka work-based learning) with employers and community partners, and engaging instructional practices. Further, these efforts need to be offered as seamlessly as possible among multiple organizational partners.

Developing an effective individual pathway will necessitate the development of these other components beyond classroom instruction. The advantage of building a Pathways System is you don't do the same development work over and over again for each pathway. Instead, you develop these assets systematically and with thoughtful intention. You create efficiencies, focus, and coordination among your initiatives, and you provide for a scalable approach to reach more and more learners and employers over time.

The Pathways System Framework™ is flexible enough to be used in multiple contexts.

◊ First, the Pathways System model should be used within an individual school to better structure the pathways work.

◊ Next, the model can also be used within a school district to enhance coordination and planning among multiple schools and the school district leadership.

◊ Third, the Pathways System model can be utilized on a regional basis, helping organize the work of multiple school districts, career technology centers, colleges, industry coalitions, businesses, and other partners.

Here is the definition of a Pathways System, followed by more detailed descriptions of each of the components of a Pathways System:

> *A Pathways System is the coordinated interaction of key components – career development, pathway programs, dynamic teaching and learning, employer and community engagement, and cross-sector partnerships – designed to develop a high level of career and life readiness among youths and adults in schools, colleges, workforce programs and the across the broader community, resulting in enhanced workforce competitiveness and community prosperity.[6]*

In building a Pathways System, you create a plan of action relating to each of the components of the Pathways System Framework™. These components are discussed below:

I. CAREER AND LIFE READINESS

In a Pathways System, the unifying goal of all partners is to develop "Career and Life Ready Learners," individuals who possess a mix of knowledge, learning skills, problem-solving and creativity, interpersonal skills, executive skills, career navigation skills, and civic engagement understanding that prepare them for success in postsecondary education, the skilled workplace, and citizenship. Pathways System partners work to ensure that learners are provided with experiences and education that lead to success in postsecondary education, economically viable career pathways, and personal effectiveness in a 21st century economy.

Career and Life Readiness (explained further in Chapter 5) includes the development of the following:

1. Applied knowledge
2. Effective relationships skills
3. Executive skills
4. Transition knowledge and skills
5. Career navigation skills
6. Financial literacy
7. Civic engagement

2. CAREER DEVELOPMENT

In a Pathways System, all learners experience meaningful and expansive career development. Their parents or guardians are actively engaged in the process. A well-planned career development program encourages students to identify personal aptitudes and interests, explore career options through multiple methods, and make informed postsecondary education and training decisions. In the K-12 system, these efforts begin early, intensify in the middle school years, and become even more focused during high school. Postsecondary partners utilize an aligned career development framework for their adult learners.

3. PATHWAY PROGRAMS

In a Pathways System, education and training partners coordinate the development of a range of Pathway Programs for youth and adult learners. A Pathway Program is a sequence of interconnected academic and elective classes revolving around a career or subject theme, integrated with experiential learning and close connections between secondary and postsecondary education, training, and/or apprenticeships. Pathway Programs are designed to address workforce needs and support the development of Career and Life Readiness knowledge and

> ### Program Exploration
>
> Students begin to explore available Pathway Programs while in middle school or early high school and then choose a program in which to enroll.

skills for each learner.

For K-12 systems, students begin to explore available Pathway Programs while in middle school or early high school and then choose a program in which to enroll. Each school offers Pathway Programs that address a variety of student interests as well as prominent career opportunities in the region and state. In systems that have regional career and technical education centers, their programs are linked to programs at the partnering high school, and when open enrollment options are offered, students may choose among multiple schools. Each Pathway Program is seamlessly connected to postsecondary education and/or a training program.

4. EMPLOYER-COMMUNITY ENGAGEMENT

In a Pathways System, employers and community organizations are essential partners, helping to provide students with skill development and career development experiences in the workplace and bringing highly relevant work-based activities, content, and role models into the classroom. The Pathways System outlines practical and specific ways that employers and community organizations can connect with students and impact each Pathway Program.

5. DYNAMIC TEACHING AND LEARNING

In a Pathways System, teachers and faculty members employ evidence-based instructional practices that are highly engaging, rigorous, and relevant to each Pathway Program. Teachers continue to implement important required curricular reforms, and all Pathway Programs emphasize problem-based, project-based, and inquiry-based learning. Targeted professional development, teacher externships, peer collaboration, and instructional coaching provide ongoing teacher support.

6. CROSS-SECTOR PARTNERSHIPS

In a Pathways System, partners from K-12 and postsecondary education, employer organizations, community volunteers, and workforce and economic developers are organized into a Pathways Partnership. The Pathways Partnership convenes a Leadership Team to provide strategic input on the direction and responsibilities of all partners involved in implementing the Pathways System. Together, they identify the key knowledge, skills, and attributes that help youth and young adults succeed in education, the workplace, and civic life. All aspects of the Pathways System reflect these shared career and life readiness goals.

Section 3. Discussing and Defining Career Pathways

In the introductory chapter, I shared the definition of a Pathway Program that we use in this book and in our work. Here it is again:

> *A Pathway Program is a program of interconnected academic and elective classes revolving around a career or subject theme. The program is integrated with experiential learning and close connections between secondary and postsecondary education, training, and apprenticeship. The program is designed to support the development of Career and Life Readiness for the learner, so that the individual can successfully enter and advance in a career path.*[7]

In Appendix 1, the legislative definitions of Career Pathway used in the Workforce Innovation and Opportunity Act (and likely to be included in the next iteration of the Perkins Act) are provided. The federal definition covers the same concepts that are addressed in our definition of a pathways system, but like typical legislative language, it has multiple descriptive phrases that somewhat integrate the concepts of an individual Pathway Program with components of a Pathways System.

Until recently, there wasn't any sort of nationally recognized definition of a "Career Pathway." While the federal definition of career pathway needs to be attended to, in program design and implementation, I believe it will be easier to use the complementary but distinct definitions of Pathway Program and Pathways System.

Meanings attributed to "Career Pathways"

In day-to-day conversation about education reform, it is common for people to use the words "career pathways" but to actually attach slightly different meanings to the term. I have identified at least three ways that the term "career pathways" is commonly used, each with slightly different implications.

First, a Career Pathway can be the **individual's identified area of interest**, that is, the career field in which the individual wants to learn about or pursue as a career. The interest can be somewhat vague and exploratory in nature (i.e. "my pathway is health services") or it can be more specific and focused (i.e. "my pathway is respiratory therapy").

Second, a Career Pathway (or career path) can be a way of thinking about **how an individual moves from one job to another to another within a career field**, advancing along a "Career Pathway." Particularly for the adult learner, the emphasis on a Career Pathway is not on just preparing the learner for an entry-level job, but it is also on clarifying how an individual might advance from one job to the next in a Career Pathway. The Career Pathway would be documented by the different jobs within the pathway, and the pathway would explain the skills, knowledge, experience, and credentials the individual needs to appropriately advance in that pathway.

Finally, the term "Career Pathway" can be a **short-hand reference for the education and training experience that the youth or adult learner experiences** (i.e. "they enrolled in a Career Pathway.") That's the way we use the term in this book, except that I apply the term "Pathway Program" to help clarify that this is an organized education and training experience. In this usage, we would say that a well-designed Pathway Program (the educational experience) would prepare an individual for entry into and advancement through a Career Path (the occupational experience).

Building from this definition, there are 12 elements to the Pathway Program organized around four themes: Program Structure, Program Leadership, Program Alignment, and Program Connections.[8]

Note: In Appendix 1, we share the references to other organizational program standards from which the NC3T model was synthesized and adapted.

Pathway Program Components

Theme I. Program Structure

1. *Pathway Program Interconnected Structure.* The Pathway Program is organized and presented to students as a well-defined, multi-year program of themed courses interconnected with academic core courses and experiential learning activities.

2. *Student Access.* The Pathway Program is accessible and marketed to students of varying achievement levels, including students who have Individualized Education Programs or limited English language proficiency.

3. *Cohort Scheduling.* Students in the Pathway Program are scheduled as a cohort and enrolled in as many classes together as possible.

Theme II. Program Leadership

4. *Pathway Program Advisory Committee.* The Pathway Program has an active employer-led Advisory Committee comprised of experts from the field; this committee reviews curriculum, expected skills and knowledge, and equipment, and it coordinates employer involvement in the program.

5. *Pathway Program Instructional Team.* The Pathway Program Instructional Team consists of teachers of career- or themed-classes,

teachers for academic subjects, and staff from the counseling department, collaborating to develop cross-curricular projects and lessons and to track and address the progress of students within their Pathway Program cohort.

Theme II. Program Alignment

6. *Alignment with Workforce Needs and Opportunities.* The Pathway Program is developed in alignment with in-demand careers that lead to family-sustaining earnings.

7. *Alignment with Standards.* The Pathway Program is aligned to applicable standards for Career, and Life Readiness, including relevant standards established by the state for academic knowledge and skills and technical skills.

8. *Alignment with Cross-Curricular Connections.* The Pathway Program Instructional Team identifies cross-curricular connections between required academic courses and career-themed elective courses, and it creates resources for cross-curricular and integrated instruction.

9. *Alignment with Industry-Based Credentials, Certifications, and Technical Skills Assessments.* The Pathway Program leads to clearly identified college credit, technical skill assessments, and/or industry-recognized certifications, delivered with support for students to know about these options and access them.

Theme IV. Program Connections

10. *Experiential Learning, Community-based Experience, and Student Leadership.* Pathway Program students participate in organized and relevant job shadows, mentorships, field trips, career-related clubs, and skill competitions, as well as in classroom based interactions with guest speakers and individuals coaching student projects. Students develop leadership skills through school- and community-based leadership experiences, volunteerism, and competitions.

11. *Seamless Connections with Postsecondary Institutions and Regional Career and Technical Centers.* The Pathway Program at a high school is aligned with and coordinated with Pathway Programs offered by postsecondary education partners and/or regional career and technical education centers. The high school-based Pathway Program is designed in collaboration with postsecondary partners to allow for a smooth transition of the student from secondary to postsecondary education and training, while minimizing duplication of content among programs.

12. *Postsecondary Dual Enrollment and Articulation Agreements.* The Pathway Program is supported by articulation agreements among high schools and postsecondary education partners, enabling students to earn dual, concurrent, and articulated credits and skills credentials at reduced or no-cost tuition rates for the secondary student.

Section 4. Frequently Asked Questions about Pathways

What are the benefits of offering Pathway Programs?

A Pathway Program provides learners with much greater relevance to their educational experience. They experience relevance through exploring careers, learning about their own aptitudes and interests, and learning about a career field that matches to those aptitudes and interests. Further, they experience relevance by seeing their career field in the real world through work-based learning and by working on projects connected to real employers and community needs. They also experience relevance by seeing the connectivity of all their classes when their teachers work in teams to coordinate learning experiences around the shared theme.

Students also experience strong relational connections. They experience connections with a group of students who share their interests, working with these same students over a period of time in a sequence of courses and extra-curricular activities. These connections give every student a sense of belonging and importance in their school and community. They experience connections with teachers who care about them as

> **Program Relevance**
>
> A Pathway Program provides learners with much greater relevance to their educational experience. Through greater relevance and relational connections, students experience engagement.

people and who help develop their knowledge and skills in their chosen area of interest. Finally, they connect with other adults – employers and community members – who are investing in them by providing work-based learning and community-based learning experiences and by modeling what effective adult life looks like.

Through greater relevance and connections, students experience engagement. They are engaged in the intellectual life of the school, they are engaged in the relational life of their school and community, and they are engaged with the developing their future selves.

What if students change their minds – will they be locked into a Career Pathway if they don't like it?

Most schools that offer Pathway Programs allow students to change their pathway (or the academy) at least one time during high school. Allowing students to change pathways multiple times does create some scheduling challenges because if too many upper level students are starting a new pathway and want to enroll in an introductory pathway course, they may block a younger student from taking a seat in that class. To make sure the introductory courses are accessible to the younger students, if a school allows students to change their career focus multiple times, those students should probably be enrolled in a "general studies" Pathway Program to complete their graduation requirements.

Offering a pathway exploration process during middle school or in ninth grade is a good strategy to minimize switching among pathways. If students have a substantive opportunity to "try out" a number of pathways for a few days or a few weeks, they are more likely to select a Pathway Program that is a good fit. Further, if all the Pathway Programs are centered around core transferable knowledge and skills, even if the school limits students' ability to switch among programs, they will graduate with a strong set of skills that will prepare them well for the next level of education and training.

Isn't it unrealistic to ask 15-year-olds to make a career decision?

Yes. Most youth at 15 or 16 years old are not mature enough and do not have enough life experiences to make a firm decision about a career. Of course, some youth are very focused early on toward a specific career. But these students are the exception.

A Career Exploration Decision

When students select a Pathway Program for their high school experience, they and their parents should understand they are making a "career exploration decision," not a "career decision.".

The pathways model does not ask a youth to make a firm career decision. Really, at the high school level, a Pathway Program is an applied form of career exploration. In fact, in the career development four-stage model shared in this book, the high school level is called "Career Application." When students select a Pathway Program for their high school experience, they and their parents should understand they are making a "career exploration decision," not a "career decision."

Are Pathways Programs just preparing students for low-skilled careers instead of college?

For many of us, the last time we saw a "vocational program" was when we ourselves were in high school. Much has changed in recent years, and programs have advanced significantly, reflecting changes in technology and the skills needed in the workforce. For example, school leaders and instructors make sure that automotive technician programs adapt as automotive technician jobs become more technology intensive, with computer analysis tools, hybrid engines, electric motors, and self-driving technologies requiring the use of both "head and hands."

Also, remember that Pathway Programs are not only based on CTE programs. Some Pathway Programs cover liberal arts, journalism, performing and fine arts, social service and social justice, and so on. Many high-tech, high-demand sectors like communications and information technology (computers), engineering, and advanced manufacturing fall under the CTE umbrella but still require a college degree. So, CTE already is focused on a range of occupations requiring varied levels of education and training. In fact, according to the U.S. Department of Education, about 75 percent of CTE students who take three or more related CTE courses already attend some form of postsecondary education and training.[9]

> ## Multiple Destinations
>
> To maximize student options, Pathway Programs should be designed with three potential destinations (or off-ramps and on-ramps): an industry-recognized certification, an associate degree, and a bachelor's degree..

Most importantly, effective Pathway Programs should be designed with three potential destinations (or off-ramps and on-ramps) for every pathway: an industry-recognized certification, an associate degree, and a bachelor's degree. This design makes the Pathway Program relevant for the learner who wants to go as quickly as possible into the job-market and also for the student who wants the full college-university experience. In a robust program, the multiple destinations force stronger program design so that students develop immediately marketable skills as well as the deeper theoretical knowledge needed for higher levels of education, career advancement, and leadership in their chosen fields.

Is preparing students for a job really the mission of schools?

From the earliest days of public education, two values have been in tension: the need for the individual to be a productive working member of society and the aspiration to prepare an individual for a life of learning and personal growth. Education has veered between two extremes: one extreme of tracking students into clearly delineated social and work roles and the other extreme of only focusing on general knowledge and skills, devoid of career relatedness.

At one extreme, education that doesn't prepare individuals with an eye to the workplace doesn't serve society well because a large number of individuals won't become self-sufficient members of society. The evidence in Chapter 3 suggests that our current k-12 education system has largely veered to the extreme that only focuses on general academic knowledge and skills. On the other hand, if education only has a short-term focus on training for immediate employment, the education experience becomes too narrow, and individuals won't be adequately equipped to adapt to the relentless pace of change that has become the norm in our society and workforce.

The tracking model of the mid-20th century made the mistake of training some youths for jobs rather than also preparing them to be learners who could better adapt to the changing needs of the workplace. In a regimented tracking model, only the college-track students were held to high expectations for abstract reasoning and problem solving. Other students were readied for low-skilled or semi-skilled employment, and when the world started changing rapidly in the 1970s and 80s, many of these workers couldn't adapt.

In today's economy, which values higher-level thinking and problem solving as well as marketable technological and business-process skills, we need a fusion of the two approaches. The two goals – developing adaptive learners and preparing for careers – are not incompatible, in fact they are both essential. Educators and the community-at-large are responsible for holding the two values in a productive tension.

What is the difference between Career Clusters, CTE, Career Pathways, and Pathway Programs?
As described in Appendix I, several of these terms have similarities, but each one has a specific, distinct meaning. Career Clusters are groupings of occupations and career specialties, and the primary purpose of the Career Clusters model is as an organizing tool for making decisions about curriculum, instructional design, and career development.

Career and technical education (CTE) means a sequence of educational courses that has a specific career focus and is designed to develop the academic and technical skills related to that career area. States that receive federal Perkins Act funding must apply the minimum definition of CTE used in the federal law and can also add tighter state criteria.

A Career Pathway is a broad term that may carry several meanings, depending on the user's intent. By federal definition, a Career Pathway is a course of study that also includes other elements that we associate with a

Pathways System, like employer engagement, career development, and student supports. The term Career Pathway can also mean, depending on the user's perspective: 1) an individual's identified area of career interest; or 2) the jobs and skills one holds as her or she advances from one job to another to another within a career field.

A Pathway Program (sometime referred to as a Career Pathway, a pathway, an academy, or a program of study) is a specific sequence of courses consisting of coursework, experiential learning (also known as work-based learning), and connections to postsecondary education and training. The Pathway Program is developed around a theme (not only a career), which can be a recognized CTE program or a broader theme like science research, social services, journalism and new media, etc.

What if our school is too small to offer stand-alone Pathway Programs or to separate students into cohorts?
The size of a school, large or small, does not affect its ability to implement a version of the Pathways System framework, since the framework components are relatively flexible.

One issue a smaller school faces is how many elective courses can be offered. The number of electives will be constrained by the need to have adequate enrollment in each course and to have enough qualified teachers.

The small school, with lower enrollment, will face the challenge of creating Pathway Programs that engage a sufficient number

> ## Pathways: A Flexible Model
>
> The size of a school, large or small, does not affect its ability to implement a version of the Pathways System framework, since the framework components are relatively flexible.

of students. To engage a critical mass of students for the pathway, which is about 20 to 25 students at each grade level, the small school may need to opt for "blended pathways" that bring together several concepts into a cross-disciplinary pathway, like "21st Century Business and Technology," which combines elements of business, marketing, information technology, and graphic media.

Finally, a small school, particularly one that is rurally isolated, may need a different approach for business engagement. The school may not find many employers and they may not always match up to the pathway focus the school has chosen. As such, the student connections to those employers may need to focus more on broad employability skills rather than on career specific skills. This smaller number of employers may require an integrated employer advisory committee rather than individual committees for each Pathway Program.

What if we don't have enough time to teach career competencies with all the demands for standardized testing?

A review of state academic standards, many of which are derived from the Common Core State Standards, will show that the standards are solid and reflect many of the knowledge and skills needed for workplace and life success. But the academic standards alone do not fully reflect the attributes that will make someone successful in college, career, and life. That's why we urge every Pathways Partnership to define, adopt, and implement a holistic definition of Career and Life Readiness, similar to the definition we offer in Chapter 5 of this book.

Testing, however, is another matter. Assessment of student learning is a natural and valuable part of instruction, and standardized assessments bring needed uniformity of expectations, particularly for students who have historically been held to low expectations and low levels of instruction. Still, accountability systems that only focus on academic testing will skew instruction and use of school-time to focus narrowly on core content. Instead, a balanced accountability system should also take into account the whole range of college, career, and life readiness. Until national and state policies are modified accordingly, visionary educators will need to swim against the tide of testing requirements to ensure that students are the focus of teaching and learning and that testing is recognized as part of the equation but is not the only thing that matters.

Aren't academic teachers and faculty members really supposed to focus on teaching subject matter, not take responsibility for career and life readiness?

From the earliest days of American secondary schools, teachers have been isolated as subject matter experts, teaching specialized courses. Given the complex nature of subject matter, subject experts are essential, and the resulting delivery model is understandable.

A Student-focused Culture

School and college leaders will need to build a new culture, one that recognizes the value of specialized content but also that challenges every teacher to take responsibility for developing the student as a person - with the transferable knowledge, skills, and competencies he or she will need for success.

The downside, however, is that the whole student gets lost in this equation.

Teachers have been conditioned to think that their only responsibility is to teach subject matter. School and college leaders will need to build a new culture, one that recognizes the value of specialized content but also that challenges every teacher to take responsibility for developing the student with the transferable knowledge, skills, and competencies he or she will need for success.

At the high school level, teachers in pathways-oriented schools often talk about the camaraderie and renewed sense of passion they discover when they work together on behalf of students. But undoubtedly, some teachers and college instructors see themselves as only concerned about their field of expertise. Teachers and instructors with this narrow mindset should be encouraged to develop a broader conception of their job, but if they refuse to accept the new role, they should be encouraged (or required) to move on to another school or another career.

If most of the jobs of the future haven't even been created yet, why should we focus on career preparation?
This notion about how most of the jobs of the future haven't been invented yet is an education myth, with no basis in reality.

Occasionally, I talk to educators who attended a conference and heard a speaker say, "The jobs our children will do haven't even been invented yet." As an example of how this idea gets circulated, consider a researcher and writer who focuses on learning technology. She included a statement in her 2011 book purporting that "65% of children entering grade school this year will end up working in careers that haven't even been invented yet."[10] Next, this interesting factoid was picked up and re-stated by another opinion writer in the New York Times.[11] The problem is, this "fact" has no basis in research. While there is a citation hearkening back a well-researched U.S. Department of Labor report from 1999, FutureWork, the "fact" is nowhere to be found in the actual report.[12] This is a telling example about how interesting, but inaccurate statements, make their way onto education futurist circuit. The danger with statements like "the jobs of the future haven't even been invented yet," is that they subtly undermine the will to help students really prepare for the future.

Let's take the statement at face value and look at a practical example: The 65 percent of the youth who started 1st grade in 1999, and the jobs they could pursue in 2016. At the time of this writing, those first graders would be about 23 years old. Look at the vast number of jobs that today's young workers hold – retail, information technology, manufacturing, marketing, sales, finance, accounting, teaching, public safety, the skilled trades. These jobs did exist in 1999. So, the statement on its face is not credible.

Yes, there will be some jobs in the future that don't exist right now. As an example, take a look at the jobs a group of futurists at the education organization CST have come up with:

◊   Robot Counselor (a technology advisor for the purchase of personal robotics),

◊   Rewilder (a natural scientist),

◊   Garbage Designer (engineer specializing in waste management),

◊   Neighborhood Watch Specialist (drone operator for domestic & neighborhood security)

◊   Simplicity Expert (an organizational specialist)

◊   Healthcare Navigator (a health social worker/advisor)

◊   Nostalgist (an interior designer working with elderly patients)

◊   Telesurgeon (surgeon using robotic surgery)

◊   Solar Technology Specialist (energy specialists that manage solar power installations and systems),

◊   Aquaponic Fish Farmer (Agriculture specialist integrating fish farming and crop management). [13]

The titles for the jobs of the future are fun to think about. But looking more closely, most of them are simply outgrowths of current industry sectors that utilize emerging technologies. And even if they do emerge as new jobs, it doesn't mean that the vast preponderance of current jobs are going to disappear. More realistically, as we've seen in fields like automotive technology, and heating/ventilation/air conditioning, marketing, and countless others, current jobs are going to morph into new forms through the relentless advance of technology, particularly with robotics, artificial intelligence, and the "internet of everything." Devices and jobs related to them are going to be increasingly digitized, automated, and connected through wireless internet connectivity. Jobs of the future won't be entirely new careers, but they will generally require a higher level of knowledge and sophistication to carry out. That's why Pathway Programs should include career-focused content but also be designed develop transferable Career and Life Readiness skills and knowledge.

Is this pathways movement driving a corporate agenda in our schools?
The American economy is incredibly diverse, with a range of businesses that are small, medium, and large in scale. Sweeping generalizations about a "corporate agenda" are difficult to substantiate. While about 30 percent of jobs still require a high school education or less, and many large corporations

employ these workers, education should not be focused on these types of jobs. Rather, the jobs that are growing and are providing good earnings are those that require thinking, problem solving, and communications skills accessed by a range of postsecondary education and training. The Pathways System approach engages the full range of employers from small or medium companies to larger global corporations but still recognizes the larger societal goal of preparing all learners with career

> ## Balancing short-term vs. long-term employer needs
>
> The Pathways System approach engages the full range of employers from small or medium companies to larger global corporations but still recognizes the larger societal goal of preparing all learners with career, and life readiness.

and life readiness. The concerns of educators worried about a "corporate agenda" should be addressed, but those concerns should not cut off rational discussion about the need to build a Pathways System.

* * *

In this chapter, we have defined Pathway Systems and Pathway Programs and we have addressed common questions about the pathways model. In subsequent chapters, we will delve into the details of building a Pathway Program, and then how to develop a Pathways System.

But remember, the primary purpose of education is to prepare individuals for further education and training, career, and life success. This involves re-orienting education around the individual instead of only focusing on the structure and the system. Next, we need to be clear about answering the question – what does it actually mean to be ready for career and life success?

Volusia County Schools Career Academies

Quick Look

Since the early 2000's, Volusia County Schools have launched dozens of career academies integrated into the district's ten high schools. During the 2014-2015 school year, nearly 4,000 students were enrolled in a career academy. Covering a wide range of career clusters, career academies include agriscience, aviation, communications, health services, marine science, and engineering, among others.

Program Detail

Volusia County Schools, located in Central Florida (Daytona Beach), serves over 61,000 students; it is the state's thirteenth largest school district and one of the largest employers in the county. The district's student population is diverse with 61 percent eligible for free or reduced lunch and over five percent participating in the English as a Second Language program.

Approximately 20,000 students attend the district's ten high schools, and about 4,000 students are enrolled in the district's 34 career academies. Through its controlled enrollment policy, students attend schools within their geographically assigned zone but may request a zoning variance to attend a school of their choice.[14] Covering a wide range of career clusters, career academies include agriscience, aviation, communications, health services, marine science, and engineering.

Career academies include rigorous academic courses integrated with career-related electives. Students learn about multiple careers within their career cluster through classroom instruction, guest speakers, and relevant school clubs or organizations. Students participate in work-based experiences such as field trips, job shadows, and internships. Career academy teachers also have opportunities to participate in a workplace externship experience, and by doing so they receive professional development credit.

Generally, each high school offers a choice of at least three career academies. However, students may request a zoning variance to attend a school offering the career academy of their choice. Should a student cease enrollment in the out-of-zone career academy, he or she is required to return to the assigned zoned school. Transportation to out-of-zone schools is not provided.

Advisory Committees and Career Connection Cadre

For each career academy, there is an Advisory Committee comprised of community and business volunteers who provide curriculum and equipment recommendations, help connect students with workplace learning opportunities, assist with organizing externships for teachers, and offer support in finding business members to act as guest speakers. Overall, Advisory Committees ensure the quality and relevance of each career academy.

There is also a county-wide group called the Career Connection Cadre, involving about 60 organizations, including the Volusia County Schools, Daytona State College, the region's Workforce Development Board, and members of the business community. Members of The Career Connection Cadre offer opportunities for job shadowing, internships, and cooperative education placements. A designated member from each career academy's Advisory Committee participates in The Career Connection Cadre partnership.[15]

Dual Enrollment

Each career academy has postsecondary dual enrollment and industry certification options. In addition, students may take approved dual enrollment courses on a part-time basis during or after school and throughout summer breaks. Dual enrollment students do not pay registration, matriculation, or laboratory fees; textbooks are also provided at no cost.

Marketing the Career Academies

For several years, each career academy was individually responsible for marketing its program to students, but as the number of academies grew, the approach proved inefficient. In 2006, Volusia County Schools began offering Career Academy Showcase events.[16] All middle school students and their families are encouraged to attend and thousands do so each year. To help students and parents navigate through the vast amount of information, a High School Showcase guidebook is presented at showcase events.

During showcase events, every career academy hosts a table, staffed by academy teachers and students, to provide more detailed information about its program and to sign up students and parents to attend open house events at the individual schools. During the career academy registration process, students may apply to three academies, indicting their order of preference. Although the district is unable to guarantee placement, most students are enrolled in one of their three selections.

Results

Volusia County Schools, beginning with its earliest efforts to connect rigorous academic content with career relevance, has created a strong model of high quality and well-organized career academies spanning a wide range of career clusters. Student achievement results from the class of 2015 illustrate the positive outcomes of the district's career academies:

◊ 185 students earned an AA/AS degree through dual enrollment

◊ Students took 5,428 dual enrollment courses

◊ Students earned 4,801 college credits through dual enrollment

◊ Students who took the ACT (American College Test) increased by 11 percent, and the average composite score exceeded the state average

◊ 3,417 students enrolled in Advanced Placement courses[17]

#

Chapter Five

Career and Life Readiness

Section 1. The Value of Defining Career and Life Readiness

Steven Covey, in his widely regarded book, *The Seven Habits of Highly Effective People*, said that the first habit of effectiveness is to "Begin with the End in Mind." Thus, a critical first step in creating an effective Pathways System is to begin with "the end in mind."[1]

Isn't the true "end in mind" of our education and workforce efforts to develop a person (a learner) who has the capacity for competitive skilled employment and who can be an asset to their employer, family and community? Thus, the true aim of education is to develop individuals who are ready for postsecondary success, for career success, and for life success, a learner who is Career and Life Ready.

Most readers would agree that this Career and Life Readiness is an appropriate goal for education. Why then is it a happy accident when a young person graduates fully ready for career and life success? Why is it that so many young people complete high school but are seriously lacking in some of the knowledge, skills, and attitudes that contribute to true success.

First, of course, we know that the family is indispensible. In a positive family environment, many of the key values and interpersonal competencies children need are introduced and reinforced. We also recognize, that in a very diverse society, some parents are poorly equipped with these competencies, and thus, aren't passing them along to their children.

Most schools don't have a clear definition of what Career and Life Readiness is. Even if we want to take a broader perspective of developing the whole person, not just teaching curriculum, if we don't have clear target for Career and Life Readiness, we can't hit the mark.

Whether we like it or not, schools – as the one common social institution that every youth experiences – have an important role in upholding and strengthening, or instilling for the very first time, key values and competencies that students will need for career and life success.

The challenge is that our schools are governed by an accountability system that is almost 100 percent targeted on the teaching and testing of content knowledge. A further challenge is that most schools (and their larger communities) don't have a clear consensus around what exactly Career and Life Readiness is. If we want to take a broader perspective in our schools and communities of developing the whole person, not just teaching curriculum, we must have a clear definition of Career and Life Readiness in order to hit the mark.

The Pathways System is meant to be a synergistic collaboration of multiple partners, including families who need to be on the same page in defining the end in mind. That's why each partner should be involved in exploring, adopting and taking action upon a definition of a Career and Life Ready Learner.

To help bring clarity to this effort, this chapter briefly summarizes the background of state and national discussions to define college and career readiness, identifies some missing pieces from these discussions, and then brings all the pieces together into an integrated model definition. Finally, I suggest some steps you can take to adopt and implement a holistic definition for use within your Pathways System.

Section 2. The Origins of "College and Career Readiness"

As noted in Chapter 1, for much of the last 125 years of American public education, high school students were categorized as either "college-bound" or "career-bound" because that reflected the nature of our workforce: lots of medium- and low-skilled workers and a small number of individuals in the management class. Beginning in the 1970s, the U.S. workplace has been requiring more of its front-line workers, including responsibility for analysis, technology use, communication skills, problem solving, and team management. The line between management and the workers has blurred significantly. While the workplace has evolved dramatically, college readiness and career readiness are still thought of as two separate concepts in most schools.

This began to change around the year 2000, when some education policymakers started using the term "college and career ready" as one phrase rather than two. The work in this direction was led by three organizations: Achieve, Inc., the Fordham Foundation, and Education Trust, through an effort called the American Diploma Project. They released their joint report *Ready or Not?* in 2004.[2] In the research phase, the analysts looked at jobs that led to a career path with advancement opportunities and a decent income, regardless of the level of post-high school education and training required. They looked at jobs for which a worker could enter the field with just a high school diploma (but which still offered good wages and career path), as well as jobs requiring two-year degrees and four-year degrees. Their analysis determined that all these "good careers" required a high level of reading, communication, and mathematical thinking. They also determined that the level of academic skills for either direct career entry or college entry was about the same. Thus, they determined that "college readiness" and "career readiness" (tightly defined to exclude low skill jobs) were the same, as it pertained to core academic skills. (By the way, the report did not address other competencies relating to college readiness or career readiness, which are addressed later in this chapter.)

Based on this finding, *Ready or Not?* argued for a higher level of expected academic skills and knowledge for all high school students. This line of research led to efforts by several states to create a preferred rigorous high school course of study, like Indiana's "Core 40," which would be required or strongly recommended as the default curriculum for all high school students.

To be clear, the findings of the report did not claim that all jobs would require a higher level of proficiency in reading, writing, and mathematics because there were and would continue to be a multitude of low-skilled jobs. But for skilled careers leading to decent earnings, the report postulated that the skill sets needed for college and career were more or less the same. This finding has been the subject of some respectful wrangling among education researchers, advocates, and policymakers, mostly over how to operationalize this conclusion. For example, one question has been whether or not all high school students should be encouraged to enroll in a particular level of mathematics, such as Algebra 2.

What is important to note, however, is that for the first time, college AND career readiness began to be used as a unified term.

The Common Core

The work of the American Diploma Project evolved as Achieve Inc. signed up states willing to align their state academic standards to the newly identified college and career readiness expectations. Next, this effort morphed into developing a set of model academic standards – the Common Core State Standards – with guidance from Achieve Inc. and endorsements by the Council of Chief State School Officers and the National Governors Association.

From its early stages of development, the Common Core was specifically designed to encourage a more applied approach to academic skills, and it broke with previous model academic standards by encouraging reading non-fiction sources, emphasizing oral communication and listening skills, and applying literacy strategies across the curriculum, not limiting application of language skills to the English and Languages Arts department of the high school.[3]

This state-led effort resulted in the construction of model academic standards for reading and mathematics that were designed to prepare students for success in higher education and future careers. When released in June 2010, the K-12 standards had these strengths:

◊   they were aligned with college and work expectations;

◊   they included rigorous content and application of knowledge through higher order skills;

◊   they built upon strengths and lessons of current state standards;

◊   they were informed by top-performing countries, so all students were prepared to succeed in our global economy and society; and

◊   they were evidence and/or research-based.[4]

Despite the great consternation that arose over the Common Core in some states, a large percentage of states have adopted some version of academic standards that approximates the Common Core, even though some of these states have declined to adopt the aligned testing regimen.

Section 3. Beyond Academic Skill Readiness

The core academic standards adopted through the Common Core movement only address literacy, math, and science. Moving beyond the general academic skills defined in the "college and career readiness" definitions, other researchers have

---

Understanding College Readiness

College readiness is more than academic knowledge and skills. Rather, it includes four distinct dimensions of college readiness: cognitive strategies, content knowledge, learning skills and techniques, and transition knowledge and skills.

worked to delve more deeply into the competencies needed for college, career, and life success.

David Conley of the University of Oregon is one of the most cited authorities on the specific issue of college readiness. He states, "A student who is ready for college and career can qualify for and succeed in entry-level, credit-bearing college courses leading to a baccalaureate or certificate, or career pathway-oriented training programs without the need for remedial or developmental coursework."[5]

Conley's work suggests that college readiness is more than academic knowledge and skills. Rather, he identifies four distinct dimensions of college readiness:[6]

1. **Key cognitive strategies.** Students must be able to formulate, investigate, and propose solutions to non-routine problems; understand and analyze conflicting explanations; evaluate the credibility and utility of source material; think analytically and logically; and exercise precision and accuracy.

2. **Key content knowledge.** The content knowledge expectations all identify a "manageable set of big ideas, concepts, and organizing principles that form the structure of each academic subject area, and they emphasize the importance of students making connections among the big ideas. This focus on the structure of knowledge enables students to scaffold their understandings in a way that post-secondary education can build on."[7]

3. **Key learning skills and techniques.** Students must be able to "plan their time carefully… study independently in informal and formal study groups… [and] seek help from academic support services."[8]

4. **Key transition knowledge and skills.** Students need to know how to choose a college, apply to college, seek financial aid, and adjust to college life. This process "requires a tremendous amount of specialized knowledge. Students must learn to match their personal interests with college majors, understand financial aid programs, apply and submit necessary information on time, and understand that college will be different than high school."[9]

To help students become college ready, Conley recommends the schools adopt four principles:

◊ Create and maintain a college going culture.

◊ Align the core academic program with college readiness standards.

◊ Teach key self-management skills.

◊ Prepare students for the complexity of applying for college.

Defining Career Readiness Beyond Academic Skills

While the Common Core and other state standards focus on the literacy and math skills needed for a career, the standards do not address in any significant way the skills and knowledge that employers often talk about, like work ethic, teamwork, and customer service. As I like to say, "there are some skills that help you get hired: and there are some skills, if you DON'T have them, get you fired."

For over 20 years, a variety of organizations have been articulating these workplace-related skills. Some people call them "soft skills," supposedly because they represent the "soft side," interpersonal and intrapersonal, perhaps difficult to measure. But the term "soft skills" seems to diminish their critical importance. Other alternative terms used are "employability, workplace, professional, and personal success" skills.

In his remarks about career and technical education in 2011, Secretary of Education Arnie Duncan recognized the importance of these skills. He said, "there's a lot of talk these days about the need to boost college and career readiness. But the truth--and I include myself here--is that most of the current debate is about college readiness. *Too often, career readiness is an afterthought* (emphasis added). A career ready student must also have knowledge and skills that employers need from day one. This means having critical thinking and problem-solving skills, an ability to synthesize information, solid communication skills, and the ability to work on the team."[10]

Developing Consensus on Employability Skills

Several times in meetings I have attended with educators and employers to discuss career readiness, I have heard an employer say, "I just want someone who shows up on time and looks me in the eye." While this statement reflects a real frustration the employer is experiencing, the reality is that an employer really wants much more than just timeliness and interpersonal confidence. And for educators to change their practice, they need much more specificity on what employers need and expect.

Fortunately, there are many useful resources to bring clarity to this question – What exactly do employers want and need?

The modern era discussion about employability skills began in 1990 with the U.S. Department of Labor's SCANS Report (Secretary's Commission on Achieving Necessary Skills). The Commission was charged with the task of determining the skills that young people need to succeed in the world of work.[11]

Next, about the same time that Congress enacted the No Child Left Behind Act in 2001 with its narrow focus on accountability for reading and math skills, a new organization was formed called the Partnership for 21st Century Skills, now known as the Partnership for 21st Century Learning (P21).[12] P21, guided by dozens of multi-national companies and business organizations, articulated a broad set of knowledge and skills – so-called "21st Century Skills." While P21 members recognized the value of core academic skills, they also called for a broader set of competencies, summarized into what they dubbed the "4 C's":

◊ Critical thinking and problem solving

◊ Communication

◊ Collaboration

◊ Creativity and innovation

Since that time, these efforts have been followed up by numerous other employer groups, educational organizations, professional associations, and governmental entities, all of which have identified key workplace and employability skills. In fact, there is an overabundance of reports, all with slightly different terminology.

To develop a common language and understanding about employability, the U.S. Department of Education Office of Career, Technical and Adult Education (OCTAE) commissioned the creation of the Employability Skills Framework (the Framework). This effort brought together a diverse group of the career and technical education (CTE), adult education, workforce development, and business organizations to work out the details of the Framework.

According to the Employability Skills Framework, employability skills are general skills that are necessary for success in the labor market at all employment levels and in all sectors. These skills, which may be taught through the education and workforce development systems, fall into three broad categories:

◊ **Applied Knowledge** – the thoughtful integration of academic knowledge and technical skills, put to practical use in the workplace.

◊ **Effective Relationships** – the interpersonal skills and personal qualities that enable individuals to interact effectively with clients, coworkers, and supervisors.

◊ **Workplace Skills** – the analytical and organizational skills and understandings that employees need to successfully perform work tasks.

A full explanation of these categories can be found at the Employability Skills Framework site (http://cte.ed.gov/employabilityskills/). Given the high quality of this resource, I have included it my integrated definition of Career and Life Readiness, explained in the following section.

Missing Competencies Needed for Career and Life Readiness

The Employability Skills Framework is comprehensive and provides an excellent synopsis of the skills needed for workplace success but is not intended to address every competency that a youth needs to be ready for life. By design, that framework is just focused on employability.

Other competencies should also be considered that a well-rounded person will need in order to have a productive and meaningful life (family and citizenship).

Through our analysis of multiple resources, and looking beyond just postsecondary education and the workplace, we see four missing elements: Career-Specific Technical Skills, Career Navigation Competencies, Financial Literacy, and Civic Awareness and Commitment.

We offer these competencies, as follows:

1. **Career Specific Technical Skills.** This represents the career-specific knowledge and competencies that are particular to a specific occupational field. These can either be acquired through a specialized education and training program, an apprenticeship program, on-the-job training, or some combination of all of these.

2. **Career Navigation Skills.** Career Navigation skills involve knowledge about the economy, knowledge about career fields and occupations, and self-awareness, all of which are required for a youth or adult to choose a career focus, identify necessary education and training, develop marketable career-specific technical skills, secure employment in a career field, grow and advance in a career, and make successful transitions to a different career field when necessary.

3. **Financial Literacy.** Financial literacy is the knowledge, skills, and mindset to take individual responsibility for personal economic well-being, including finding and applying financial information, setting financial goals, saving, utilizing financial services, meeting obligations, and building and protecting wealth. I utilize the competencies identified by the Jump$tart Coalition© for Personal Financial Literacy.[13]

4. **Civic Engagement Skills.** Civic engagement skills involve the knowledge, skills, and mindset to take individual responsibility for executing the rights and responsibilities of citizenship in a participatory democracy.

So, given the significant overlap in thinking about core academic skills, employability skills, college readiness, and the additional competencies we have identified, I believe it makes sense to eliminate the overlap between the models, and create one integrated framework for Career and Life Readiness. That is what we present next.

Integrated Framework for Career and Life Readiness

Career and Life Readiness means that an individual has the knowledge and skills necessary for success in postsecondary education, economically viable career pathways and personal effectiveness in a 21st century economy.

> ### An Integrated Definition
>
> It makes sense to eliminate the overlap between the models for employability, college readiness, and life readiness, and create one integrated framework for Career and Life Readiness.

Readiness includes the following elements:[14]

1. Applied Knowledge

Applied knowledge is the thoughtful integration of academic knowledge and technical skills put to practical use in the context of postsecondary education, training, apprenticeship, and the workplace.

Applied academic skills enable individuals to put skills based on academic disciplines and learning to practical use in education and workplace settings. These skills include the following:

◊ Reading
◊ Writing
◊ Using mathematical strategies and procedures
◊ Using scientific principles and procedures

Critical thinking skills enable individuals to analyze, reason, and solve problems. These skills include the following:

◊ Thinking critically
◊ Thinking creatively
◊ Making sound decisions
◊ Solving problems
◊ Reasoning
◊ Planning and organizing

Career-related technical skills enable individuals to enter an occupation or career pathway that requires an entry-level of knowledge and skills specific to that occupation or career pathway. These skills and knowledge include the following:

◊ Understanding key concepts about the occupation, career pathway, or industry

◊ Understanding essential safety concepts and procedures relative to the occupation or career pathway

◊ Using tools and technology applications proficiently as required for entrance into the occupation or career pathway

2. Relational Skills and Personal Attributes

Relational skills and personal attributes are interpersonal skills and personal qualities that enable individuals to interact effectively with instructors, fellow students, clients, coworkers, supervisors, and family members.

Interpersonal skills enable individuals to collaborate as a member of a team or work independently, as appropriate, communicate effectively, maintain a positive attitude, and contribute to the overarching goals of the workplace. These skills include the following:

◊ Understanding teamwork and being able to work with others

◊ Responding to customer needs

◊ Exercising leadership

◊ Resolving conflicts through negotiation

◊ Respecting individual differences

Personal Qualities contribute to effective relationships in college, career, and life. These skills include the following:

◊ Demonstrating responsibility and self-discipline

◊ Adapting and showing flexibility

◊ Working independently

◊ Demonstrating a willingness to learn

◊ Demonstrating integrity

◊ Demonstrating professionalism

◊ Taking initiative

◊ Displaying a positive attitude and a sense of self-worth

◊ Taking responsibility for professional and personal growth

3. Executive and Communication Skills

Executive and communication skills are the analytical and organizational skills and the understandings that learners and employees need to successfully perform tasks and carry out projects in postsecondary education, training, apprenticeship, and the workplace.

Executive skills are the abilities individuals need to successfully accomplish work tasks. These skills include the following:

◊   Managing time and other resources effectively
◊   Understanding, evaluating, and using a variety of information
◊   Communicating effectively with others in multiple formats (speaking, writing, listening)
◊   Understanding relationships among the components of a system
◊   Applying information technology appropriately and effectively

Technology use skills enable individuals to successfully perform work tasks in today's technology-driven workplace. These skills include the following:

◊   Understanding technology and its appropriate uses
◊   Using technology efficiently and effectively

Systems thinking skills enable individuals to successfully perform work tasks by understanding relationships among the components of a system. These skills include the following:

◊   Understanding and using systems
◊   Monitoring systems
◊   Improving systems

Communication skills enable individuals to successfully perform work tasks by communicating effectively with others in multiple formats. These skills include the following:

◊   Communicating verbally
◊   Listening actively
◊   Comprehending written material
◊   Conveying information in writing
◊   Observing carefully

Information use skills enable individuals to successfully perform work tasks by understanding, evaluating, and using a variety of information. These skills include the following:

◊ Locating information
◊ Organizing information
◊ Using information
◊ Analyzing information
◊ Communicating information

Resource management skills enable individuals to successfully perform work tasks by efficiently and effectively allocate resources. These skills include the following:

◊ Managing time
◊ Managing money
◊ Managing materials
◊ Managing personnel

4. Career Navigation Skills

Career navigation skills enable individuals to understand and act on information that affects their career objective. This knowledge allows them to grow and advance in a career and make successful transitions to a different career field when necessary. These skills include the following:

◊ Developing an awareness of personal temperament, skills, and strengths

◊ Maintaining knowledge of industries, sectors, careers, and pathways

◊ Recognizing cross-sector transferable knowledge and skills

◊ Utilizing postsecondary search, application, and financing resources

◊ Developing the ability to network with others, perform job searches, complete job applications, interview for a position, and negotiate a job offer

◊ Managing a personal career path

◊ Engaging in ongoing skill development

5. Postsecondary Transition Knowledge and Skills

Postsecondary transition knowledge and skills enable individuals to choose a college, apply to college, seek financial aid, and adjust to college life.[15] These skills include the following:

◊ Analyzing postsecondary options based on career awareness

◊ Assessing postsecondary costs, financing options, and return on investment

What is career and life readiness?

Career and Life Readiness means that an individual has the knowledge and skills necessary for success in postsecondary education, economically viable career pathways and personal effectiveness in a 21st century economy. Readiness includes the following elements:

1. **Applied Knowledge**—the thoughtful integration of academic knowledge and technical skills, put to practical use in the context of postsecondary education, training, apprenticeship, and the workplace.

2. **Effective Relationships**—the interpersonal skills and personal qualities that enable individuals to interact effectively with instructors, fellow students, clients, coworkers, supervisors, and family members.

3. **Executive Skills**—the analytical and organizational skills and understandings that learners and employees need to successfully perform tasks and carry out projects in postsecondary education, training, apprenticeship, and the workplace.

4. **Postsecondary Transition Knowledge and Skills**—the knowledge and skills needed to choose a college, apply to college, seek financial aid, and adjust to college life.

5. **Career Navigation Skills**—the knowledge about the economy, career fields and occupations, and self-awareness that is required for a youth or adult to choose a career objective, identify necessary education and training, develop marketable career-specific technical skills, secure employment in a career field, grow and advance in a career, and make successful transitions to a different career field when necessary.

6. **Financial Literacy**—the knowledge, skills, and mindset to take individual responsibility for personal economic well-being, including finding and applying financial information, setting financial goals, saving, utilizing financial services, meeting obligations, and building and protecting wealth.

7. **Civic Engagement**—the knowledge, skills, and mindset to take individual responsibility for executing the rights and responsibilities of citizenship in a participatory democracy.

◊ Applying for admission and matriculating to postsecondary education

◊ Developing an individual role and identity in the postsecondary setting

◊ Advocating for personal needs with administration and faculty

6. Financial Literacy

Financial literacy enables the individual to take responsibility for personal economic well-being.[16] These skills include the following:

◊ Finding, evaluating, and applying financial information

◊ Setting financial goals and planning how to achieve them

◊ Developing income-earning potential and the ability to save

◊ Using financial services effectively

◊ Meeting financial obligations

◊ Building and protecting wealth

7. Civic Engagement Skills

Civic engagement skills enable the individual to take responsibility for executing the rights and responsibilities of citizenship in a participatory democracy. These skills include the following:

◊ Developing awareness of major national, state, and local governance issues

◊ Understanding the timelines and trends of U.S. and global history and the implications of history pertaining to current civic issues

◊ Committing to civic involvement, including voting

◊ Participating in civic-minded and community-based organizations

Section 4. Developing, Communicating, and Implementing the Career and Life Readiness Definition

Some of the attributes of Career and Life Readiness lend themselves to measurement through written assessments, but many will be clearly difficult to directly evaluate in a completely objective, non-biased way. Perhaps general proxy assessments are sufficient (some scores on assessments and some measure of activities, experiences, and effort). Most important is that the students themselves understand and buy into the importance of these attributes and attitudes and that we create a way for them to set goals, keep score, and monitor how well they are progressing.

In order for school districts and/or communities to turn this compilation of competencies into a usable tool, they should develop and adopt a definition of Career and Life Readiness and utilize it among all stakeholders by communicating the definition and bringing value to it.

Developing a Definition

There are essentially two approaches to developing a definition: top down or consensus building. I suggest using a modified consensus building approach. Don't start from scratch and recreate the work of dozens of committees and commissions over the last 30 years. Instead, have your Pathways System Leadership Team convene a short-term committee to gather and explore college and career readiness resources, such as the Integrated Framework for Career and Life Readiness.

Stakeholders may include teachers, students, family members, guidance counselors, local postsecondary faculty and leaders, regional employers, workforce development agencies, and community organizations.

> **Getting Youth Buy-in**
>
> The most important factor in defining Career and Life Readiness is that we help our youth understand and buy into the importance of these attributes and attitudes, and that we create a way for them to set goals, keep score and monitor how well they are progressing.

Create a draft definition using the integrated definition I have shared here and/or other tools and models. Using in-person focus groups and online survey tools, ask multiple stakeholders to share their perspectives and feedback to further refine the definition. Share and refine as many times as you believe are necessary to get as close as possible to consensus. Make sure, however, to give strong credence to the perspective of the employer community, and try to avoid loading the definition down with education jargon. If the document sounds like an academic exercise that is too technical or esoteric, it will lose its value as a general audience communication and engagement tool. You want this definition to speak to students, parents, teachers and employers. It needs to make sense to all these key stakeholders.

Using all this gathered input, present a revised definition to the Pathways Leadership Team for adoption as the definition that will used by all partners within the Pathways System Initiative.

Communicate the Career and Life Readiness Definition

Facilitating a consensus building activity around Career and Life Readiness is the first and most important step in communicating the definition. Once the definition has been adopted, additional action steps for communication can include the following:

◊ Create (or have students create) visually appealing written materials (brochures, posters, and web-sites).

◊ Present the definition to all stakeholders at appropriate meetings and invite meaningful discussion regarding how the definition may impact their organization's engagement with students.

◊ For teaching and guidance staff, review the definition during a professional development or faculty meeting. Request that participants form small groups and discuss questions such as these:

  ◊ How might this definition impact my instruction?
  ◊ How might this definition impact the relationship I build with students?
  ◊ How can I present this definition to my students?

◊ Conduct a similar presentation at a school board meeting or parent forum event and include business/community partners. Encourage teachers to discuss the definition with students.

◊ Include the definition on all communications, including websites, brochures, and reports.

◊ Post the definition in the school lobby, offices, and classrooms.

◊ Provide definition posters to local employers, workforce agencies, and community organizations.

◊ Refer to the definition throughout strategic planning and when new initiatives are under consideration.

◊ Review the definition periodically and make changes as needed.

Bringing Value and Importance to the Definition

Unless the definition of Career and Life Readiness is implemented into the school in a meaningful way, it will have little or no impact. There are two important activities to bring value: integrate the definition into the taught curriculum and bring recognition opportunities to students who excel in exhibiting Career and Life Readiness.

Integrating into the School Culture

Working in mixed teams of administrators, teachers, and guidance counselors, develop a student self-assessment rubric based on the definition; list the desired attributes and outcomes of a Career and Life Ready student. This rubric may be distributed and explained to all eighth grade students who will use it to assess their personal development of the attributes throughout their high school years.

Recognizing Student Attainment of College and Life Readiness

Here is a good story of how a school district is bringing visibility and value to their definition of Career and Life Readiness.

The Greater Clark County Schools in south Indiana have developed a college and career readiness program called PRIDE. The acronym means the following:

◊ Persistence – persevere through challenges, problem solve

◊ Respectfulness – access and serve others, possess a positive attitude, communicate clearly

◊ Initiative – self-start, think critically

◊ Dependability – demonstrate academic readiness, reliability, responsibility, and teamwork

◊ Efficiency – be organized, punctual, and self-managed.

The district began the initiative at the high school level and invited students to voluntarily seek a College and Career Readiness Work Ethic Certificate based on the PRIDE attributes. To earn the certificate, the students commit to demonstrating a level of achievement in nine domains, based on the PRIDE criteria. This includes a commitment to carry out six hours of community service; maintain a good GPA, attendance rate, and discipline; and be certified by three teachers as to attainment of all nine components. In the graduation ceremony, the students who earn the certificate receive visible recognition through a brightly colored sash. Further, the district also recruits local employer partners to provide hiring consideration and increased pay to Work Ethic certificated students. The program is now being adapted and applied at the middle and elementary school levels, so similar incentives for work ethic and recognition exist at each education level. The message about the broad aspects of college and career readiness are communicated and taught in Grades K-12.[17]

How do we teach Career and Life Readiness Skills?

In recent decades, in the literacy field, research has proven the value of direct (or explicit) instruction for some students. Even for students who can intuitively learn to read with fluency, understanding the structure and rules of reading can further strengthen their reading skills. A similar strategy may be brought to bear in developing Career and Life Readiness competencies. Some students obviously are wired with the well-developed social and emotional skills needed for school and workplace success. But even for students who have strong natural social-emotional intelligence, some of these competencies – like career navigation, financial literacy, and transitions knowledge – will be easier to understand with an explicit instructional model.

There are several important approaches to consider:

1. Offer a stand-alone course like "Freshman Academy" or "Career and Life Development." Similar programs like AVID (an acronym for Advancement Via Individual Determination), which explicitly build many of these competencies for students from first-generation college-going families, have demonstrated positive outcomes for students.[18]

2. Embed Career and Life Skills in a regularly scheduled Student Advisory period, a frequently scheduled version of a home-room.

3. Most importantly, gain teacher and counselor buy-in and embed a common approach to Career and Life Readiness expectations in every classroom. As a school-wide approach, students will realize, "Wow, they really mean it, and perhaps I better start paying attention!"

* * *

With a shared definition of Career and Life Readiness, the focused purpose of education, the school-based team with its employer and community partners is ready to begin designing a high-quality Pathway Program that is explicitly designed to facilitate the full range of Career and Life Readiness attributes for students. In this next chapter, you will discover the key elements of such a Pathway Program and the action steps you can follow to develop new or strengthen existing Pathway Programs in your schools.

Part II

How to Design a Pathway Program and Pathways System

Chapter Six

Designing the Pathway Program

Section 1. Strategic Decisions

In Chapters 2 and 3, we explored the reasons for a Pathway System and the evidence of its value. In the previous chapter, we created a definition for Career and Life Readiness that all stakeholders can endorse and work together to implement on behalf of youth and adult learners. In this chapter, we focus on how to develop a Pathway Program.

First, there are a number of strategic decisions to make, such as the number of Pathway Programs, the scale of implementation across the school, and the timeframe for implementation.

Strategic Decisions about Pathway Programs

Establishing a Campus-based Leadership Team

Each Pathway Program needs direction, attention, support and accountability from leaders who themselves are held accountable for program success. To oversee the creation, implementation, and continuous improvement of a Pathway Program, the school executive should designate one or more individuals with administrative authority to take responsibility for the Pathway Program through both the design and implementation phases. This is the Campus-based Leadership Team, and it is based within each school, giving overall guidance and accountability for the Pathway Program on that campus.

Note: Other leadership and organizational teams are discussed in Chapter 7, which relates to Pathways System design beyond the individual school.

Web-Based Resources

You can visit our website to access case studies, background resources, and forms and templates related to the Pathways Program work referenced in this chapter. Visit **www.powerandpromiseofpathways.com**.

Addressing Key Workforce Skill Gaps

Utilizing regional workforce information, the Campus-based Leadership Team should assess the overall enrollment and completion of current and proposed Pathway Programs against current and projected workforce needs. The Campus-based Leadership Team needs to identify if there are key programs that are missing from the current offerings and make a priority for program start-ups to address these needs. For example, some of the highest demand sectors across the country that are underserved in the high school settings are information technology, health care, engineering, and advanced manufacturing.

School-wide Approaches to Pathways

Early on in the process of exploring Pathway Programs, the Campus-based Leadership Team needs to answer the following questions:

◊ **How pervasive will Pathways be within the school?** Will we build the capacity to serve all students within a pathway model, or will many students continue to enroll in a general high school course of study? In the scenario where programs are not utilized by all students, the Pathway Programs are often referred to as either "pocket academies" or "pocket pathways," meaning they are inserted into one "pocket" of the school's portfolio of offerings. In contrast, if the Pathway Programs are meant for all students, they are usually referred to as "wall-to-wall."

◊ **How many Pathway Programs can the school accommodate?** For a three–year structure (grades 10-12), assume 75 to 90 students per program spread across three grades of the school while freshman students participate in a freshman seminar and freshman academy program. If you run a four-year Pathway Program, assume 25 to 30 students per grade level, for a total of 100-120 students. A school of 900 students in grades 10-12 could offer about 10 Pathway Programs.

◊ **Will the school offer a collection of stand-alone Pathway Programs, or organize the Pathway Programs into larger academies?** Academies, which could each contain a number of related Pathway Programs, could include the following:

  ◊ Academy for Health and Human Services
  ◊ Academy for Advanced Technology
  ◊ Academy for Arts, Entrepreneurship, and Humanities

◊ **Will the school offer a Freshman Experience or Freshman Academy** (or correlated 8th grade activity)? The Freshman Academy or Freshman Experience is a way of organizing 9th grade students into common classes, and even a separate section of the building, as a strategy to ease the transition into high school and facilitate exploration of the school's Pathway Programs.

◊ **How quickly will the transition happen?** This is an especially important decision if the school intends to go "wall-to-wall." Launching all Pathway Programs simultaneously has advantages, as fewer students will remain in a general track while others enjoy the benefits of the Pathway Programs. Still, on the side of quality implementation, starting small with a few programs for the more willing Instructional Team members has benefits because the first Instructional Teams will gain experience that they can share with the subsequent Instructional Teams.

By the way, there is no empirical evidence I know of that favors the all-at-once approach versus the phase-in approach, so the Campus-based Leadership Team will need to exert its judgment about what local factors are most important. Either way, the program start-up phase should not drag on beyond three years, or it will be difficult to manage the competing cultures of Pathways and general track students.

Addressing the false dichotomy between college-prep and career-prep

Perhaps you are expecting possible backlash from the affluent parents of "college-prep" students. The school should anticipate confusion and legitimate concerns and address them early in the outreach process. See the Frequently Asked Questions in Chapter 4 for ideas on how to address common questions. Whatever you do, if you choose to phase in Pathways or allow students to opt out of Pathways, you should work with all your staff to ensure that non-Pathways students are not labeled as the "college-prep" kids, while the students

> ## No College-Prep vs. Career-Prep Labels
>
> Whatever you do, if some students are allowed to opt out of pathways, those students CANNOT be labeled as "college-prep" kids while the students enrolled in the Pathway Programs are referred to as the "career prep kids." These kind of labels will undermine your pathways programs from the start.

enrolled in the Pathway Programs are labeled "career prep" students. If you allow this to happen, higher performing students and their parents will shun Pathway Programs and continue to opt for a generic high school program. Rather, ensure that all of your programs allow students to take the essential university-admissions required academic courses. The California Partnership Academy model, for example, encourages students to take university-admissions required courses, and a larger percentage of those students take the university-recognized courses than the student population at large, showing that blending a career-prep and college-prep mindset is possible.

Assure parents that Pathway Programs will fully prepare their children for college and university while also enhancing their children's education with an applied learning experience. Instead of being on the defensive, communicate that some of the Pathway Programs offer, in fact, more rigorous and better preparation than a traditional high school program because they offer long-term culminating projects and experiential learning (similar to college projects and college co-op). Also, as you design the mix of Pathways offerings, make sure to create some Pathway Programs that require, or at least strongly suggest, higher levels of math and science course-taking and that explicitly include Advanced Placement courses.

Determining how to collaborate with part-day career centers

Your region may already have a career and technology center that provides CTE services to students on a part-day basis. Center-based programs often offer equipment-intensive labs (like culinary, construction, automotive) and programs that could not be offered and fully enrolled by just one school. These programs are an excellent resource, but they have a long history of operating as a distinct alternative to the generic high school curriculum. To incorporate the career and technology center (tech center) into a seamless Pathways System requires fresh thinking from leaders of both the tech center and the school district.

> ## Integrating the Career Technology Center
>
> Incorporating the career and technology center (tech center) into a seamless Pathways System will require fresh thinking, from leaders of both the tech center and school district.

Here are some factors to consider. First, the part-day tech center model usually serves one group of students in the morning and another group of students in the afternoon. Some tech centers offer their programs in three levels (typically for 10th, 11th, and 12th graders) and some offer the programs in just two levels (typically for two consecutive years beginning in 10th or 11th grade).

In working with a part-day tech center, you need to design some Pathway Programs that connect into the offerings of the center, perhaps serving about 20 percent of your upper level students. The large majority of your pathway programs will be run entirely within your home school environment, serving the other 80 percent. For the tech center programs that are offered as three levels, students should begin attending the tech center as 10th graders. But for the programs that are only two levels and two years in length, how do you handle this? You could have students begin the tech center experience in 10th grade and finish in 11th grade and then participate in a dual-enrollment, entrepreneurship, or extensive work-based learning experience in 12th grade. Or alternatively, your school could provide a 10th grade preparatory experience (such as principles of leadership and entrepreneurship) and then have students enroll in the technology center for 11th and 12th grades.

A somewhat sticky situation may arise if the tech center offers a program (like computer science or pre-engineering) that is not hugely expensive and that you believe should be offered within your high school. If all the local feeder schools followed your lead and withdrew students from the tech center, that program at the tech center would fold. Without constructive discussion and fair warning, this switch might be perceived as unfair to the tech center.

A final consideration is the potential use of the tech center facilities to extend the experience of the high school-based programs, but just on an occasional basis or for a time limited project or learning unit. In many places, tech centers are under pressure to increase the number of program completers taking two or more levels of a program, and often there is an accountability system incentive driving program completion. Because of this pressure, directors of technical centers may resist opening up the labs for students who will not be program "completers." Still, the very expensive labs and specialized equipment can be a valuable part of a local Pathway Program. If the tech center leadership wants to position the center as a local resource, then a creative, collaborative solution can be reached. However, if the leaders of either the tech center, the school district, or both, see themselves as competitors fighting for students and the dollars that follow students, they will miss the opportunities for creative solutions, and ultimately, programs and students will suffer.

In summary, changing to a Pathways System approach will require a change of perspective but will also allow for creative collaboration about how programs and facilities can be modified to accommodate them.

Creating a timeline for program start-up

Creating a new Pathway Program will take about a full school year, given the other duties and responsibilities that administrators and teachers have. During this 12-month period, administrators make key program and personnel decisions, design the program structure and curriculum, and communicate extensively with teachers, employers, potential students, and their parents. Here is a sample timeline.

Start-up Planning Timeline for Pathway Program

Economic/Workforce Analysis to Identify Program Needs Conduct economic and workforce analysis, review of teacher interests, and review of student career interest inventories; identify one or more programs to be launched; designate programs for the start of the next school year.	September-November
Form a Program of Study Advisory Committee Identify school, employer, higher education, and parent representatives; establish a schedule of meetings and define members' roles and responsibilities; form task forces (e.g., expanding partners, technical curriculum, facilities, equipment).	November-March
Identify/Prepare Program of Study Instructional Team Select a Lead Teacher, other teachers (career and academic), school and district administrators, and a counselor; provide professional development.	November-December
Clarify Roles and Responsibilities for Design Phase Ask the Pathway Program Advisory Committee to identify and validate key skills and knowledge in the industry, and plan and coordinate employer and community engagement; advise the Pathway Program Instructional Team to design curriculum, assure secondary-postsecondary-employer alignment, create an internal process for planning and student support, and develop roles for employer and community engagement.	November-February
Coordinate the Pathway Program within the High School and College Inform the entire school staff, orient counselors, arrange cohort scheduling, schedule Pathway Program classes, and coordinate with union leaders; integrate information into relevant career development or freshman seminar classes. Also reach out to potential college partners early in the process.	December - March

Start-up Planning Timeline for Pathway Program

Recruit and Select Students Create basic Pathway Program information to share with students and counselors; distribute information to all freshmen, accept and screen applications, hold interviews and parent meetings, identify and schedule students, and plan summer activity.	January-April
Develop Curriculum (especially Level 1) Have the teachers lead, draw on employers for technical input, examine related state standards, conduct Internet searches, visit other schools with Pathway Programs, and develop integrated curriculum ideas; design program scope for three levels of high school and additional postsecondary levels leading to relevant certifications and degrees.	February-August
Prepare Facilities and Equipment Adapt a classroom as "home base," prepare necessary space, and obtain and install necessary equipment.	April-August
Plan Motivational Activities Identify activities that will make the Pathway Program appealing, including what types of student monitoring and rewards will be used.	June-August
Plan Experiential Learning Program Schedule companies that will participate and identify topics of most interest, develop a calendar of events for these activities.	July-August
Welcome First Cohort of Students	August-September

Adapted from: Planning Guide for Career Academies, by Charles Dayton, Coordinator Career Academy Support Network UC Berkeley[1]

Section 2. Creating a Pathway Program

In this section, we examine more closely the twelve key elements of a Pathway Program, organized under four themes. Following each discussion, several reflection questions are provided, helping you determine the current status of that element within your organization. Finally, possible action steps are listed to jumpstart planning and implementation.

A Pathways Program is a program of interconnected academic and elective classes revolving around a career or subject theme. It is integrated with experiential learning and close connections between secondary and postsecondary education, training, and apprenticeship. The program is designed to support the development of Career and Life Readiness for the learner, so that the individual can successfully enter and advance in a career path.

Theme I. Pathway Program Structure

1. Pathway Program Interconnected Structure

Description

The Pathway Program is organized and presented to students as a well-defined, multi-year program of themed courses, interconnected with academic core courses and experiential learning activities.

Discussion

A Pathway Program, as described here, results from active planning and careful attention to all aspects of the 12 components of a Pathway Program, organized into four key themes:

◊ Structure

◊ Implementation Teams

◊ Alignment

◊ Connections

Shifts in Planning and Coordination

One of the biggest shifts that will happen relating to planning and coordination will be reorganizing disparate elective classes into a recommended sequence of courses that constitute a Pathway Program. Pathway Programs introduce and reinforce key knowledge and skills across the three-plus year sequence of courses. In the past, teachers offering these themed electives may have built each individual course from scratch, reflecting a personal interest or passion, and getting them to let go of some valued activities or projects may be difficult. That's why starting with identification of the program knowledge and skills and then working backwards to sketch out the sequence of courses is helpful. Through the Pathways System, teachers of the themed classes will definitely gain more than they relinquish, and using the backwards-mapping process, they will probably be pleasantly surprised as to how many of their resources and projects can be maintained in the new structure.

Curriculum Sequencing

Inside the high school, one of the biggest curriculum shifts that will happen will be reorganizing disparate elective classes into a recommended sequence of courses that constitute a pathway.

Offering the Pathway Program as a sequence will also affect the way student course scheduling happens. Students at the upper levels in high school tend to fill out their course schedule with electives (since they have finished most required academic courses in 11th grade); this approach to scheduling may need to be modified so that pathway students in the earlier grades are given first priority to introductory courses. This is necessary so that those younger students can begin progressing through the Pathways sequence.

Another shift is to incorporate the content of academic classes and experiential learning/student leadership directly into the Pathway Program development process. Cross-curricular and experiential learning are no longer add-ons that are nice to have; rather they become an integral part of the curriculum. Through the process, the program curriculum map extends beyond just the themed courses. It covers the themed courses, the academic cohort courses, and the experiential learning/student leadership component.

The Design Team Process

To create a Pathway Program, the Program of Study Advisory Committee and the Pathway Program Instructional Team will need to work closely together as a short-term "Design Team." In working together, the Campus-based Leadership Team should establish specific roles for each of the two entities.

The primary role of the Pathway Program Advisory Committee is to identify and validate key skills and knowledge in the industry and plan and coordinate employer and community engagement for the Pathway Program. The primary role of the Pathway Program Instructional Team is to design curriculum, assure opportunities for secondary-to-postsecondary planning and coordination, create internal processes for academic and social-emotional supports for students, and develop roles for employer and community engagement.

When there are joint Design Team meetings, the Pathway Program Advisory Committee should take the lead with their responsibilities but also be given briefings on the work of the Instructional Team, with the opportunity to ask clarifying questions and provide input, and vice versa.

Self-Assessment
◊ Do we have access to a regional workforce analysis to identify what are important industry sectors and career clusters for our region, even if those businesses are not located directly in the service area of our school?

◊ What concentrations of related electives do we already have in place, such as business, finance and marketing, information technology, agriculture, foreign languages, fine arts, performing arts, etc.?

◊ If our students already take a career interest/aptitude assessment, have we aggregated to create a school-wide picture of what programs students might find interesting?

◊ Do we already have courses that are arranged as a sequence of related courses?

◊ Do we have any well-established student clubs, such as robotics or future health care professionals, that demonstrate that interest in a potential Pathway Program could be developed?

Action Steps
☐ Create a design process, drawing upon the expertise of the Pathway Program Advisory Committee and the Pathway Program Instructional Team.

☐ Clarify Roles and Responsibilities for the design phase. Designate the primary roles and responsibilities of the Pathway Program Advisory Committee and the Pathway Program Instructional Team.

☐ Begin the design phase by securing model program standards (see Common Career Technical Core[2]), and validating those standards with an industry-sector group and/or the Program Advisory Committee.

☐ Schedule introductory meetings between secondary and postsecondary faculty to discuss the programs and courses that already exist and how communications will be maintained during the design phase and during program launch.

❐   Build a specific timeline for addressing each of the other components of the Pathway Program into the sequence, with particular attention to standards alignment; integration of experiential learning; and alignment to certifications, assessment, and dual enrollment credits.

2. Student Access

Description

The Pathway Program is accessible and marketed to students of varying achievement levels, including students who have Individualized Education Programs or limited English language proficiency.

Discussion

Designing the Pathway Program so that all students have access to its content and outcomes is one of the most important and often challenging aspects of the design phase. While some courses may require pre-requisites, the Pathway Program, if possible, should accommodate, be marketed to, and welcome students with special learning needs, students with limited English proficiency, and students of either gender. The Pathway Program description and the descriptions of each course should clearly state the expected competencies and effort required. School counselors and other support staff should guide students to select a Pathway Program that aligns with their current level of academic achievement and with their motivation to succeed.

Self-Assessment

◊   Are detailed descriptions of each Pathway Program available to students and parents or guardians? Do these program descriptions include information explaining the level of academic proficiency recommended for the program?

◊   Are some Pathway Programs limited to students who have taken pre-requisites, achieved certain GPAs, or fulfilled other academic performance criteria? Are these criteria fixed or are exceptions allowed?

◊   What are the academic and social supports available to help marginally qualified students access the program?

◊   For a Pathway Program already in place, do the students represent the diversity of the student body? If not, to what do you attribute this?

Action Steps

❐   For a Pathway Program already in place, review the demographics of its student enrollment to determine if it represents diversity. If not, determine and address the root causes.

❐   Use qualified students or employer volunteers who are non-traditional to that career field to share information during student recruiting activities.

❏ Review the way in which students learn about Pathway Programs to discern whether specific student groups are targeted for or guided to certain programs. If necessary, develop and execute a recruitment and retention plan for the Pathway Program. Be sure to address ways in which students will be encouraged to enroll in a Pathway Program that is non-traditional for their gender.

❏ Provide teachers with professional learning relating to differentiated instruction, helping them understand that lower-achieving students may be able to reach success in their program with appropriate support.

❏ Ensure that the Pathway Program takes full advantage of academic and social supports available within the school, and identify unmet needs.

3. Student Cohort Scheduling
Description

Students in the Pathway Program are scheduled as a cohort and enrolled in as many classes together as possible.

Discussion

Student cohort scheduling is a distinctive feature of an effective Pathways System. As part of a pathway program or career academy cohort, students gain a greater sense of belonging and build deeper relationships with peers who share common career interests and goals. Cohort scheduling also makes it easier to offer Pathway Program-related presentations and pathway-related activities.

It may, however, be difficult to schedule student cohorts for certain classes. For example, there may be a limited number of students available to fill an advanced math class, so both cohort and non-cohort students will be enrolled. Each year, when the master schedule is created, make every effort to utilize Pathway Program cohort scheduling as much as possible.

Self-Assessment

◊ Does the school currently schedule students in cohorts? If not, what challenges should be anticipated when creating cohort scheduling?

◊ Are there other schools in our region or state that utilize cohort scheduling, from which we can gather information?

◊ If full cohort scheduling is not an option, what other extra-curricular experiences might Pathway Program students engage in to create a sense of community?

Action Steps

☐ Ensure that individuals responsible for creating the school's master schedule are directly involved in their school's Pathways Leadership Team.

☐ Explore and review the current master schedule to identify ways it can be modified to work with the Pathways System (e.g., common planning time for Instructional Teams and cohort student scheduling).

☐ Examine schedules from other schools, both regionally and nationally, looking for structures that may be adapted to your context.

☐ Prioritize scheduling Pathway Program classes first when drafting a new master schedule and then fitting other classes around the Pathway cohort classes.

☐ For each Pathway Program, identify at least one core academic class that could be "paired" with that program for shared cohort scheduling. (For example, an engineering Pathway Program could work to schedule most or all of its students in the same upper-level math course.)

Theme II. Pathway Program Implementation Teams

4. Pathway Program Advisory Committee

Description

The Pathway Program has an active employer-led Advisory Committee comprised of experts from the field; this committee reviews and provides input on curriculum, expected skills and knowledge, and equipment, and it coordinates employer involvement in the program.

Discussion

The Pathway Program Advisory Committee is essential to ensuring that each Pathway Program authentically aligns with up-to-date career practices; it is the program's link to the actual world of work. The Pathway Program Instructional Team should utilize the expertise of Advisory Committee members by encouraging open and honest dialogue regarding program improvements and future growth. The Pathway Program Advisory Committee should be chaired and led by an employer rather than a member of the Pathway Program Instructional

---

Employer Leadership

Providing true leadership responsibility for employer partners sends an important signal about the role of employers in the program; rather than just being a rubber stamp for what the school or teacher intends to do, employers are active co-creators of the program.

Team. Active leadership of employer partners sends an important signal about the role of employers in the program; rather than just being a rubber stamp for what the school or teacher intends to do, employers are active co-creators of the program. Advisory Committee members should meet at least four times annually, and members of the Pathway Program Instructional Team are encouraged to participate in all meetings.

> ### Joint Efforts for Employer Engagement
>
> When feasible, it makes sense for high schools, regional career technology centers, and local colleges to work together to recruit and engage business partners.

When feasible, high schools, regional career technology centers, and local colleges should work together to recruit and engage business partners. Since the Pathway Program is meant to be a secondary-to-postsecondary sequence of courses, operating a joint committee makes sense. Operationally, each committee meeting agenda could focus first on shared issues that affect all programs, and then spend time working on school-specific issues. It may make sense to have subcommittees that break out for these smaller, school-focused discussions.

Self-Assessment

- *Is an active Pathway Program Advisory Committee in place for the Pathway Program? If so, is it functioning in a productive manner or does it need to be re-evaluated? If not, why not?*

- *Has a regional industry-sector working group been formed? From this working group, can members be recruited to serve on the school's Pathway Program Advisory Committee?*

- *Does a partner organization, like a community college or regional technical center, already have a standing Program Advisory Committee? Can that committee interact with programs at both the secondary and postsecondary levels?*

Action Steps

☐ Identify regional industry-sector working groups from which Pathway Program Advisory Committee members can be recruited.

☐ Identify Pathway Program Advisory Committees working at a local college or school district and explore creating a shared Advisory Committee.

☐ Create a written Pathway Program Advisory Committee description that includes the key objectives and functions, required number of participants, minimum number of yearly meetings, and roles and responsibilities of the members.

☐ Invite volunteers representing the full range of occupations and industries served by the Pathway Program to an informational meeting that explains the role and expectations of Advisory Committee members.

☐ Invite employer volunteers to join the committee and designate a chairperson.

☐ Ask committee members to take responsibility for recruiting additional committee members.

☐ Establish dates, time, and location for meetings in the coming year.

☐ Within the first several meetings, create annual strategic improvement goals and action steps for the program, and regularly discuss and monitor progress toward the goals. Identify action steps for both the Instructional Team as well as for the Pathway Program Advisory Committee.

☐ Create an annual progress report for the Pathway Program and report to the Campus-based Leadership Team.

5. Pathway Program Instructional Team

Description

The Pathway Program Instructional Team consists of teachers of career- or themed-classes, teachers for academic subjects, and staff from the counseling department, collaborating to develop cross-curricular projects and lessons and to track and address the progress of students within their Pathway Program cohort.

Discussion

Instructional Teams may be organized in two basic ways. Schools with many Pathway Programs typically cluster these into broad academies or institutes. In this case, an Instructional Team typically works with students from within one entire academy. In schools with only a handful of unrelated Pathway Programs, different Instructional Teams should be assigned to work with students from each Pathway Program.

In either case, it is essential that Instructional Teams

> ## Instructional Team Time
>
> It is essential that Instructional Teams have consistent common planning time, ideally once or twice weekly, but at least once every other week.

have consistent common planning time, ideally once or twice weekly, but at least once every other week. During this time, team members work from a consistent meeting protocol, established by the pathway leadership team, that stipulates the amount of meeting time dedicated to students' social and emotional needs and the amount of time to focus on curriculum and program coordination. During time devoted to students' social and emotional needs, teachers may use the school's established Response-to-Intervention (RIT) strategies or Positive Behavior Interventions and Supports (PBIS) with individual students or may hold meetings directly with a student and his or her parents/guardians.

Instructional Team meetings include time devoted to making Pathway Program instructional decisions and identifying opportunities for cross-curricular integration. Using a Pathway Program curriculum map, Instructional Teams collaborate to coordinate lessons for the upcoming weeks.

Self-Assessment

◊ Do teachers currently work as part of an Instructional Team? If so, describe the function and process of the Instructional Team approach. If not, what challenges do you anticipate in forming Instructional Teams and how might they be overcome?

◊ Has the instructional staff received sufficient training in functioning as an Instructional Team, identifying and addressing students' social and emotional needs, selecting and administering behavioral and academic interventions, and developing cross-curricular integration? If not, what training is needed first and who has the knowledge and expertise to provide it?

Action Steps

❑ Determine the way in which Instructional Teams may be formed. Include teachers and counselors in these discussions and announce the plan to the entire staff.

❑ Survey core academic and elective teachers and counselors to determine which Pathway Program Instructional Team they prefer to join based on interest and expertise.

❑ Determine how common planning time for Instructional Teams can be integrated into the master schedule.

❑ Identify and reserve professional learning days to offer Instructional Team professional development, common planning time, and teacher externship experiences.

❑ Invite teachers and other staff members to create a school-based protocol for Instructional Team planning time, drawing from and adapting existing resources.

Theme III. Alignment

6. Alignment with Workforce Needs and Opportunities

Description

The Pathway Program is developed to align with in-demand careers that lead to family-sustaining earnings.

Discussion

Ensuring that Pathway Programs are aligned to workforce needs and career opportunities that lead to family-sustaining earnings is a challenge. First, without a clear mechanism and criteria by which to identify workforce and community needs, making an objective decision about what programs to offer is difficult.

Second, developing meaningful connections between business and education will require ongoing effort. Some employer-led organizations simply are not experienced in working with education or do not have an internal structure in place to engage with education partners. If the chamber of commerce or a business and industry coalition isn't already organized and knocking at the door of education, developing the platform for collaboration might take some time.

Third, traditions in schools run deep and resources are limited. Current programs often reflect student and staff interests, yet these may need to be modified or phased out to make room for Pathway Programs that more closely align with workforce trends. Initially, these new programs, such as engineering, mechatronics, and advanced manufacturing, may not be as popular with students, so a targeted awareness-building process should begin as soon as the program is identified for launch.

Self-Assessment

◊ Were current Pathway Programs selected with an eye to workforce needs and career opportunities or more by student and teacher interests?

◊ Are new Pathway Programs under consideration, and if so, what criteria were used to select them?

◊ Have school leaders used an analysis of workforce and economic needs in making programmatic decisions?

Action Steps

❐ Identify the Pathway Programs to be implemented over time. These Pathway Programs should address high priority local and regional needs but also be broad enough to engage the full range of student interests and state and national career opportunities.

❏ Interpret workforce and economic data and review the ways in which they may impact the Pathway Program courses; determine if there are courses missing or current courses that are no longer relevant.

❏ Encourage teachers to use relevant economic and workforce data with students during career development and awareness conversations and lessons.

❏ Consider including the data on the school district website as part of the Career and Life Readiness message.

7. Alignment with Standards
Description
The Pathway Program is aligned to applicable standards for Career and Life Readiness, including relevant standards established by the state for academic and technical knowledge and skills.

Discussion
In designing a Pathway Program, begin with the end in mind. Early in the planning phase, identify and clearly articulate the knowledge, skills, and attributes that learners in the Pathway Program are expected to acquire. To help accomplish this, the planning team, which includes members from both secondary and postsecondary schools as well as employer partners, can draw from resources such as the Common Career Technical Core (a national resource), applicable state academic and/or technical standards, industry standards, and the Career and Life Readiness expectations developed by the Pathways leadership team. After reviewing these resources, the program team creates a master list in which expectations for the Pathway Program are identified and used to guide the development of a Pathway Program sequence of courses. From this point, each course may be further defined by the identification of specific standards and competencies to be taught, the assessments to be administered, and the options for dual-enrollment, Advanced Placement, and industry-based credentials.

Self-Assessment
◊ When was curriculum last aligned with standards?

◊ Was the Pathway Program aligned to just academic standards or just technical standards, or was it aligned to a mix of Career and Life Readiness standards?

◊ How are teachers trained to know and utilize standards?

◊ How are students made aware of standards?

◊ Does the school have a systematic process for updating curriculum? If so, has it been effective? Why or why not?

Action Steps

☐ Identify the standards most relevant to the Pathway Program. If an Advisory Committee has not yet been formed, consider asking business members about industry standards related to the Pathway Program.

☐ Provide teachers with professional learning time to analyze the standards. Invite teachers to brainstorm ways in which these standards may impact the Pathway Program curriculum and instruction.

☐ Locate a school that has the Pathway Program in place and ask if they are willing to share their curriculum and standards alignment.

NOTE: National model career technical standards (Common Career Technical Core) can be found at the Advance CTE website. http://www.careertech.org

8. Alignment Across Courses

Description

The Pathway Program Instructional Team identifies cross-curricular connections between required academic courses and career-themed elective courses, and it creates resources for cross-curricular and integrated instruction.

Discussion

When developing cross-curricular connections among high school courses, a number of innovative approaches help students see the linkages between different disciplines. To accomplish this work most effectively, teachers are given professional time and sufficient guidance to fully understand the standards and to create a curriculum map for their course. Once teachers share and review the curriculum maps developed by fellow Instructional Team members, they can meet to identify areas of overlap and begin to develop learning units that connect the content and skills within their Pathway Program courses. As an example, the Volusia County School District in Florida has developed a very thoughtful process of curriculum mapping through which teachers explain their curriculum to one another and then look for the natural cross-curricular connections. Note: See the Promising Practice Profile for more details about Volusia County School District's career academies.

Self-Assessment

◊ Do teachers currently collaborate to develop integrated or coordinated learning units? If so, describe the process and outcomes.

◊ Have teachers received any training on curriculum mapping, creating integrated units, and integrating standards?

◊ Do students have the opportunity to engage in cross-curricular projects and to present their projects to fellow students or community members?

Action Steps

☐ Develop or approve a protocol for cross-curricular coordination, and in a multiple-Pathways school, create a common protocol.

☐ Provide teachers with the training needed to develop curricular maps, providing relevant examples. Encourage teachers to draft a curriculum map and share with Instructional Team members.

☐ Provide teachers with training needed to develop integrated learning units.

☐ Create larger cross-program projects for students to work together utilizing the strengths and knowledge of several Pathway Programs.

9. Alignment with Industry-based Credentials, Certifications, and Technical Skills Assessments

Description

The Pathway Program leads to clearly-identified technical skill assessments, and/or industry-based credentials, delivered with support for students to know about these options and access them.

Discussion

Since the passage of the Perkins CTE Improvement Act of 2006, under the direction of state oversight agencies, local schools and colleges have expanded the use of technical skill assessments in each career and technical education program. In some industry sectors like information technology, there are credentials that many prospective employees are expected to hold. In other sectors, such as health care, there are many required state-issued licenses. State licenses often require a minimum number of instructional hours and practice and also set a minimum age for earning the license. High school CTE programs also use their own assessments that are created to reflect industry standards and expectations but are not necessarily recognized by the industry itself.

One common misconception about industry-based credentials is that business and industry uniformly recognize these credentials and require them for employment. In fact, many businesses do not know about or require an employee to have a particularly industry-based credential, even though a national or regional industry association helped to develop and administer the assessment.

Self-Assessment

◊ Do any current courses or programs offer students opportunities to earn industry-based credentials? If so, list the credentials.

◊ Is there any relevant policy in place to require or encourage the use of industry-based credentials in Pathway Programs?

Action Steps

❏ Identify the available industry-based credentials and technical assessments associated with each Pathway Program. The state Department of Education may offer guidance and recommendations.

❏ Involve the Pathway Program Advisory Committee in recommending the industry-based credentials or state-endorsed licenses appropriate for students to earn in each Pathway Program.

❏ Identify the knowledge and skills associated with the credentials and ensure that these skills are embedded in the curriculum.

❏ Identify possible sources of external funding to help pay the cost of credentialing assessments that otherwise the student must purchase.

❏ Share study guides or assessment information with Pathway Program teachers and encourage them to brainstorm ways in which their courses can be modified to address the skills these resources highlight.

Theme IV. Connections to the Community and Partner Organizations

10. Experiential Learning, Community-based Experience, and Student Leadership

Description

Pathway Program students participate in organized and relevant job shadows, mentorships, field trips, career-related clubs, and skill competitions as well as school-based interactions with guest speakers and individuals coaching student projects. Students develop leadership skills through school- and community-based leadership experiences, volunteerism, and competitions.

Discussion

Experiential learning is an umbrella term for activities that help students connect with employers and others in their community and gain real-world or close to real world experiences. The term incorporates terms like workplace learning, work-based learning, work-and-earn learning, community-based experiences, and simulated workplaces. Work-place learning and work-and-earn learning are activities where individuals go into the workplace for extended periods, doing real work and sometimes being paid. Work-based learning is work that has a strong connection to the world of work, either by the student visiting the workplace through a site tour, a short-term job shadow, or an internship. Work-based learning can also include activities that bring the world of work into the classroom through a company-based project or scenario or the simulation of a work-setting.

The biggest operational question to consider here is scalability. As more schools and colleges aim to involve their students in experiential learning, creating experiences for all students will become increasingly challenging since the number of business and community organizations that will be willing and able to provide experiential learning for young people will always be limited. To create scalability where every student is getting a meaningful experiential learning opportunity, we will have to be realistic about these limitations in capacity of outside organizations.

Experiential learning can be a process or system of experiences in the community with employers, where the student has the opportunity to see and understand a workplace. In the Academies of Nashville initiative, for example, they define experiential learning as a four-year sequence of learning: Freshman year involves a career development fair and college visit; sophomore year includes an industry-related field trip; junior year offers a job shadow experience; and senior year requires a capstone project, which can include an internship or employer mentorship. Note: See the Promising Practice Profile for more details about the Academies of Nashville.

As another example, Souderton Area High School in Souderton, Pennsylvania has developed an expansive experiential learning program (they call mentorship), where many students secure short-term and medium-term mentorships relating to their career interest in the community. Some students are able to fulfill the mentorship requirement by leading working teams inside the school, such as managing the in-school television and media program, or by producing work for outside non-profit organizations. Note: See the Promising Practice Profile for more details about Souderton's Mentorship program. Experiential learning also takes into account the mature structure of career technology student organizations. Leadership in student government organizations and the National Honor Society can also count when connected to a project of community service. Most importantly, the definition of Career and Life Readiness and the outcomes associated with that should be embedded into all experiential learning opportunities. The coaches and sponsors of these experiences should be briefed on what the Career and Life Readiness expectations are and then be led through a planning process to identify where and how those readiness skills can be developed and how they will be reported on and documented.

Self-Assessment
◊ Have we established the expectation that, within a certain time frame, all students will participate in experiential learning activities?

◊   What school-wide initiatives, programs, and/or clubs are in place to help students develop leadership skills and/or provide learning experiences within the community?

◊   Are there employer organizations in our region that are already coordinating experiential learning opportunities?

Action Steps

☐   Survey students to determine their interest and potential commitment to workplace learning opportunities.

☐   Meet with Advisory Committee members to determine how they can assist with organizing experiential learning opportunities for students.

☐   Meet with the school district solicitor to identify and resolve potential liability and security issues.

☐   Draft an experiential learning protocol that answers the following questions:

   ◊   How will students arrange for experiential learning or will the school assign a staff member to develop and oversee a program?

   ◊   How will students be accountable for the experience? For example, will they be required to report on their experience in some way?

   ◊   What kind of training or tips will be offered to businesses that volunteer to host these experiences?

☐   Review the student organizations currently offered to ensure that all career clusters are included. Review the effectiveness and engagement of student organizations and, if necessary, make improvements that will increase student involvement and enthusiasm.

11. Seamless Connections with Postsecondary Institutions and Regional Career and Technical Centers

Description

The Pathway Program at a high school is aligned with and coordinated with Pathway Programs offered by postsecondary education partners and/or regional career and technical education centers. The high school-based Pathway Program is designed in collaboration with postsecondary partners to allow for a smooth transition of the student from secondary to postsecondary education and training, while minimizing duplication of content among programs.

Discussion

Ideally, students should be able to begin a Pathway Program in high school, earning early college credits and/or certifications, and continue the program at a postsecondary institution where a degree or additional certifications may be attained. A well-planned Pathway Program offers students various "exit points" throughout the postsecondary experience. For example, a student who transitions from a high school Pathway Program to the partnering community college Pathway Program, may exit after one year, earning an industry license. Alternatively, the student may choose to remain at the community college for two years, earning both the license

---

Multiple Pathways "Exit Points"

A well-planned Pathway Program offers students various "exit points" throughout the postsecondary experience.

---

and an associate degree. Finally, the student may apply the associate degree to the Pathway Program offered at a university where a bachelor's degree is attainable.

Of course, developing a Pathway Program at this level requires high levels of commitment and collaboration among all partners. Administrators from each of these organizations need to decide together on protocols and approaches for the collaboration among their staff and throughout the courses they offer within the Pathway Program. Each of these organizations should consider signing a memorandum of understanding or memorandum of cooperation about how they will create the seamless connections between their institutions.

Self-Assessment

◊ If Pathway Programs are in place, have partnerships with postsecondary programs been established, enabling students to begin the program in high school and continue at a postsecondary institution? If not, how might this work begin?

◊ Does the school partner with a regional career and technical school? If so, describe the collaboration including the number of available career and technical programs and the number of students attending.

Action Steps

❏ Assign an administrator or staff member to oversee all aspects of partnerships with regional career technology centers and local colleges.

❏ Reach out to regional career technology centers and local colleges to communicate an interest in developing joint Pathway Programs. Learn about the programs they currently offer to identify overlap with the high school's Pathway Programs.

❏ Network with other high schools to learn about their involvement with postsecondary Pathway Programs; if feasible, replicate their programs and agreements.

12. Postsecondary Dual Enrollment and Articulation Agreements

Description

The Pathway Program is supported by articulation agreements among high schools and postsecondary education partners, enabling students to earn dual, concurrent, or articulated credits and skills credentials at reduced or no-cost tuition rates for the secondary student.

Discussion

State funding for dual enrollment, or the lack thereof, will impact the way in which high school students can earn early college credits. In some locales, community colleges are experiencing a general decline in enrollment since waning of demand for education and training that spiked at the beginning of the 2007-2009 Great Recession. While funding for dual enrollment credits may be tight, the college may have an extra incentive to collaborate in developing Pathway Programs, if they perceive the opportunity to create a pipeline of motivated, well-prepared students to enter their programs. On the other hand, individual college instructors may worry that by encouraging high school students to earn dual enrollment or articulated credits for 101 level courses while enrolled in high school, this arrangement could reduce the number of first-year students enrolling in their 101 courses at the college campus. While all institutions of higher learning have a commendable public mission, they also contend with financial realities and the need to drive program enrollments and fill classes. As such, it is important to build partnerships that can openly recognize these organizational concerns, and problem-solve around the potential competition for students' tuition.

Self-Assessment

◊ Do students currently have opportunities to earn college credit while in high school? If so, are these opportunities available to a wide variety of students, or are they mostly available to high achievers? Are these opportunities highly marketed to students? What percentages of students taking dual enrollment courses actually earn college credit?

◊ Is a school administrator or staff person clearly identified as the key contact for postsecondary institutions? If not, who might assume this responsibility?

◊ What challenges do we need to overcome to increase the number of early credit options offered to students?

Action Steps

❑ Identify one person to assume the responsibility of securing and negotiating dual and articulated agreements with postsecondary partners.

❏   Set an annual goal to increase the number of dual enrollment
    agreements.

❏   Become informed about state dual enrollment policies and funding.

❏   Review the way in which students learn about currently offered dual
    enrollment opportunities. Is there a need for increased marketing and
    communications?

❏   Determine how curriculum will be reviewed as it is aligned with dual
    credit options.

Maximizing the Impact of a Pathway Program

A Pathway Program can provide a powerful learning experience that
deepens learning and strengthens motivation and confidence for a learner.
With creative and dedicated teachers, creating a high quality Pathway Program
is very doable, but often, one or two select programs within a large, generic
high school become an "island of excellence in a sea of mediocrity."

Creating high quality at scale is more challenging. That's why schools need to
adopt the Pathways System Framework™ and join a Pathways Partnership. The
Pathways System includes the activities, policies, and structures that support
each individual Pathway Programs and also builds organizational connections
among schools, colleges, employer organizations, and other partners, helping
enhance the impact of Pathway Programs and reducing the "re-invention of
the wheel" for each Pathway Program. The Pathways System structure allows
the community to offer a portfolio of Pathway Programs and related services,
growing into a "Pathways for all" model.

* * *

*In the next chapter, we explain in detail the development of the Pathways
System and the components of the Pathways System Framework™.*

Mountain Home High School Career Academies

Quick Look

Mountain Home High School (MHHS), now known at the Mountain Home High School Career Academies, is a high school in rural Mountain Home, Arkansas, that operates a wall-to-wall academies program that serves every student with career development, Pathway Programs, and extensive community involvement through the mentoring program.

Program Detail

Mountain Home High School Career Academies serves 875 students in grades 10 through 12. In 2001, school leaders began to implement a career academies model, at the conclusion of an intense three-year period that involved research, site visits to model schools, and targeted professional development for staff. According to Principal Ms. Dana Brown, two key factors drove this decision: an increasing dropout rate and community concerns regarding the future of the local workforce.

Wall-to-Wall Academies

A key decision facing the Mountain Home administration when planning was whether to structure the school with stand-alone Pathway Programs that served a portion of the total school population or as a wall-to-wall academy model that required every student to choose an academy Pathway Program. After conducting research and site visits to schools with career academies, the team recommended a wall-to-wall academy model.

At the beginning of the 2003-2004 school year, Mountain Home implemented three career academies, which remain in place today: Communications, Arts, and Business (CAB), Agriculture, Construction, Manufacturing, and Engineering (ACME), and Health and Human Services (HHS). Every student at the school enrolls in a Pathway Program within one of the academies, based on a combination of student learning style and career interest. Students take both core academic classes and career-related Pathway Program classes within their academy and may gain exposure to other academies through electives. At the end of each year, students can opt to change academies, though fewer than two percent choose to change their academy.[3]

Mountain Home has also worked with the school district's junior high school to develop a "freshman transition bridge." Ninth grade students take a mandatory, semester-long course designed to help students make a smooth transition into the high school's career academies.

Business and Community Involvement

Representatives from local businesses actively participate in the school's Academy Homeroom Advisory Groups and individual businesses sponsor students through internship programs. In addition, several local businesses provide guidance and support for various clubs and activities at the school. Since 2005, the school has operated a successful community and business mentoring program. Mountain Home staff documented this program in an informative guidebook, *Bridging the Gap: A Community Mentoring Program for High School Homeroom Advisory Groups.*[4]

Real World Application and External Connections

All academies include short and long term career-related projects. For example, CAB students may work with CAB Productions, an MHHS student-run business that provides hands-on experience in the entertainment industry from lights and sound, performance, event planning, marketing, and finance.

While enrolled at MHHS, eligible students have the opportunity to earn concurrent college credit from Arkansas State University Mountain Home and through Advanced Placement courses. Other opportunities for MHHS students to expand learning and transition into postsecondary education and/or the workforce include Navy Junior Reserve Office Training Corp (NJROTC), Senior Capstone Projects, Senior Internships with local business partners, transitioning into the workforce through certificate/license programs from ASUMH Technical Center in the areas of Mechatronics, CNA, Automotive, Welding, and HVACR, and participating in the redesigned work permit program that allows students that currently work to continue while completing coursework to graduate.

Results

Since implementing the career academy model in 2003, MHHS has seen a dramatic increase in student achievement, including improved attendance and graduation rates, decreased dropout rate, and increased achievement on state exams and ACT tests. In 2009, all three of MHHS's career academies achieved "Model Status" from the National Career Academy Coalition.[5]

#

Chapter Seven

Designing the Pathways System

Section 1. The Process for Building a Pathways System

Developing an effective Pathway Program takes a good deal of work, but most of that effort is directed from the school in which the Pathway Program is located. In contrast, a Pathways System takes longer to build because it has more moving parts. A Pathways System within an individual school is simply an extension of one or more Pathway Programs, but a larger Pathways System requires engaging a larger set of organizations working at a community or regional level.

In this section, we describe the process for Pathways Systems development among multiple partners. The process is organized into five phases: Explore, Convene, Envision, Commit, and Act.

PHASE 1: EXPLORE. Build Awareness and Interest

(Approximate timeframe: one to six months)

During the Explore phase, numerous stakeholders learn about and become interested in participating in the Pathways System. Typically, one or two local individuals find out about the Pathways model, conduct some self-directed study, and then begin to introduce the concept to others in their community. The local initiators may invite outside experts to visit their community and explain the Pathways model through a workshop-style meeting and/or a series of small group meetings. The

---

Web-Based Resources

You can visit our website to access case studies, background resources, and forms and templates related to the Pathways Program work referenced in this chapter. Visit **www.powerandpromiseofpathways.com**.

PATHWAYS SYSTEM DEVELOPMENT PROCESS

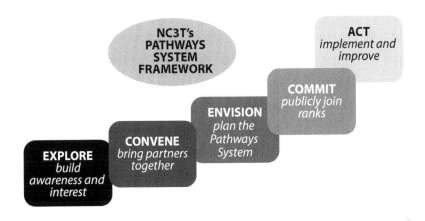

local initiator may also invite local partners to participate in an informational webinar or purchase a book to learn more.

Action Steps

☐ Organize meetings with other stakeholders to discuss what kind of Pathways-related changes are needed.

☐ Gather information to build the case for change:

  ◊ General student achievement

  ◊ Graduation rates from high school

  ◊ Percent of high school students enrolling in postsecondary education and training after high school

  ◊ Percent of postsecondary students completing a program, and general level of student debt

  ◊ Documented information about skills gaps within employer firms

  ◊ Documented information about current and projected skilled workforce shortages

☐ If necessary, commission a workforce and skills gap analysis for the region.

☐ Find an expert organization, like NC3T, and invite them to visit the community to provide information and facilitate exploratory discussions about the Pathways model.

❏ Include all relevant stakeholders:

◊ K-12 superintendents, regional career technology school directors, school board members, and school principals

◊ College presidents and deans

◊ Workforce system directors

◊ Business and industry organizations (sector specific and also chamber of commerce)

◊ Employers of varying sizes

◊ Youth-serving organizations

◊ Community-based foundations

❏ Identify other schools, colleges, and communities that are implementing notable Pathways-related initiatives, and schedule visits to see their work in person.

PHASE 2: CONVENE. Bring Partners Together

(Approximate timeframe: Three months from the start of this phase)

During this phase, partners begin to discuss and plan the initial structure for a Pathways System.

Action Steps

❏ Create initial written materials describing the purpose of the Pathways model, with attention to the student and workforce outcomes.

❏ Establish broad outcomes for the initiatives – workforce quality, reduced skill-gaps, higher postsecondary completion rates. These can be modified over time but need to be discussed early on.

❏ Convene a "launch meeting" to outline responsibilities, introduce new partners, and ensure that all members have a clear understanding of the Pathways System and the Pathways System Development Process.

❏ Engage a non-biased expert facilitation to run kick-off and planning meetings, if needed.

❏ Appoint key planning structures:

◊ Intermediary Organization, the organization and point of contact to serve as the convener

◊ Pathways Partnership Leadership Team

◊ Pathways Communications Team

◊ Campus-based Leadership Team

◊ Other task forces or working groups

☐ Create initial communication materials for all stakeholders to use and develop a communications plan.

☐ Identify regional strengths relevant to a Pathways System using a tool like NC3T's *Design Specifications and Asset Inventory.*

☐ Gather and review regional economic, workforce and education data. Organize and share with all stakeholders.

PHASE 3: ENVISION. Plan the Pathways System

(Approximate timeframe: Three to 12 months from start of this phase)

The Envision Phase is when the bulk of the planning work occurs. The partners identify specific outcomes; set goals, strategies and action steps, assign work to organizations and people; and establish timelines. Throughout the Envision Phase, new stakeholders continue to get involved; they need to be brought up to speed on earlier thinking and decisions, and they need to be given the opportunity to provide meaningful input.

Action Steps

☐ Organize a kick-off Envision meeting to review results of the *Design Specifications and Asset Inventory* and the economic and education data. Utilizing this data, the Pathways Partners identify strengths and gaps relevant to their Pathways System.

☐ During the Envision meeting, create tentative Pathways System goals. These may include the following:

◊ The adoption a Career and Life readiness definition

◊ The general structure of the Pathways System (i.e., the number of Pathway Programs to be offered, what schools and colleges will offer, how career development will be organized, how early college credits/ industry certifications will be offered)

Early Implementation

During the early stage of partner engagement and planning, some proposed initiatives may gain widespread support among partners, such as beginning employer engagement with established programs. These activities can be planned and implemented even while the broader Envision Phase continues. Partners should be cautious, however, that the activities launched as "early implementation" do not consume so much energy and focus that the Envision Phase grinds to a halt, or that the initiative becomes so firmly entrenched it cannot be modified or redirected as the bigger plan takes shape.

◊ Specific ways in which business and industry members will partner with K-12 staff and students

◊ The out-of-classroom career development and experiential learning that students will be offered

◊ The way in which the Pathways System Initiative will be communicated to all community members

☐ Convene campus-based design teams to plan the launch and expansion of freshman academies, Pathway Programs, career development, and employer engagement for the school.

☐ Create cross-cutting teams to work across school districts and colleges, sharing strategies and resources and negotiating which factors should be consistent across sites and which can be customized for each site.

☐ Identify the key metrics that each stakeholder will use, establish benchmark performance, and set targets for improvement.

☐ Begin early implementation of initiatives around which there is strong consensus.

PHASE 4: COMMIT. Publicly Join Ranks

(Approximate Timeframe: Two to four months from start of this phase)

During the Commit phase, all the Pathway Partners will formally commit themselves to the vision, goals, strategies and action steps identified for developing and implementing the Pathways System. The Pathways Partnership Leadership Team will finalize the Pathways System Implementation Plan, and in a public event (conference, press event, town-hall meeting), the Pathway Partners will formally announce the plan and their respective roles and responsibilities. The event should be carefully scripted with guidance from the Pathway System Communications Team, and each participant must be committed to "staying on script."

Action Steps

☐ Draft, gather input, modify, and finalize the Pathways System Implementation Plan.

☐ Share the draft Pathways System Implementation Plan with all stakeholders, taking feedback into account as the plan is finalized.

☐ Select the date, time, and venue for the commitment event; create materials to share with the public and the press, and create talking points for the representatives of the Pathways Partnership.

☐ Unveil the finalized Pathways System Implementation Plan through at least one public event and multiple communications platforms.

PHASE 5: ACT. Implement and Improve

(Approximate timeframe: Ongoing upon initial adoption of the Pathways System Implementation Report and the annual Pathways System Progress Report)

During the Act phase, all stakeholders carry out the day-to-day work called for in the Pathways System Implementation Plan. During the Act Phase, stakeholders monitor activities and measure progress using agreed-upon metrics. Based on the degree of progress measured, the stakeholders update goals and modify the Pathways System Implementation Plan on a regular basis. The Pathways Partnership releases an annual Pathways System Progress Report to the community that looks back at past implementation and also identifies selected improvement goals and strategies for the future.

Action Steps

❐ Stay in contact with the stakeholders, prompting them to report on their progress, using both metrics and qualitative measures.

❐ Meet regularly to assess implementation progress.

❐ Make revisions and updates to the Pathways System Implementation Plan at least annually.

❐ Prepare and share the Pathways System Progress Report to the public at least annually.

❐ Convene all stakeholders at least annually to share progress and urge forward progress. Convene smaller stakeholder groups on a quarterly basis to help maintain operational connections.

Section 2. Components of the Pathways System

As previously described in Chapter 4, a Pathways System is defined as follows:

A Pathways System is the coordinated interaction of key components – career development, pathway programs, dynamic teaching and learning, employer and community engagement, and cross-sector partnerships – designed to develop a high level of career and life readiness among youths and adults in schools, colleges, workforce programs and the across the broader community, resulting in enhanced workforce competitiveness and community prosperity.

An effective Pathways System exhibits six characteristics:

1. **Career and Life Readiness.** Partners define the mix of applied knowledge, technical skills, employability skills, and other competencies that prepare individuals for success in postsecondary education, the skilled workplace, and personal life.

2. **Career Development.** Learners gain the knowledge and skills to make informed choices about careers and related education and training.

3. **Pathway Programs.** Pathways programs at the secondary and postsecondary levels are aligned with workforce demands and are structured to help develop Career and Life Readiness skills.

4. **Employer and Community Engagement.** Employers and community partners help students experience the workplace and build positive relationships with employer mentors.

5. **Dynamic Teaching and Learning.** Research-based educational practices engage learners in rigorous and active learning, and educators continue to grow in their skills and knowledge.

6. **Cross-Sector Partnerships.** Partnerships among K-12 education, postsecondary education, workforce systems and other entities create sustained collaboration to develop the local Pathways System.

Overview of the Pathways System Framework™

System Component 1. Career and Life Readiness

◊   Applied Knowledge

◊   Effective Relationships

◊   Executive Skills

◊   Postsecondary Transition Knowledge and Skills

◊   Career Navigation Skills

◊   Financial Literacy

◊   Civic Engagement

System Component 2. Career Development

◊   Comprehensive Career Exploration Resources and Guidance System

◊   Student Career and Education Plan

◊   Preparation of Students to Choose Among Pathway Programs

◊   Engagement of Parents and Family Members

System Component 3. Pathway Programs

Program of Study Structure
◊ Program of Study Interconnected Structure
◊ Student Access
◊ Cohort Scheduling

Program of Study Leadership
◊ Program of Study Advisory Committee
◊ Pathway Program of Study Instructional Team

Program of Study Alignment
◊ Alignment with Workforce Needs and Opportunities
◊ Alignment with Standards
◊ Alignment through Cross-Curricular Connections
◊ Alignment with Industry-based Credentials, Certifications, and Technical Skills Assessments

Program of Study Connections
◊ Experiential Learning, Community-based Experience, and Student Leadership
◊ Seamless Connections with Postsecondary Institutions and Regional Career and Technical Centers
◊ Postsecondary Dual Enrollment and Articulation Agreements

System Component 4. Employer and Community Engagement
◊ Well-defined Employer and Community Connections
◊ Business and Industry Experiences for Faculty and Staff

System Component 5. Dynamic Teaching and Learning
◊ Curriculum Supported by High Quality Teaching and Learning
◊ Literacy Across the Curriculum
◊ Academic, Social, and Program Supports
◊ Professional Development Planning

System Component 6. Cross Sector Partnerships
◊ Pathways Partnership Leadership Structure
◊ Campus-based Leadership Teams
◊ Pathways Partnership Intermediary Designation
◊ Communications Tools and Resources

◊   Definition and Implementation of College, Career, & Life Readiness

◊   Industry Sector Collaboration

◊   Utilization of Shared Metrics

◊   Pathways System Implementation Plan and Community Progress Report

◊   Reporting, Acquisition and Transcription of Dual, Concurrent, and Articulated Credit and Other Skills Credentials

◊   Alignment of Administration, Policy, and Funding

In the remainder of this chapter, I describe in detailed each of the six components of the Pathways System Framework™, with a description, a discussion, self-assessment questions, and action steps to focus work on each component.

System Component 1. Career and Life Readiness

In a Pathways System, the unifying goal of all partners is to develop Career and Life Ready Learners, individuals who possess a mix of knowledge and skills that prepare them for success in postsecondary education, the skilled workplace, and citizenship. Pathways System partners work to ensure that learners are provided with experiences and education that lead to success in postsecondary education, economically viable Career Pathways, and personal effectiveness in a 21st Century economy.

Career and life readiness (explained in Chapter 5) includes the development of the following:

1. Applied knowledge

2. Effective relationships skills

3. Executive skills

4. Postsecondary transition knowledge and skills

5. Career navigation skills

6. Financial literacy

7. Civic engagement

Description

Members of the Pathways Partnership adopt a shared definition of Career and Life Readiness. The definition (either locally developed or adapted from state government guidance) should include or address the following skills, knowledge, and attributes: applied knowledge and skills, personal relationship skills, executive skills, transition knowledge and skills, career navigation skills, financial literacy, and civic engagement. All members of the Pathways Partnership take an active role to implement the shared definition. *Students understand the Career and Life Readiness expectations and monitor their personal progress and development.*

Discussion

The true aim of education and training. The ultimate aim of education and training in the Pathways System is to develop learners who are Career and Life Ready. This is the organizing principle to which all parts of the pathway partnership should be focused, because it will help develop learners and workers who are more adaptable, creative, and responsive to the demands of postsecondary education and the skilled workplace. Career and Life Readiness (CLR) is the common language for organizing the work of Pathway Partnerships.

In a Pathways System, the unifying goal of all partners is to develop Career and Life Ready Learners, individuals who possess a mix of knowledge, learning skills, problem-solving and creativity, interpersonal skills, executive skills, career navigation skills, and civic engagement understanding that prepare them for success in postsecondary education, the skilled workplace, and citizenship.

Most education and workforce organizations have either a formal or informal set of "readiness" expectations, but often these expectations are vaguely stated or too narrowly focused, not inclusive of the whole person. Most likely, the learners themselves are not aware of these definitions and expectations, and they have no personal ownership over what the definition means to them.

Early on, the Pathways Partnership Leadership Team needs to convene a working group to explore current definitions of readiness and create a more holistic definition of CLR that can be embraced by all the partners.

Implementing CLR across the Pathways Partnership. While different education and workforce partners have identified readiness factors, there usually is no operational method to pass along this responsibility to classroom instructors, adults working in extra-curricular clubs and projects, and employer partners involved with education.

Over the life of the Pathways System Initiative, each member of the partnership will adopt and endorse the CLR expectations, and then delineate exactly how their organization will leverage its expertise and capacities to support development of CLR for the learner. To implement the definition, teachers and instructors should be engaged and challenged to discover how they can embed these concepts into classroom instruction. Employer and community partners should also identify how their work-based learning experiences can develop and reinforce aspects of CLR. Student organizations, drama clubs, performing arts teams, community college leadership programs, academic societies, and business-industry coalitions all have important roles to play.

The biggest culture-shift will be one that moves the focus of schools and colleges from being content-centered to one that is learner-centered. The learner-centered approach uses effective content instruction as a means to develop Career and Life Readiness. It doesn't mean abandoning content, but to reframe the purpose of content instruction as contributing to the development of the whole person.

Measuring the development of CLR. It is critically important that learners actually understand the CLR definition and are actively thinking and working toward their personal development. For students to understand and embrace their own responsibility to develop personal Career and Life Readiness, the CLR Task Force can work with schools and colleges in the partnership to develop a model individual portfolio tool. Using the portfolio tool, students can track the development of their own Career and Life Readiness.

CLR should be measured in all the different learning environments, and those experiences should be documented in the learner's CLR Portfolio. While accurate measurement of these competencies is important, educators should resist the instinct to rely solely on a standardized assessment; they should include a mix of real-life scenarios and applications to demonstrate competencies. In addition, standardized measures can serve as reasonable proxies for some of the competencies.

Shifting to a people-driven approach. Focusing the school on Career and Life Readiness will be a significant departure for many teachers and instructors. Through tradition and practice, some instructors believe that their responsibility is only to teach subject matter or job-specific skills. They may react against this new approach saying, "I was hired to teach math or science or agriculture, not to be a social services counselor." The biggest culture-shift will be one that moves the focus of schools and colleges from being content-centered to one that is learner-centered. The learner-centered approach uses effective content instruction as a means to develop CLR. It doesn't abandon content but instead reframes the purpose of content instruction as contributing to the development of the whole person.

Self-Assessment

- *What types of definitions of "readiness" already exist, formally or informally, among the Pathway Partners? (Most schools and colleges will have identified some lists of competencies and expectations in mission and vision statements or in organizational strategic plans).*
- *Is a shared definition of Career and Life Readiness (by whatever term used) already developed? If so, how is it used and in what ways is development of these skills measured? Is the definition holistic or too narrow?*

Action Steps

☐ Review Chapter 5 as a resource to guide the development of a shared CLR definition.

☐ Form a CLR Task Force to review partner definitions, create a draft working definition, and through a consultative process, adopt a shared definition of CLR.

☐ Broadly communicate the resulting CLR definition. For example, create posters and encourage teachers and businesses to display them, post the definition on the school's website homepage, and create a press release for local media outlets.

☐ Develop and pilot the use of a rubric to measure and a portfolio to document student acquisition of CLR skills. Engage students directly setting goals for development of their own readiness.

☐ Where feasible, integrate the definition into capstone or graduation projects, requiring students to reflect on the ways in which they are Career and Life Ready.

System Component 2. Career Exploration and Planning

In a Pathways System, all learners experience meaningful and expansive career development. Their parents or guardians are actively engaged in the process. A well-planned career development program encourages students to identify personal aptitudes and interests, explore career options through multiple methods, and make informed postsecondary education and training decisions. In the K-12 system, these efforts begin early, intensify in the middle school years, and become even more focused during high school. Postsecondary partners utilize an aligned career development framework for their adult learners.

2a. Comprehensive Career Development System and Resources
Description

The school district or college has in place a career development system that spans all grade levels and clarifies relevant roles and responsibilities of counseling staff, teachers, and administrators. Students engage in career interest assessments, career-related learning activities both in school and within the community, and interactions with adults working in business and industry. Career development activities, resources, and counseling procedures are aligned with state and/or local standards. Parents or guardians are actively engaged as important partners in the career development process. A Career Development Committee oversees this work. Appropriate materials are prepared that provide information about the local and regional economy and high-priority career sectors.

Discussion

The need for substantive, effective career development is acute, given the clear data that millions of youth and young adults–even academically prepared youths–are enrolling in college, switching majors multiple times, and dropping out without completing their college programs. One study estimated that 46 percent of students change their major at least one time.[1]

At the K-12 level, the effective Career Development system is built on the foundation of a systemic and age-appropriate approach to career awareness, career exploration, career application, and career management skill preparation.

Unfortunately, in many K-12 education systems, career development is an overlooked and uncoordinated set of activities. At the postsecondary level, career development resources often exist, but many of the less motivated and less engaged learners do not actively take advantage of these resources. Rather, learners may have a vague notion of a career interest, or remember some classes that they enjoyed during high school, and decide on a declared major without a great deal of thought. Youths may not really know how that major will lead to specific career opportunities and how many jobs actually exist their selected field of study.

The best reality check as to whether a career development system is getting the desired results is this – find typical students in the hallway or another informal setting and ask them to talk about their career interests and how that connects to their plans for the future. If in most cases, the students can answer confidently and without hesitation about their thinking and options, then you have an effective career development model. Given this reality check, most schools are not hitting the mark. Typically, even when individual schools are working on the problem, there is not a cohesive integrated K-12 approach to career development.

In contrast, an effective Career Development System encompasses four stages that help students move from the abstract to the experiential:

◊ Career Awareness

◊ Career Exploration

◊ Career Application-Immersion

◊ Career Management

At the K-12 level, the effective Career Development system is built on the foundation of a systemic and age-appropriate approach to career awareness, career exploration, career application, and career management skill preparation that is seamlessly integrated with learning about postsecondary education options and developing students who "know how to go" to postsecondary education (selection, application, and financing).

At the postsecondary level, community-colleges and four-year colleges and universities ensure that all students give serious attention to career development, first when they enroll, and then throughout the course of their program.

For an in-depth explanation of this approach, go to Chapter 8: Exploring and Planning for Careers, which shares key strategies that can be deployed and a year-by-year model sequence of activities.

Self-Assessment

◊ In what ways do our districts (K-12) or college partners provide career development for all students?

◊ What are the responsibilities of teachers and school counselors in facilitating career development?

◊ Are there state-provided or other career development resources that should be incorporated?

Action Steps

☐ Create a Pathways System Career Development Team to help planning and implementation of system-wide expectations and resources for career development.

☐ Form a campus-based Career Development Team to development and implement a career development system and curricula.

☐ Develop a Career Development framework, aligned with state requirements and professional organization standards, that identifies the broad topics and experiences students in each grade level will have.

☐ Ask each Pathway Partner organization to adapt and apply the framework in its organizational setting. Include activities and experiences that engage employers and community organizations.

☐ Conduct an asset inventory of career development activities and curricula currently in place. Identify gaps and prioritize the most immediate needs.

☐ Review career development curricula and programs used at other schools, colleges and workforce system providers.

☐ Create and distribute industry sector and career-related brochures to students, parents, community, and staff.

☐ Ensure that accommodations and adaptations for special education students and English language learners are embedded in the system.

☐ Provide guidance staff, teachers, and faculty time to collaborate for developing lessons and related activities.

2b. Student Career and Education Plan
Description

Every youth, by grade eight, has developed and begins to maintain a personalized Career and Education Plan integrating career development with planning for high school course taking, postsecondary education, and other forms of training. The plan is developed with parental or guardian input, and it is reviewed and modified at least annually.

Discussion

As of 2015, 29 states and the District of Columbia had enacted requirements for the use of a Career and Education Plan (under a variety of names depending on the state).[2] The purpose of a Career and Education Plan (CEP) is to create a process for career development and to link this to a student's planning for high-school-level courses and college-level courses. A CEP should be the core deliverable within the school systems career development program.

At the college level, interest in strongly encouraging or requiring career development is also growing. Decisions about career development requirements are made on a campus-by-campus basis, and there does not appear to be any national data about how many colleges require career development activities by students. College programs like ASAP,[3] which require a career development plan as part of a comprehensive set of supports, demonstrate student retention and program completion that is much higher than for the general student population.

Self-Assessment

◊ Does every student, by grade eight, develop a personalized CEP that integrates career development with planning for high school course taking, for further education and training, and for career entry? If so, how do students develop the CEP, how often is it reviewed, and how are parents or guardians involved?

◊ Does every newly enrolled college or adult education student develop a personalized CEP that integrates career development with planning for further education and training?

◊ What schools or colleges within the Pathways Partnership have a career development system that is well-organized and yielding positive results?

Action Steps

❏ Review examples of individualized CEPs, focusing on those that have a six-to-ten-year window.

❏ Create an individualized CEP plan with teacher, guidance staff, and parent input.

❏ Provide professional development for teachers and counseling staff on the way in which the plan will be used.

❏ Provide an overview of the plan's purpose and procedures to all students and parents.

❏ Make information about the CEP on each school's website.

❏ Review the individualized CEP with the student annually to determine its effectiveness and if revisions are necessary.

❏ Incorporate use of the CEP into the school or college's system for comprehensive career development.

2c. Preparing Students to Choose Among Pathway Programs
Description

In the K-12 sector, counselors from middle and high schools collaborate to introduce students to high school Pathway Programs, review results from career development assessments and inventories, and also review regional employment and hiring data to helping students and their parents make informed enrollment decisions.

Discussion

For the typical 13- or 14-year-old, career development is an abstract concept because what lies immediately ahead for the 8th or 9th grade student is three or four more years of required academic classes, with a schedule that is randomly filled in by a smattering of disconnected elective classes. The actual high school experience has little to do with the student's career development goals.

By contrast, offering Pathway Programs at the 9th or 10th grade levels creates a needed immediacy to questions raised through career development. Therefore, as the Pathway Programs are launched in a Pathways System, students need a way to learn about the available Pathway Programs and make informed enrollment decisions. Of course, enrollments will be determined by the number of seats available in a particular Pathway Program as well as whether or not the school district allows for open enrollment of students from other schools in the district or from neighboring districts.

Pathways System leaders should consider marketing (or awareness building) to encourage enrollment in all programs, but especially for the high-skill, high-wage programs for which sometime enrollments are too low.

Most youths only know about careers that are popular in the media – lawyering, doctoring, entertainment, sports, and perhaps culinary, custom automotive, space exploration, and other miscellaneous jobs. The occupations that actually offer the greatest sustained opportunities – health care, computer technology, and engineering – may seem too difficult or lack the "cool and fun" factor of popular programs like culinary and cosmetology, among others. Pathways System leaders need to consider marketing (or awareness building) to encourage enrollment in all programs, but especially for the high-skill, high-wage programs for which sometime enrollments are too low. Students and parents need a number of opportunities to learn about the programs available at the secondary and postsecondary levels, particularly for the programs that require stronger academic preparation and personal effort.

Effective pathway leaders take this challenge seriously by starting early to engage elementary and middle school students and their parents. Schools conduct regular student and family tours of the high school allowing visitors to see several of the Pathway Programs in operation as well as having youth ambassadors from the high school come to the middle school or the 9th grade freshman academy to talk with students about the programs. Schools can also offer a Pathway Program fair or expo on a district-wide basis or a school-by-school basis. Some schools also offer summer-camp versions of their programs, opening up the school to younger students, to give an advance peek at how the program looks and feels.

Self-Assessment

◊ What type of collaboration happens between middle school and high school staff to help students make Pathway Programs selection decisions?

◊ How do students considering postsecondary education learn about the Pathway Programs that relate to their expressed area of career interest? Are campus tours only a general introduction to the campus, its amenities, and the college application process, or do the tours also focus on learning about programs related to the students' career interests?

Action Steps

❐ Embed information about the high school Pathways System into the middle school career development experience. Consider sharing Pathway Program-related videos created by high school students.

❐ Arrange for all middle school students to visit the high school and local career technical center and tour each of the Pathway Programs at each.

❐ Require all freshmen to complete a one semester or full year freshman seminar course. Provide multiple opportunities for freshmen to experience and learn about each of the Pathway Programs.

❐ Train junior and senior students at the high school, or college students already enrolled in a Pathway Program, to serve as tour guides for program open house and student orientation activities.

2d. Engaging Parents and Family Members
Description

Students and their parents, guardians, or influential family members have opportunities to learn about postsecondary options and how to make postsecondary decisions that are related to the identified career interests of the student. Extensive effort is made to engage students from families that have not participated in postsecondary education and to provide targeted support for specific areas such as understanding the application process and financing options.

Discussion

Research indicates, and experience confirms, that the role of parenting teens is very different than the parenting younger children.[4] As the role of parenting changes, the way that schools interact with parents must also change. The Ferris University study on career advisement suggests that, for high school students, their parents still are the most influential people in helping them make a career decision.[5] A great amount of work needs to be done in learning how to activate parents in their new role.

Pathway system leaders must actively innovate with new approaches so they can help parents both raise aspirations of the students and help them make the most appropriate personal decision based on their aptitudes, their achievement preparedness, their work ethic, and their career aspirations.

Parents and family members without postsecondary success also need focused help to understand the college search, application, and financing process. This awareness-building effort needs to start early so that economically disadvantaged families understand that postsecondary education is not a pipe-dream for their child. Almost all parents want their child to enroll in postsecondary education, but if they have been convinced by media stories that college is too expensive, or that it's too demanding for their child, then they might unwittingly send contradictory messages.

Self-Assessment

◊ What learning opportunities for students and parents are offered regarding postsecondary options?

◊ What materials are developed that specifically address the role of parents and family members in supporting the student's career and postsecondary decision-making?

Action Steps

❏ Blend college awareness and college access activities with career development.

❏ Invite postsecondary financial aid experts to speak with students and parents.

❏ Organize student visits to community colleges, colleges/universities, and technical colleges.

❏ Facilitate an engaging college and career event for parents and students at least once a year. After a brief informative presentation, invite parents and students to stay and talk with representatives of regional businesses and postsecondary institutions.

❏ Explore how to use "parent advisors" to assist other parents in the student aid and student advising process.

System Component 3. Pathway Program

In a Pathways System, education and training partners coordinate the development of a range of Pathway Programs for youth and adult learners. A Pathway Program is a sequence of interconnected academic and elective classes revolving around a career or subject theme, integrated with experiential learning and close connections between secondary and postsecondary education, training, and/or apprenticeships. Pathway Programs are designed to address workforce needs and support the development of Career and Life Readiness knowledge and skills for each learner.

Students explore available Pathway Programs while in middle school or early high school and then choose a program in which to enroll. Each school offers Pathway Programs that address a variety of student interests as well as prominent career opportunities in the region and state. In systems that have regional career technical centers, their programs are linked to programs at the partnering high school, and when open enrollment options are offered, students may choose among multiple schools. Each Pathway Program is seamlessly connected to postsecondary education and/or training and apprenticeship programs.

See Chapter Six for an in-depth review of decisions to be made by the Campus-Based Leadership Team and the process for creating a high quality Pathway Program.

System Component 4. Employer and Community Engagement

In a Pathways System, employers and community organizations are essential partners, helping to provide students with skill development and career development experiences in the workplace and bringing highly relevant work-based activities, content, and role models into the classroom. The Pathways System outlines practical and specific ways that employers and community organizations can connect with students and impact each Pathway Program.

4a. Well-defined Employer and Community Connections

Description

Each Pathway Program offers students a variety of employer- and community-based learning opportunities with a strong expectation that students will participate in workplace tours, job shadows, internships, and community-based service learning. Pathway Program teachers engage business and community volunteers for guest lecturing, advising, mentoring of student teams, and coaching and judging of student projects.

Discussion

Too often, individual teachers and faculty members are given the entire responsibility to determine what kind of employer involvement they can develop for their Pathway Program. Most teachers have very little time to develop these processes, but some teachers have stronger community and employer connections and are more naturally entrepreneurial than others. Thus, while some programs have strong connections, many others may have very weak community and employer involvement. The Campus-based Leadership Team and/or Pathways Partnership should work to create clear policies, processes, and expectations that students will participate in workplace tours, job shadows, internships, and community-based service learning.

> *Too often, individual teachers and faculty members are given the entire responsibility to determine what kind of employer involvement they can develop for their Pathway Program. Most teachers have very little time to develop these processes.*

Roles for employers fall in the following categories with supporting strategies:

Help Students Build Career Understanding
◊   Host a Table at a Career or Industry Fair
◊   Offer a Work-Site Tour
◊   Grant a Career Interview
◊   Offer Resume Writing and Mock Job Interviews Support
◊   Invite Students to Join Employer at a Work Event

Facilitate Classroom Presentations and/or Lead Small Group Discussions
◊   Talk to Students About Their Career or Industry Sector
◊   Talk to Students About a Specific Technical Skill or Use of Equipment
◊   Talk to Students About General Workplace Skills and Culture
◊   Talk to Students About Career Exploration and Career Navigation

Assist Students with Career or Leadership Projects
◊   Act as an Expert Judge
◊   Act as Project Coach
◊   Assist Teachers with Career-Related Units of Study

Offer Experiential Learning Opportunities Outside of School
◊ Host Student Job-Shadows
◊ Host Student Internships
◊ Host Teacher Externships

Support Program Improvement and Advancement
◊ Serve on a Program Advisory Committee
◊ Act as an Advocate
◊ Collaborate in a New Program Start-Up or Restructuring
◊ Provide Program Resources
◊ Share Professional Expertise

Self-Assessment
◊ Does the school or Pathways Partnership have established procedures or processes to assist teachers with securing business and community volunteers?

◊ Does the school have established training and/or security clearance procedures in place for business and community volunteers?

◊ Do employer-led organizations or industry-based organizations in the community have designated staff and processes for creating connections to K-12 or postsecondary education? If so, describe the involvement.

Action Steps
☐ Create a role for the Intermediary Organization or industry-based organizations to coordinate employer and community involvement across the entire Pathways System.

☐ Designate one or more staff members at each school to coordinate with the Intermediary Organization and to lead employer and community involvement for their campus.

☐ Create a written, clearly stated description of each volunteer role that includes tips for engaging with high school students; distribute to all volunteers and post on the Pathways Partnership or school website.

☐ Create an orientation session for new volunteers emphasizing student privacy laws; offer orientation session several times a year.

☐ Establish expectations for the number of times each Pathway Program Instructional Team should engage with a volunteer each school year.

☐ Train teachers how to effectively work with employer partners; ensure that student privacy laws and student safety laws are reviewed with staff.

❑ Develop a process and directions for volunteers to easily obtain required security clearances.

❑ Determine the minimum number of experiential learning activities students will have each year.

❑ Develop protocols and procedures for staff to follow when arranging these experiences.

❑ Share student experiences with the community to build Pathways System awareness.

❑ Explore development or purchase of a web-based technology tool to facilitate the scheduling and connection to employer volunteers.

4b. Business and Industry Experiences for Faculty and Staff
Description
Teachers from each Pathway Program are encouraged to participate in relevant job shadows and teacher externships.

Discussion
Often, teachers and counselors have very little professional employment experience outside of the education sector. To create a Pathways model that makes the culture shift away from a content-only approach, these teachers and counselors need to experience, first-hand, what the modern workplace looks and feels like. This business-related learning experience is often called a teacher externship or teacher job shadow, and it is among the best ways for teachers to get connected to the relevance of the workplace. Through a teacher externship, staff can gain a deeper understanding of how employability skills, career-specific skills, and general academic knowledge and skills, play out in the workplace.

> *Through a teacher externship, staff can gain a deeper understanding of how employability skills, career-specific skills, and general academic knowledge and skills, play out in the workplace.*

Self-Assessment
◊ Are teachers and other staff required or offered support to participate in a teacher externship or teacher job shadow?

◊ How many teachers and faculty members are involved in these activities, and how often?

◊ Is there any funding for stipends and recognition for participating teachers and faculty members?

Action Steps

☐ Involve teachers and faculty members in developing a teacher externship or teacher job shadow program drawing upon existing program models in other school districts.

☐ Create written protocol and procedures detailing the structure and expectations of the program.

☐ Invite Pathway Program Advisory Committee members to offer their companies as pilot sites for the externship program.

☐ Structure the program so that Pathway Program Instructional Team members can experience the externship together.

☐ Strongly recommend that Pathway Program Instructional Teams develop cross-curricular units on what they learned through the externship.

☐ Create a feedback process so host companies and teachers are able to reflect upon and improve the externship experience.

☐ Provide teacher stipends and teacher recognition opportunities for the teachers who choose to participate.

System Component 5. Dynamic Teaching and Learning

In a Pathways System, teachers and faculty members employ evidence-based instructional practices that are highly engaging, rigorous, and relevant to each Pathway Program. Teachers continue to implement important required curricular reforms, and there is an ongoing emphasis on problem-based, project-based, and inquiry-based learning in all Pathway Programs. Targeted professional development, teacher externships, peer collaboration, and instructional coaching provide ongoing teacher support.

5a. Curriculum Supported by High Quality Teaching and Learning
Description

Pathway Program teachers work to implement high quality curriculum in core academic content areas such English language arts, mathematics, and science as well as in other required and elective courses; they utilize evidence-based instructional approaches such as project-based, problem-based, and inquiry-based learning.

Discussion

In a Pathways System, the program is built around standards, but not just standards relating to technical knowledge and skills. They also include the important knowledge, skills, and attitudes that cut across any program, and which are developed through a variety of disciplines.

A growing body of evidence (see Chapter 3) demonstrates the importance and impact of both active learning, which activates student curiosity and intellectual engagement around problems, projects, questions, and challenges, and social-emotional learning, which helps students monitor and regulate their own emotions.

Active Learning

For active learning, teachers can employ a range of techniques with specific definitions and strategies. These include: Project-based learning-using a project to organize and connect learning among multiple disciplines and to demonstrate learning; problem-based learning-helping students learn to frame and address problems where the scope of the problem and the information needed is not spoon-fed to them; inquiry-based learning-posing a big question that the student is given to answer; and challenge-based learning-issuing a challenge to address a pressing phenomenon, whether it is social, environmental, technical, or international in nature. These strategies, when delivered with careful planning and structure, lead learners to be more resourceful in finding and vetting pertinent information, to retain more of what they have learned, and to be able to apply their knowledge in new settings.

Active learning strategies, when delivered with careful planning and structure, lead learners to be more resourceful in finding and vetting pertinent information, to retain more of what they have learned, and to be able to apply their knowledge in new settings.

Active learning contrasts sharply with the way education was delivered to many of us. I well remember the classroom of the 1960s and 70s where students were asked to fill out simple worksheets using only a textbook as an information source; where students did all their work – reading, taking tests, and writing reports, in isolation from other students; where memorization of names and dates and labels was paramount; where solving a mathematical problem with only one well-rehearsed algorithm was the norm; or when listening to a lecture was for the purpose of taking notes and then answering test questions based on the lecture. One of the premier organizations providing professional development to teachers in the use of Project-based learning is the Buck Institute for Education.[6]

Social-Emotional Learning

Social-emotional learning helps students understand the range of and source of their emotions, based upon the evidence that having a better connection with emotions helps remove unseen barriers to learning. For example, Dr.

John Medina, author of the book "Brain Rules," points out students who bring a high level of emotional stress from their homes, neighborhoods, and peer relationships literally cannot think clearly.[7] Learning to understand, monitor and regulate these emotions helps the individual clear their mind and focus on the work of learning.

Toolkit of Teaching Strategies

Teachers and education advocates are prone to take ideological positions and engage in "education culture wars." I am not arguing for veering to an ideological extreme and completely excluding the use of "traditional" methods. Mature teachers recognize there is time and place for sharing foundational information as quickly and efficiently as possible. There is an appropriate way for the teacher to deliver information and expound on ideas through a lecture. Students, through memorization, should master basic arithmetic facts so they don't have to waste intellectual energy on recalling basic equations. Students need to know the rules of decoding text (phonics) and develop a broad, basic vocabulary so they can focus on understanding, not just on the mechanics of reading.

Whatever the mix of strategies employed, the end game is for students to internalize knowledge and develop the creativity, problem-framing and problem-solving skills so they face the challenges of the real world with confidence.

Whatever the mix of strategies employed, the end game is for students to internalize knowledge and develop creativity, problem-framing, and problem-solving skills, so they face the challenges of the real world with confidence. Today's world is information rich, but understanding and wisdom are rare. We need to develop true thinkers, not just individuals who believe there is a right answer and a wrong answer to every question. Teachers who work to develop their craft are always learning, testing, and experimenting with techniques for teaching and learning.

Self-Assessment

◊ Is teaching and learning in the school only focused on mandates related to core academic standards and teacher evaluation protocols, or are staff members actively seeking to understand and apply research-based instructional strategies?

◊ What professional development relating to these instructional strategies has been provided?

◊   Is professional development actually changing practice in the classroom? Why or why not?

Action Steps

☐   Gather, review, and discuss research and resources to deepen understanding about dynamic teaching and learning.

☐   Identify the instructional practices, like active learning, social-emotional learning, literacy strategies, and curriculum integration, that teachers will be encouraged to use and those that will be rolled out through school wide initiatives.

☐   Provide ongoing professional development opportunities for teaching staff to learn and hone these approaches.

☐   Utilize highly skilled instructional coaches when feasible.

☐   Organize learning walks so that teachers can see peers utilizing the instructional approaches.

5b. Literacy Across the Curriculum

Description

The school sets expectations and monitors implementation of teaching and learning strategies that strengthen students' literacy skills; this expectation is shared among teachers in all subject areas.

Discussion

Over the past 15 years, the concept of literacy-across-the-curriculum has been growing in sophistication and implementation in many secondary schools. For most school systems, the thinking about reading has been "learn to read" in Grades K-3 and then "read to learn" in grades 4 and beyond. What this approach has failed to recognize is that basic decoding skills, word identification, and vocabulary acquisition are important foundations but that reading comprehension skills must continue to develop as students progress through school.

One of the discoveries among literacy researchers and practitioners has been that in order for students to access higher levels of information and content, they need to continue to strengthen their reading comprehension strategies and apply those in the different disciplines.[8] Reading within each discipline – literature, history, mathematics, science, and career programs – requires specialized vocabulary and comprehension strategies that are tailored to that discipline.

This finding has led to updating of academic standards across many states, standards that add a new emphasis on strategies for understanding non-fiction text, such as in social studies and technical education. A strong pathway system must be built with an explicit literacy-across-the-curriculum approach

Self-Assessment

◊ Do teachers explicitly teach or model a range of literacy strategies within their content area? If so, provide one or two examples and the ways in which school administrators monitor this expectation.

◊ What kind of professional development relating to these literacy strategies has been provided?

Action Steps

❑ Provide teachers with professional development opportunities to increase their understanding and use of literacy strategies.

❑ Utilize highly skilled instructional coaches or reading specialists when feasible.

❑ Promote the understanding that all teachers share a responsibility in helping students attain and utilize literacy strategies tailored to their discipline.

❑ Provide teachers with relevant professional articles and tip sheets pertaining to literacy integration.

5c. Academic, Social-Emotional, and Program Supports

Description

Students who struggle to meet academic and social expectations are given a variety of supports, including but not limited to tutoring, customized online remediation, and online credit recovery options. For some older students who are participating in work-based learning or early college credit programs, child care, transportation services, and incidental educational expenses may also be addressed.

Discussion

Another important component of the teaching and learning framework for Pathways is the development of academic, social-emotional, and program supports. For students to be able to access high-level content, they will need continuing academic support. Some of the program research demonstrates that when academic supports are provided concurrent to a student's participation in a relevant career-themed course, the academic instruction yields better results (See Chapter 3 for information about the I-BEST program and integrated CTE/literacy and CTE/math programs). The key factor in this type of concurrent support is motivation and relevance. If students are motivated to learn the content they find in the themed or career-related classes and see how the learning skills will be applied in that learning environment, then they will be more open to investing time and energy to strengthen their learning skills (reading comprehension, writing, and mathematics problem solving).

In addition, many, perhaps most, students need social and emotional support, particularly if they are from situations of distress, family trauma, or concentrated poverty. In today's environment, school leaders should presume that many students come to school with some level of emotional distress and trauma. Brain research clearly demonstrates that stress and trauma interfere with learning. Learners need to develop strategies to help them introspectively process the thoughts and emotions in a positive way. These social emotional supports can unlock the paralysis in their psyche so that they can focus on learning.[9] And to be honest, many teachers also struggle from their own life and relational challenges. They too need to strengthen their own capacity to deal with stress; building these social-emotional strategies into the learning environment will produce healthier, happier teachers too!

If students are motivated to learn the content they find in the themed or career-related classes... they will be more open to investing time and energy to strengthen their learning skills (reading comprehension, writing, and mathematics problem solving).

Finally, some older students participating in extended work-based learning or early college credit programs, need specialized supports that are specific to their life and financial situations. Learners may need financial assistance for transportation to and from their Pathway Program and work-based learning experiences, and young parents may need childcare services that are safe, enriching, and affordable. Students at both secondary and post-secondary levels may also need financial support to cover expenses such as books, materials, uniforms, and the cost of industry-based certifications.

Self-Assessment
◊ Do we offer effective academic supports for struggling or at-risk students?

◊ Do we offer support to help students develop social-emotional competence?

◊ Are students able to get to their work-based learning experiences or a college campus? If not, what steps can be taken to improve this?

Action Steps

☐ Explore remediation strategies that integrate relevant applications of reading, mathematics and other subjects, particularly utilizing strategies that are integrated with the student's identified career development interests.

☐ Implement scheduling options that allow students to access both academic remediation and Pathways-themed courses, not being forced to forego something that is inherently motivating for something that is difficult and demoralizing.

☐ Survey students and staff to determine the most immediate support needs that can be addressed at a campus level.

☐ Review the current process of identifying students in need of support and the way those supports are provided. Identify and begin to address gaps.

☐ Ask Instructional Teams or department members to brainstorm and share the academic and social support challenges that students face and ways in which these needs can be met.

☐ Form a committee to review support tools and resources, both no-cost and for purchase, and identify the ones that may meet the needs of students.

5d. Strategic Professional Development

Description

The professional development needs of administrators, teachers, and counselors are identified; a systematic plan to provide professional development is in place. Professional development includes a focus on alignment of secondary and postsecondary curricula, development of integrated academic and technical content, strong content knowledge among teachers, and active learning strategies.

Discussion

Professional development for teachers is something that everyone agrees is important to the development of high-quality instruction. However, based on numerous discussions I have had with administrators and teachers, in actual implementation, professional development is often planned and carried out in an ad hoc manner.

Before the start of the school year, administrators usually set aside one or two days of professional development, and two or three more days are built into the school year calendar. Most of the professional development that precedes a typical school year opening of school may be focused on what should really be called 'technical assistance' or 'operational training,' such as learning about new rules and regulations and how to use new software systems.

By contrast, the more productive approach is to create a professional development plan in direct response to the identified professional growth needs of individual teachers and other staff members. This means that administrators first must identify the competencies needed for good teaching.

School administrators create a professional development plan in direct response to the identified professional growth needs of individual teachers and other staff members.

Next, they must either formally or informally assess how well-developed those competencies are for each teacher. This leads to the development of a personalized professional growth plan for each staff member. Next, the administrators look at the aggregated needs of staff derived from the sum of the personalized professional growth plans. From there, when there are common needs, the administration can create professional development opportunities (perhaps in small groups by targeted needs) that will address these needs. Of course, for very specialized professional growth needs, the administrator tries to provide the opportunity for teachers to access online learning and off-campus workshops and conferences, given budget and staffing constraints.

In the same way that students need to understand the competencies for Career and Life Readiness, teachers should understand and own their own professional growth needs, and the school leaders should set expectations and create the supports for that professional growth.

Within the Pathways implementation system, a number of professional development activities are commonly needed, including the following:

◊ Managing effective Advisory Committees

◊ Creating business and school partnerships

◊ Upgrading career development systems

◊ Helping counseling professionals and teachers understand current career opportunities and workforce trends

◊ Communicating, branding, and conducting outreach for the Pathways System

◊ Designing a freshman seminar and freshman academy

◊ Developing the capacity of the leader

◊ Managing the master schedule for Pathway Programs and academies

◊ Designing the Pathway Program

◊ Using "Guided Pathways" models (like ASAP) at the postsecondary level

◊ Developing teacher externships

◊ Practices for effective Instructional Teaming

◊ Creating meaningful work-based learning/experiential learning

Self-Assessment

◊ Are teacher competencies identified and discussed, leading to personalized professional growth plans?

◊ Is a school-wide professional development plan in place? If so, how often is it updated, and who takes the lead in ensuring it is followed?

◊ Is there a structured process for identifying and providing professional development needs for all staff?

◊ Is the professional development plan guided by needs identified through a teacher competency model or by self-identified teacher interests and preferences?

Action Steps

❐ Conduct an asset inventory of current professional development opportunities (required and voluntary) available to teachers, counseling staff, and administrators.

❐ Develop an annual or multi-year comprehensive professional development plan.

❐ Invite or require teachers to develop individualized professional development plans.

❐ Ensure that professional development opportunities include a focus on the alignment of secondary and postsecondary curriculum, the development of academic and technical skills integration, an increase in teachers' content knowledge, and evidenced-based instructional approaches.

❐ Offer voluntary professional development at various times including before school, during lunch ("Lunch and Learn"), after school, and during summer break.

❐ Encourage the use of professional learning communities and peer-led professional development, tapping into on-site teacher and administrator expertise.

❐ Invite or require staff members that attend professional conferences to share what they have learned upon their return at upcoming staff development meetings.

System Component 6. Cross-Sector Partnerships

A Pathways System brings together members from K-12 and postsecondary education, employer organizations, community volunteers, and workforce and economic developers, organized as a Pathways Partnership. The Pathways Partnership convenes a Pathways Partnership Leadership Team that provides strategic input on the direction and responsibilities of all partners involved in implementing the Pathways System. Together, they identify the key knowledge, skills, and attributes that help youth and young adults succeed in education, the workplace, and civic life. All aspects of the Pathways System reflect these shared Career and Life Readiness goals.

6a. Pathways Partnership Leadership Structure
Description
Comprised of leaders from multiple stakeholder groups (including K-12 education, postsecondary education, employers and employer-led organizations, workforce development, economic development, and community-based organizations), the Pathways Partnership provides strategic guidance and advocacy for the Pathways System. The Pathways Partnership creates other working groups as needed to carry out detailed planning around specific components of the Pathways System Implementation Plan. Members of the Pathways Partnership meet regularly during initial development of the Pathways System Implementation Plan and at least twice annually to monitor and sustain its success.

Discussion
The Pathways Partnership represents all the various stakeholders involved across the region, and at regular intervals the entire group of organizations should convene to give feedback and approval to key decisions and also to provide public support and endorsement to the Pathways System initiative. To accomplish the work of the Pathways Partnership, the partners need to delegate planning and decision making authority to the Pathways Partnership Leadership Team and also guide and support the work of other committees.

Pathways Partnership Leadership Team (PPLT)
The Pathways Partnership Leadership Team (PPLT) is a subset of the Pathways Partnership, being identified and selected from within the Pathways Partnership. It has the following responsibilities:

◊ The PPLT decides on key goals and parameters related to the Pathways System. Decisions include identifying the high priority programs that should be offered at the secondary and postsecondary levels and deciding how communications will be carried out.

◊ The PPLT engages additional leaders from education, workforce, employment, and elected leadership to actively and visibly build understanding and buy-in to the Pathways System and also helps push through barriers to Pathways System implementation, such as policy, funding, and entrenched practices. The PPLT also ensures that appropriate planning and implementation teams are in place to carry out the goals of the Pathways System initiative.

◊ The PPLT coordinates with the regional Industry Sector Working Groups and local programs to ensure that all school Pathway Programs are treated equitably and receive the support they need for success.

◊ The PPLT will meet regularly during initial Pathways System design (probably once or twice monthly). Once the system is developed and in operation, the PPLT should meet as often as necessary, but at least quarterly to monitor and sustain its progress and success.

Intermediary Organization

Within the Pathways Partnership, one organization is identified as the "Intermediary Organization." This organization works closely under the guidance of the PPLT and takes the lead role in convening all the Pathways System partners, inviting new partners, documenting decisions, drafting and finalizing the Pathways System Implementation Plan, and monitoring and reporting progress.

Campus-based Leadership Team (CBLT)

As discussed in chapter 6 relating to the development of an individual Pathway Program, each partner school district superintendent will appoint one or more Campus-based Leadership Teams, consisting of the chief administrator from each school or college campus as well as other administrators, teachers, and faculty the administrator chooses. The Campus-based Leadership Team (CBLT) will coordinate with the Pathways Partnership Leadership Team (through the Intermediary Organization), and lead planning and implementation at the campus level, making recommendations regarding issues such as number of students who will participate in Pathway Programs, the grade levels at which Pathway Programs will be offered, the way in which students will learn about and enroll in Pathway Programs, and the way in which Pathway Programs will be organized. The CBLT also configures and appoints individuals to several additional campus-based committees:

◊ Campus-based Career Development Committee-A team to coordinate and plan for a comprehensive approach to career development, connecting the work of the Counseling Department, with academic and pathway-based classes.

◊ Campus-based Pathway Program Instructional Team-the team of instructors that designs the Pathway Program and regularly meets to coordinate curriculum integration and attention to the learning needs of students in a Pathways Program cohort.

◊ Campus-based Pathway Program Advisory Committee-The employer-led team that provides input to Pathway Program content and also helps coordinate employer and community involvement with the Pathway Program.

Industry Sector Working Groups (ISWG)

At the regional level, one or more industry-sector working groups (ISWG) are identified and/or convened to help coordinate that industry sector's collaboration with the Pathways Partnership. The ISWG collaborates with education and workforce partners to provide up-to-date information on specific career trends, anticipated changes in demand, emerging technologies, and on-the-job skill requirements. While many ISWGs are self-organized and self-governed, the PPLT invites them to collaborate with the Pathways Partnership and to meet as often as necessary but not less than twice annually.

> *At the regional level, one or more industry-sector working groups (ISWG) are identified and/or convened to help coordinate that industry sector's collaboration with the Pathways Partnership.*

Career and Life Readiness Task Force

The PPLT convenes a working group to explore current definitions of Career and Life Readiness and develop a model definition of CLR that can be embraced by all the partners.

Pathways Communications Team (PCT)

The PPLT forms a Pathways Communications Team to create shared communications tools (talking points, branding messages, brochures, and web-based information) and provides coordination and training to ensure that all pathway partners are communicating similar messages to various stakeholders and using multiple communications channels.

Pathways System Career Development Committee

The PPLT creates a team of secondary, postsecondary, and workforce system professionals to identify resources for career development, establish shared principles and approaches for career development, and share promising practices that can be adapted or replicated among participating organizations.

Self-Assessment

◊ Is there an existing working group that might lead our Pathways System work or should a new leadership team be formed?

◊ Have any of the identified committees or working groups already been formed? Who within our K-12, postsecondary, workforce, and economic development sectors might know about existing entities?

◊ Has any entity of state government established guidance or expectations for the outcome of Pathway Programs or for Pathway Systems?

◊ Are community-wide committees or working groups in place that could lend support to or collaborate with the Pathways Partnership?

Action Steps

☐ Form an initial planning team that includes leaders from K-12 education, postsecondary education, employer organizations, parents, and community organizations.

☐ Draft a Pathways Partnership fact sheet for potential members.

☐ Draft a suggested organizational chart for the Pathways Partnership.

☐ Develop a draft Pathways Partnership Leadership Team (PPLT) description that includes its key objectives and functions, frequency of meetings, roles, expectations, and responsibilities for team members.

☐ Ask the planning group to nominate and select members of the Pathways Partnership Leadership Team, consisting of 7-11 members.

☐ Schedule and announce meeting dates and facilitate a kickoff meeting of the PPLT.

☐ The PPLT designates or elects a member of the PPLT as the Chair.

☐ Adopt necessary bylaws or procedures; appoint committees and working groups; take accurate meeting notes and document decisions; create a protocol for internal communications among the Pathways Partners.

6b. Campus-based Leadership Teams
Description

A Campus-based Leadership Team (CBLT) is formed for each campus and decides on key issues related to its Pathways System. Decisions include identifying the desired number of students who will participate in Pathway Programs, the grade levels at which Pathway Programs will be offered, the way in which students will learn and make decisions about Pathway Programs, and the way in which Pathway Programs will be organized.

Discussion

The Campus-based Leadership Team can either be designated by the school district or can be self-organized, as happens when an individual school implements a Pathway Program. Chapter 6 includes an explanation of the strategic decisions the CBLT needs to make, such as how to target workforce skills gaps, offer school-wide or "pocket" Pathway Programs, decide how many programs and how many students for each, decide whether or not to use the academy structure, consider freshman academies, set the timeline for transformation, address the false college-prep vs. career prep dichotomy, and work with part-day (shared-time) career technical centers.

Self-Assessment

◊ Has a CBLT been formed? If so, describe its role and responsibilities.

◊ If a CBLT is not yet in place, has any preliminary work or visioning been accomplished?

◊ Is the CBLT working on its own to develop Pathway Programs, or is it working in conjunction with a Pathways Partnership?

Action Steps

❐ Identify members of administration, guidance, and teaching staff that have the skills, temperaments, and perspective to work effectively on the Campus-based Leadership Team

❐ Write a description of the purpose, roles, responsibilities, and time commitment for participation on the CBLT.

❐ Appoint or invite members to join the CBLT, and conduct a kick-off meeting.

❐ Review timelines for program start-up and Pathways System design.

❐ Nominate members for other campus-based teams: Pathway Program Design Team, Pathway Program Advisory Committee, Pathway Program Instructional Team, and Career Development Team.

6c. Pathways Partnership Intermediary Designation
Description

Within the Pathways Partnership, one organization should be identified as the "Intermediary Organization" to take the lead role in convening all the Pathways System partners, inviting new partners, documenting decisions, drafting and finalizing the Pathways System Implementation Plan, and monitoring and reporting progress. Ideally, the Intermediary Organization is not an education provider but is an employer-led or community-based organization.

Discussion

In Chapter 4, we briefly discussed the emergence of the "Collective Impact Movement," a field of practice for sustaining innovation and collaboration among the many education and workforce training partners and social services agencies that work within a community, helping them create more synergies and collective impact. Through the work of this movement, we learn there is an important role identified for an organization to play in helping coordinate the work of multiple organizational partners. This coordinating organization is sometimes referred to as an "intermediary" (or "backbone") organization.[10] Ideally this organization is not one of the core partners (K-12, postsecondary, workforce, etc.) that must implement the Pathway System, which makes serving as an impartial facilitator and convener of the other organizations easier. By nature of funding and policy requirements, each organization has its inherent interests, and sometimes it is difficult to disentangle an organization's interests from the larger interests of the Pathways Partnership. The intermediary role could be played by a nonprofit community-based organization with an education component, or it could be an organization such as Alignment Nashville or STRIVE Together[11] that is specifically created for the intermediary purpose to align the work and agendas of multiple organizations. This role could also be filled by a designated staff person working for an employer-led organization like a business industry coalition or a chamber of commerce that has an education/workforce component to its mission.

Be aware that in some communities, an Intermediary Organization may not be identified or even be in existence at the beginning of the Pathways System initiative. Ultimately, a community with aspirations for effective education-employer-workforce collaboration needs to help stand up such an organization. If no organization currently plays the role of the intermediary, that function may need to be assigned to one of the core partners at the outset. Responsibility for the intermediary role should be assigned to one or two specific staff members, and the Pathways Partnership Leadership Team (PPLT) should charge them with trying to represent the interests of the entire Pathways Partnership. A clear delineation between the staff members' intermediary responsibilities and other responsibilities for their employing organization should exist, so when doing Pathways System work, they are not put in the position of having to also advocate for the interest of their individual

> *If none already exists, a community with aspirations for effective education-employer-workforce collaboration needs to help stand up a new "intermediary" or "backbone" organization.*

organization. The PPLT should continue to urge and cultivate an appropriate organization to take on the role of the intermediary.

Self-Assessment

◊ Has an organization already been designated as the Intermediary?

◊ Have the responsibilities of the Intermediary Organization been put in writing?

◊ Has a staff person been designated to assume the intermediary responsibilities?

Action Steps

❐ Draft a fact sheet outlining the role of the Intermediary Organization and share with organizations you believe may be able to fill this role.

❐ Once an Intermediary Organization is secured, request that they offer two key contacts within the organization to lead this work. Introduce these people at a Pathways Partnership meeting and ensure all stakeholders know the role of the Intermediary Organization and have the contact information.

❐ Announce the Intermediary Organization's designation on the Pathway Partnership website and through other Pathways System communication channels.

6d. Communications Tools and Resources
Description

The Pathways Partnership develops and implements a broad-based communications plan aimed at internal stakeholders and the broader community. Within each partner organization, designated staff members take responsibility for implementing their component of the communications plan and articulating the positive benefits of the Pathways System for their organization.

Discussion

One of the key leadership challenges for implementing an effective Pathways System is being able to communicate with multiple stakeholders about the urgency for change, the positive vision of what change will bring, the benefits that that vision will bring to multiple stakeholders, and then the specific changes and action steps that will be necessary.

Consider the concept of "Return on Investment 360." This means that each stakeholder in the Pathways System (sitting around a 360 degree roundtable), from teachers, administrators, business partners, community leaders, and the learners themselves, has a valid area of self-interest. Every stakeholder is making an investment of time, energy, and resources, and they need to realize a "return on investment" (ROI). Further, that ROI should be clearly articulated as something that is uniquely valuable to them.

Once these factors–urgency, vision, strategy, and return on investment–have been clearly identified, they form the foundation for a communication strategy.

Change guru John Kotter of Harvard Business School says that one of the important reasons why change initiatives fail is that there is a high degree of "under-communication."[12] Leaders take it for granted that all the relevant stakeholders understand and have embraced the core concepts of the change initiative, but when communication is weak, misunderstandings fester and eventually these misunderstandings accumulate and undermine the initiative.

For effective communication to occur, the partners must create a few, easy-to-remember, messages that explain the reason for the Pathways System, and how the system strategies will help effect real change.

Therefore, within each partner organization and as a coalition of organizations, the partners must create a few easy-to-remember messages that explain the reason for the Pathways System and how the System strategies will help affect real change.

One avoidable but all-too-frequent mistake in leading change is to think about communication as a one-way activity. Building buy-in to your initiative will involve facilitating interactive discussions about the central goals and vision, discussing the urgency for change, and then asking for input on how to accomplish the changes that are necessary. Leaders should avoid the temptation to unveil detailed solutions and action plans before they have received input from the people that will need to implement these strategies or from the people (students, parents, and employers) who will be affected by them. The best way to lead a sustainable change strategy is to create a communication strategy that involves ongoing sharing and receiving of input.

This topic is described in detail in chapter 10, authored by brand management expert Pamela Daly.

Self-Assessment
◊ Have you identified the unique "Return on Investment" that each pathway partner organization cares about and put that in writing?

◊   What form(s) of communication do your partner organizations currently utilize (e.g., newsletters, journals, websites, and public meetings)?

Action Steps

☐   Assess current communications resources within the community and within the Pathway Partnership organizations. Determine ways to address gaps. For example, if a communications person is not on staff, identify who may be able to assume these responsibilities.

☐   Review Chapter 10 of this book as a resource for development of a shared brand promise and communications plan.

☐   Develop a communications plan and budget for the Pathways System Initiative.

☐   Develop a dedicated website landing page for all pathways information. Ensure that it is maintained at least weekly.

☐   Utilize social media platforms that are regularly used by key stakeholders, such as Twitter, Instagram, Facebook, and LinkedIn.

☐   Share ideas among Pathway Partners about how their internal communications can support the work of the Pathways Initiative.

☐   If any of the local schools or colleges offers a digital communications or marketing Pathway Program, consider involving students in developing materials for the Pathway System Initiative, particularly for the development of materials targeted to other students.

☐   Write and distribute timely press releases and social media posts to keep the community informed and engaged in the Pathways System Initiative.

6e. Industry Sector Collaboration
Description

At the regional level, representatives from industry sectors collaborate with the Pathways Partnership by forming Industry Sector Working Groups (ISWGs) to provide up-to-date information on specific career trends and anticipated changes. The Pathways Partnership Leadership Team coordinates meetings with the ISWGs and all related program providers; they meet as often as necessary, but not less than twice annually.

Discussion

An Industry Sector Working Group represents an industry and the individual companies that operate within that sector. For example, the many companies that operate within the aerospace industry could include aircraft design, manufacturing and maintenance, airport operations and security, and the commercial airline companies. Industry sector organizations will play an important part of any Pathways Partnership, and they should be sought out and recruited for involvement early in the process. Depending on the region, some industry sector organizations will already exist, representing the interests of important industries like manufacturing, healthcare, or transportation and distribution. The industry groups most likely to be organized are ones that have been long established in the region or that are currently facing a serious skills-gap and are having difficulty filling skilled positions.

While these industry sector organizations may already be working with some schools and colleges or workforce partners, they may not be aware of the long-term benefit of working within the Pathways System structure. The Pathways System approach offers a sustainable infrastructure for collaboration between business/Industry and education and workforce providers. Through connection to the Pathways System infrastructure, all industry sectors will be represented and will have a place at the table through the ups and downs of hiring and economic cycles. This structure will give them a consistent way to provide input on industry and hiring trends and also to provide a common language and approach for connecting business and industry to education and the workforce.

Through the Pathways System structure, companies and education systems won't have to "reinvent the wheel" every time a new industry begins to experience a skills-gap. They also won't have to completely fold up the tents every time there is an economic downturn or restructuring within an industry.

Without a Pathways System, whenever an industry begins to experience a workforce shortage, they have to establish the working relationships with each individual school district and each college. This is a time-consuming and inefficient approach because the ramp up time is too long and the output of program completers from any one program is probably not sufficient to address the overall need. Similarly, when there's an economic downturn, companies tend to turn inward as they're dealing with issues of survival and perhaps having to lay off workers. When companies face these challenges, much of that momentum for collaboration is lost.

Through the Pathways System structure, companies and education systems won't have to "reinvent the wheel" every time a new industry begins to experience a skills-gap. They also won't have to completely fold up the tents every time there is an economic downturn or restructuring within an industry.

The Pathway System infrastructure will stay in place throughout those industry ups and downs.

The Pathway Partnership Leadership Team can help create connections to existing industry-sector organizations or help convene new working groups. The goal is to have working groups that cover the full span of economic activity and careers in the region. The Campus-based Leadership Team should facilitate the work of several ISWGs for planning, launching, and improving Pathway Programs. These working groups oversee their industry's interests and needs across the entire Pathways System. They are separate in function from an individual Pathway Program Advisory Committee, which focuses on an individual Pathway Program. The ISWG should meet as often as necessary during the start-up phase, and then continue to meet at least twice annually to discuss and review important issues relative to the regional workforce talent pipeline.

While the national Career Clusters model includes 16 clusters, some of these could be consolidated to simplify local implementation. For example, the Pathways Partnership Leadership Team could create 10 working groups appropriate for their region. If a particular sector is predominant in a region, it may need to be established as a stand-alone ISWG. Below are examples of 10 working groups that incorporate the 16 Career Clusters:

◊ Agriculture, Environment and Natural Resources

◊ Business Services, Sales, and Marketing

◊ Architecture and Construction (commercial, residential, infrastructure)

◊ Education, Training, and Human Development

◊ Engineering, Design, and Manufacturing

◊ Health Care, Health Science, and Human Services

◊ Government Services, Law and Public Safety, Homeland Security, and Defense

◊ Information Technology and Communications

◊ Tourism and Hospitality

◊ Transportation, Distribution, and Logistics

Self-Assessment

◊ What Industry Sector Working Groups (ISWGs) already exist in the region?

◊ What kinds of education and workforce initiatives already exist with current ISWGs?

◊ Are there significant portions of employment sectors not represented by ISWGs?

◊ Are there state-level ISWGs that can provide connections to companies at the regional level?

Action Steps

☐ Gather a list of the region's current industry sector organizations and create a contact list for each. Reach out to at least one company and organization, and start to identify other contacts.

☐ Share information about the Pathways System and the Pathways Partnership developed by the communications team.

☐ Draft an outline of the ways in which IWSGs may participate in the planning of the Pathways System.

☐ Invite industry sector leaders to an informational session or to a Pathways Partnership meeting to learn about the Pathways System and how they can get involved.

☐ Announce all IWSG partners on the Pathway Partnership's website and through other Pathways System communications channels.

☐ Work to minimize time in meetings for industry sector partners, focus on action items and results, and ask educators to scrupulously avoid unnecessary education jargon.

6f. Utilization of Shared Metrics
Description

Each partner in the Pathways System has identified metrics to measure the level and effectiveness of his or her participation. An ongoing improvement process is established and involves teachers, administrators, and program advisors regularly setting goals, monitoring progress, and tracking improvements made for each Pathway Program and the system as a whole.

Discussion

Each of the education and workforce partners within a Pathways Partnership already has federally- and state-mandated metrics they must use to measure program effectiveness. In addition to these mandated metrics, the Pathway Partnership should also identify (and develop, if necessary) shared input and outcome metrics. These metrics should also be used to measure the role of other organizations, such as employer organizations, and the effective collaboration between systems.

Pathways Program Metrics

Within a school or college, an effective Pathway Program will be measured with an ongoing, data-driven review process. This data-driven improvement process should ask teachers, administrators, and program advisors to regularly set goals, monitor progress, and track improvements made for each Pathway Program and the system as a whole. Administrators and teachers are trained in and expected to reflect upon program data and make improvement plans that reflect data findings. In the Pathways System, the school district and postsecondary partners encourage the use of multiple sources and types of data to assess program quality and program improvement, not relying solely on data from standardized assessments.

In the Pathways System, the school district and postsecondary partners encourage the use of multiple sources and types of data to assess program quality and program improvement, not relying solely on data from standardized assessments.

During the Pathway System design process, Pathways Partners will create a data-reporting tool using variety of indicators. Some of these data are "leading" indictors, meaning they can be measured earlier and lead to the desired results; some indicators are "lagging" indicators, meaning they come later in the process. Another way to describe these measures, which we will use here, is "predictive indicators" and "outcome indicators."

SECONDARY INDICATORS, Grades 7-12
Early stage predictive indicators would be measures such as the following:

◊ The percent of students who have an academic/career plan by the 8th grade and reviewed annually
◊ The percent of the student body enrolled in a Pathway Program
◊ Enrollments for each school's Pathway Programs
◊ Day-to-day class attendance
◊ Incidents of disruptive behaviors and discipline referrals
◊ Semester-by-semester grade point averages
◊ Successful course completion

Intermediate stage outcome indicators could be the following:

◊ Percentage of students staying in their declared pathway
◊ Grade to grade promotion
◊ Percentage of students that complete dual enrollment, AP or IB courses

◊ The percent of student who complete a qualified work-based learning experience in grades 11 or 12

◊ The percent of students who complete a career-related capstone project, presented to a panel of employer and community members

◊ Percent of students who successfully complete an on-line course in high school

Longer-term outcome indicators could be the following:

◊ On-time high school graduation rates (within four years) and five-year graduation rates

◊ Year-to-year dropout incidence rates

◊ Percent of students who complete a Pathways Program

◊ Percent of students who complete three or more classes in a Career Cluster (not sequenced)

◊ Percent of students acquiring college credits in high school

◊ Percent of students earning an industry-based credential or proficient score on a Pathways-related assessment

◊ The average number of college credits that students earn in high school

◊ The percent of seniors who apply and are accepted to one or more postsecondary institutions

◊ The percentage of students in a Pathway Program who declare a major when enrolling in postsecondary education

POSTSECONDARY

Early-stage predictive indicators would be the following:

◊ The percent of new students who have an active career-education plan

◊ The percent of new students who completed a Pathways Program at a local high school

◊ The percent of new students who participate in a career planning course or seminar

◊ The percent of students who take a substantial load of credits

◊ The number and percent of early college credits earned that are recognized on the transcripts of new students

Intermediate-stage outcome indicators could be the following:

◊ The percent of students who advance from year 1 to year 2

◊ The percent of student who complete a postsecondary Pathway Program within 150% of the expected completion time

◊ The percent of students who transfer to a related-major course of study in a four-year postsecondary institution

Longer-term outcome indicators could be the following:

◊ On-time postsecondary graduation rates (3 years for a 2-year program, and 6 years for a 4-year program)

◊ Percent of students who complete a postsecondary Pathways Program

◊ Percent of postsecondary students earning an industry-based credential

◊ The post-program earnings of program completers

Program Review Process and Program Improvement Goal Setting

On a partnership-wide basis, and also on a campus-wide basis, the Campus-based Leadership Team should identify key indicators for each Pathway Program and determine what the minimum targets are for each indicator. Using these indicators, each Pathway Program Advisory Committee should work with the Instructional Team to establish program improvement goals for the Pathway Program and set performance targets using selected indicators.

At the end of the school year, or as soon as necessary data becomes available, the Pathway Program Advisory Committees should meet to conduct an annual review of program performance against the established targets. After this program-by-program analysis is complete, the individual Pathway Program Advisory Committees can establish the next year's improvement goals for the program and submit those program goals to the Campus-based Leadership Team for review and approval.

A very simple metric relating to employer engagement will be the number of volunteer hours that employers donate in a variety of activities for the pathways initiative.

The Pathways Partnership Leadership Team should review the program data for all the Pathway Programs, identify overall Pathway System goals for improvement, and include appropriate data and program improvement goals in its Pathways System Progress Report.

Cross-Sector Metrics

In addition to metrics applied to the individual Pathway Program, the Pathways Partnership Leadership Team should establish metrics to measure overall system performance. For example, a very simple metric relating to employer engagement will be the number of volunteer hours that employers donate in a variety of activities for the Pathways initiative. These hours can be calculated using the national established average of $50 per volunteer hour to determine the in-kind cash value that a company has donated. This would one of the key metrics to measure employer engagement. Another cross-system metric would be the use, acquisition, and application of dual enrollment credits onto the transcripts of incoming freshmen, so it is apparent how many of those earned credits are actually being applied to students' transcripts. The number of credits could also be converted to a dollar figure to demonstrate how much money the Pathways initiatives is saving students in college tuition. These cross-sector metrics should be included and reported in the Pathway Systems Progress Report of outcomes and goals, discussed in the next section.

Sample Cross-Sector Metrics

◊ The number of business partners who participate in Pathway Program Advisory Committees

◊ The percentage of Pathway Program Advisory Committee members who attend at least half of the Advisory Committee meetings

◊ The number of employer volunteers participating in each Pathway Program

◊ The percent of volunteers who rate their volunteer experience as a valuable experience

◊ Number of volunteer hours donated by business and community volunteers

◊ Total dollar value of volunteer hours

◊ Percent of surveyed students who rate their work-based-learning placement as a valuable experience

◊ Percent of surveyed teachers who indicate a majority of business and community volunteers fulfilled their commitments to the Pathway Program

Self-Assessment

◊ Has the school or college identified metrics to measure Pathway Program quality?

◊ What schools or colleges in the Pathways Partnership already have a proven data-based improvement model that is valued by both administrators and instructors?

◊ Do employer-led and community-based organizations already have metrics related to their involvement in education (e.g., hours volunteered, dollar value of volunteer time, number of students reached)? If so, what is the data and how is it generated, collected, and reported?

Action Steps

❑ Ask partners to share the metrics they use and suggest that partners review the metrics named in this section.

❑ Create a Pathway Program series of metrics utilizing multiple sources of student achievement data, including but not limited to state required standardized tests results, when considering the effectiveness and success of each Pathway Program.

❑ Provide each Instructional Team with a data profile specific to its Pathway Program.

❑ Engage teachers and staff in using data routinely to make informed decisions regarding instruction and curricula. Provide data-related professional development as needed.

❑ Request that partners share their annual data with the Campus-based Leadership Team.

❑ Be straightforward about growth, success, and missed targets when providing all stakeholders with a data summary each year.

❑ Compile all partners' metrics into an annual Pathways System Progress Report that is shared among all stakeholders including the community. Make this report available on the school district's and other partner's websites.

❑ Make data easy to access for all staff and ensure that individual student data is secure and not accidentally divulged.

6g. Pathways System Implementation Plan and Community Progress Report

Description

The Pathways Partnership Leadership Team works with all partners to create a Pathways System Implementation Plan that articulates the vision, goals, strategies, and action steps for developing a district-based or regional Pathways System. Metrics for all partners are gathered into an annual Pathways System Progress Report that is shared among partners and the broader community; the report is also available on an easy-to-navigate website.

Discussion

It is common for school systems and for educational institutions to create internal strategic and operational plans. Most businesses also have established operational plans and goals for growth, revenues, and profits.

Likewise, the decisions made by the Pathways Partnership should be articulated in an easy-to-understand Pathways System Implementation Plan (PSIP), a plan that is strong in its emphasis on action and measurable results. The purpose of the PSIP is to identify the goals of the initiative, the major strategies and actions that each partner organization has agreed upon, and the metrics that are being used to measure results.

The PSIP should be written in such a way to account for the existing activities that are already happening among the education partners, workforce systems, and employers who are part of the Pathways System. This helps the reader understand not only what the new actions will be, but also how prior initiatives and accomplishments are being incorporated into the Pathways System to achieve the stated goals. Each Pathway System partner should also determine how existing reports will be modified (if possible) to reflect each partner's responsibilities in the PSIP.

After the plan has been established and implementation proceeds, the Pathways Partnership Leadership Team should create an annual report to the community–the Pathways System Progress Report–that explains progress on the goals laid out in the plan.

After the plan has been established and implementation proceeds, the Pathways Partnership Leadership Team should create an annual report to the community–the Pathways System Progress Report–that explains progress on the goals laid out in the plan. The annual Pathways System Progress Report should also state the program improvement goals that each of the program committees has recommended for the upcoming year.

The ideal time to publish the plan would be at the beginning of each school year. This allows the report's authors to discuss progress of the Pathway System from the previous school year, and in a forward-looking section, describe what program improvement goals have been established and what new activities are in store in the upcoming year.

The Pathways Partnership Leadership Team should determine who will take lead responsibility for gathering information and writing the report, what the review and finalization process will be, what kind of live event will be most appropriate for release of the Pathways System Implementation Plan and the annual Progress Report, and what kind of website will be utilized to host these resources for easy access by the public.

Self-Assessment

◊ Does the community or region already develop an annual report to the community for the Pathways work?

◊ Is there an existing community education report that could incorporate the Pathways System metrics and reporting?

Action Steps

❒ Designate the Intermediary Organization to coordinate development of the Implementation Plan and the Progress Report.

❒ Create the format and timelines to develop the Pathways System Implementation Plan and the annual Pathways System Progress Report.

❒ Keep all stakeholders up-to-date on the development of the Implementation Plan and the annual Progress Report.

6h. Reporting on Acquisition and Transcription of Dual, Concurrent, and Articulated Credits, and Other Industry-based Credentials
Description

For each Pathway Program, the school district and postsecondary partners track and report the number of early college credits and other industry-based credentials earned by high school students as well as the number of early college credits transcripted to partnering postsecondary education institutions.

Discussion

In today's education environment, schools and colleges commonly offer early college credits through dual enrollment and advanced placement courses. In fact, almost 10 percent of all high school students already earn dual enrollment credits or some related form of college credit while still enrolled in high school.[13]

The real promise of early college credits is two-fold. First, the process of qualifying high school courses to count for early college credits or for the Advanced Placement program drives better program quality. For the program, aligning the high school component of the Pathway Program to postsecondary education standards raises the rigor of the high school program. This alignment can be accomplished by following an established statewide process; through a local collaboration between high school and college faculty; or through the use of nationally-developed curriculum like the College Board's Advanced Placement program, the Southern Region Education Board's Advanced Careers program, or Project Lead the Way's STEM programs

The second benefit is a personal and financial one – the student can save several hundred or thousand dollars' worth of postsecondary tuition and fees by taking early college courses and having the credits recognized by an admitting postsecondary institution.

Unfortunately, in many situations, no clearly prescribed way exists to make sure the early college credits are awarded to the student when they enroll in college. Some changes may need to be made at the state policy level to ensure that credits are honored across public institutions within the state, but at the local level, the Pathways Partnership should ensure a mechanism exists for reporting on the number of early college credits that were earned by high school students, and then they should track the number of credits that were actually awarded onto local college students' transcripts. Further, the Pathways Partnership should set targets for the average number of early college credits earned, and in the annual Pathways System progress report, report on how many early college credits were earned in each program and how many were recognized by the partner postsecondary institutions.

Self-Assessment

◊ How do the schools and partner colleges track the number of early college credits earned?

◊ Do any schools establish specific targets for the percent of students who earn early college credits and the average number of credits earned?

◊ Do any of school and college partners track and report this on a program-by-program basis? If so, how and with whom is this data shared?

Action Steps

❏ Clearly define and communicate the different ways in which students may earn early college credits. Share this information with all stakeholders and in each school's course catalog or student handbook.

❏ Use data to create a first year benchmark and set annual goals for the percent of students to earn early college credits and the average number of credits earned.

❏ Include information about early college credits in the Pathways System Progress Report, on individual school and college profiles, and on a program-by-program basis.

❏ Create a process and technology tool to ensure that earned college credits are either immediately added onto a college transcript or shared directly with college admission counselors to ensure that early college credits are credited to students when they enroll in a partnering postsecondary institution.

6i. Alignment of Administration, Policy, and Funding
Description
Members of the Pathways Partnership continuously identify administrative and funding policies within their purview (both state and local), and to the extent possible, work to ensure that such policies are either created or modified to support effective development and implementation of the Pathway System.

Discussion
As the Pathway System is being developed, a point will come where leaders will need to make funding and policy choices that will impact the success or the failure of the Pathways System Initiative. Examples of these choices include:

◊ Staff responsibilities may need to shift to address the needs of the Pathways System Initiative. Some job descriptions and evaluation instruments may need to be updated.

◊ New data may need to be collected and reported, and these data-related tasks will need to be assigned.

◊ There may be changes to the school schedule to accommodate a Freshman Academy or a weekly/daily Student Advisory program.[14]

◊ Teachers may need to receive responsibilities to facilitate the Student Advisory program, and the school or college may choose to create an enhanced approach to career development.

◊ Schools or colleges may need to hire, on a full-time or part-time basis, Academy or Pathway Program coordinators.

◊ Funding may be allocated from each of the Pathway System partners to support the role of a Pathways System business engagement coordinator working at the Intermediary Organization.

◊ Individual partners may also need to allocate funding for a campus-based business engagement coordinator.

◊ Professional development funding will be focused on necessary workshops and allowing individuals to attend conferences where they can learn certain skills and gain knowledge about Pathways System development.

The bottom line is that staffing, policy, and funding need to be aligned on an ongoing basis, and some of these alignment needs will only become apparent as the Pathways System develops.

If these necessary changes do not happen, then instructors, staff, and other partners will begin to question whether leaders are serious about the Pathway System Initiative. Without embedding these changes in each partner's organizational structure and processes in a serious way, the Pathways System Initiative cannot lead to lasting change.

Examples of such policies include the following:

◊ Fund one or more staff position(s) to coordinate employer and community involvement and to coordinate the school's Pathway Program.

◊ Allow for the efficient transfer and acquisition of early college credits.

The bottom line is that staffing, policy, and funding need to be aligned on an ongoing basis, and some of these alignment needs will only become apparent as the Pathways System develops.

◊ Maximize the utilization of instructional staff through flexible certification processes.

◊ Provide common planning time among Pathway Program Instructional Teams.

◊ Fund the development of a fully integrated curriculum.

◊ Fund teacher externship stipends.

Self-Assessment

◊ Does your organization in the Pathways System Initiative designate a staff position specifically to coordinate involvement with other Pathway Partners?

◊ Are campus-based administrators designated to manage and advocate for the Pathways System Initiative?

◊ Has the school district conducted a review of policies, staffing requirements, and funding sources that may need to be modified to implement the Pathways System Initiative?

Action Steps

❐ Brainstorm a list of immediate-need items for the Pathways System initiative that will require funding or policy changes. Identify possible funding sources.

❐ Determine who will oversee policy, funding and staffing needs among the Pathways Partners.

❐ Determine the ways in which funding, policy and staffing changes and needs will be communicated to all stakeholders with a goal of total transparency.

❏   Ensure that the Pathways System Partnership's dedicated grant writer actively looks for Pathways-related grants and funding sources.

Conclusion

Given the interconnected aspects of a mature Pathways System, as long as five years may be required to fully design and implement the first iteration of your Pathways System. Given that this is a long-term reform strategy, all stakeholders will need to understand and adopt a mindset of continuous improvement.

The effort in building a Pathways System will be well worth it. Your Pathways System will be an invaluable asset to the youth and adult learners and to the community as a whole.

The effort will be well worth it. Your Pathways System will be an invaluable asset to the youth and adult learners and to the community as a whole. It will demonstrate a shared seriousness of intent in your community toward enhancing the competitiveness of the local workforce and strengthening the Career and Life Readiness of all learners.

∗ ∗ ∗

In the next chapter, we learn about a new way of thinking about Career Development through instilling a Career Navigation mindset in our youths and adult learners.

Food and Finance High School

Quick Look

Food and Finance High School (FFHS), based in Midtown Manhattan, New York City, is a small high school, providing over 400 students a strong grounding in culinary and business management skills. The school offers extensive work-based learning and is strengthened through school-business partnerships.[15]

Program Details

According to school principal Roger Turgeon, Food and Finance High School may be the only grades 9 to 12 culinary school in New York City. The school is based in midtown Manhattan on W. 50th Street. The name "Food and Finance" is meant to highlight both the culinary skills and business skills necessary to operate a successful food based enterprise. The school has a student body of 430 students, about 90 of whom are seniors.

Partnerships and work-based learning have been a strong component of the school from its beginning in 2012. FFHS offers extensive work-based learning through internships for its students. In the 2013 school year, about 60 seniors participated in a work-based learning program experience; about 20 internships were offered in the Fall session and another 40 internships happened during the Spring session. The internships at FFHS last 16 weeks, about three hours today, or up to 180 hours.

Since most students have not reached a professional level in their cooking skills, their internship activities consist primarily of preparing ingredients for use by the professional staff. In most restaurants, preparation of ingredients happens in the morning.

Internships are offered at numerous sites across the city, mostly in mid-town Manhattan, and internships typically pay minimum wage and are paid directly by the employer. Occasionally, work-based learning funds can be accessed to help pay for the internships, but after one "free" internship session, employers are expected to begin paying their interns from their own funds.

Internship Preparation

As part of the internship experience, students are sent to the prospective sites to interview; about three students are sent to interview for each internship spot. The work-based learning coordinator believes that having students participate in a competitive interview provides two benefits: first, students get a more real-world experience of competing for the job, and second, restaurateurs get the ability to choose the best fit for their establishment.

To prepare students for successful internships, FFHS requires students to participate in a 15-hour employability skills preparation program. The program focuses on workplace expectations for customer service, appropriate interactions with supervisors and peers, the value of timeliness, and interviewing skills with extensive role-playing. The internship preparation is provided at the beginning of each semester for that session's prospective interns.

Employer Partnerships

Principal Turgeon indicated that during the first couple of years of the school's existence, he had difficulty finding business partners because the program was an unknown factor. He said that he and his leadership team went knocking on the doors of many restaurants. By the end third year, however, partnership development became easier because the school had a track record and generated positive word-of-mouth buzz. He even noted that some restaurants started calling him asking for interns. One of the school's more prominent partners is the New York-based cable channel, the Food Network, as well as some of its high-profile chefs and restaurateurs. In fall of 2012, the school formed an Industry Advisory Board to help focus on the culinary arts programs within the school. Industry Advisory Board members include some prominent chefs in the New York community. Board Members also offer internships and support fundraising for the school.

Student-Run Enterprise

The culinary arts program also allows students to operate what is essentially a student-run business enterprise. In addition to the internships, all students at all grade levels can participate in catering activities held in the school. These events allow older, more experienced students to develop leadership skills and manage younger students, creating a strong intergrade learning experience. All funds that are generated through the student activities are used to replenish the student activities funds, which are used for the benefit of students to pay for competitions and certification tests.

#

Career Street

Quick Look

Career Street is a web-based portal that connects multiple schools in Erie County, Pennsylvania with employers and organizations in order to provide meaningful career-related experiences to students in kindergarten through grade 12. Career Street allows businesses to reach a wide range of students while eliminating the time-consuming work that teachers had been dedicating to finding and establishing connections with employer and organization partners.

Program Details

According to the program's website, "Career Street is a comprehensive career development program linking businesses, nonprofit organizations, and schools to create and share experiences for students to job shadow, intern, tour companies, benefit from class speakers, and participate in career workshops and fairs. Career Street's goal is to unite employers, schools and nonprofit organizations in the pursuit of a well-prepared future workforce, and to help better prepare students for the careers they want."[16]

Career Street was developed through Erie Together, a countywide coalition of organizations, organized by three anchor partner organizations, working "to prevent and reduce poverty, elevate prosperity, and make the Erie Region a community of opportunity where everyone can learn, work and thrive."[17] Among several related issues, the partners identified a big disconnect between education and employment. Specifically, there were too many recent graduates who could not find work and too many employers who could not find skilled, prepared workers. Working together, Erie Career Street was formed to systematize the process of better connecting education and employers on behalf of students. All of Erie County school districts, along with the Catholic Diocese, have joined Career Street; 43 schools in total. The effort is organized and managed through the Erie County Vocational-Technical School Foundation, with a full-time executive director and an advisory board of community leaders.

Creating a Profile

To access the Portal's resources, school districts, employers, and organizations register and create an information profile on the Career Street website; employers and organizations indicate the type of career activities they are able to provide.

Each district designates a program liaison, typically a high school guidance counselor. When a teacher wishes to arrange a career-related experience for students, he or she contacts the district liaison with a request. The liaison accesses Career Street's interactive database to find and schedule a relevant experience. To utilize Career Street, school districts pay an annual membership fee entitling them to unlimited use of the database and reimbursement for some related costs such as bus transportation and substitute teachers. Career Street also offers mini-grants.

User-generated Resources

In summer 2015, a group of teachers came together to assist Career Street in developing resources designed to make every career experience a positive one for both students and the volunteers engaging with them. These include *Speakers in the Classroom: Tips for Speakers and Tips for Teachers; Workplace Tours: Tips for Teachers and Tips for Host Companies*; and *Presentation Talking Points*. [18]

Results

Career Street provides a highly scalable solution for students to get connected to work-based learning, for teachers to grow in their understanding of the regional workforce, and for employers and organizations to engage with school leaders and students in a meaningful and purposeful way.

From its launch in February 2014 through August 2016, Career Street has assisted employers and schools in making almost 300 matches resulting in 12,935 student experiences. Currently, over 115 employers and organizations are registered with Career Street, and together they offer 163 experiences. [10]

One Local Employer Provides a Testimonial about Using Career Street

Our experience with Career Street has been seamless and rewarding. The setup process was quick & easy, and setting up each experience has been a breeze as well. Both of the two office tours we have provided to high school students were well-received and have not taken too much time away from day-to-day business. Instead, the tours provided students with valuable information about working at a law firm and our attorneys and staff with a rewarding touch point to the next working generation. Thanks, Career Street!

Sarah Holland, Marketing Director of Knox McLaughlin Gornall & Sennett, P.C

#

Chapter Eight

Exploring and Planning for Careers

One of the major shortcomings in U.S. education is the lack of substantive and impactful career development to help youth and young adults make aspirational and realistic career choices. The research we reviewed in Chapter 2 points out dramatically how career development is lacking for at least half of America's 15 million high school students.

As I noted in the previous chapter, by 2015, 29 states and the District of Columbia had enacted requirements for the use of a Career and Education Plan (under a variety of names depending on the state).[1] In general, the purpose of a Career and Education Plan (CEP) is to document how a youth is planning to explore career opportunities, and use that goal to shape their course of study in high school and beyond.

But in exploring more deeply this requirement that 29 states and DC have enacted, we discover there are all shapes of scope, focus and quality of implementation. The results we have seen in the earliest chapters of this book indicate that most students still are not experiencing meaningful career development.

Good career development is much more than filling out an interest inventory, writing down career goals, or even creating a course schedule loosely based on an identified career interest.

An Encouragement to Counselors

In citing this evidence about career development, I do not assign blame to school counselors, because in many places, the ratio of counselors to students far exceeds the recommended ratio of 250 to 1. In some places, the counseling department is hanging on by a thread, overwhelmed by testing administration, college admissions activities, and social-emotional counseling. Impactful career development falls by the wayside, not surprisingly.

Real career development will only succeed when it becomes part of a school-wide culture that values career development as part of the school's mission. That mission must come from education leaders and administrators.

Here is the Pathways System Framework™ description for career development:

All learners experience meaningful and expansive career development, and their parents or guardians are actively engaged in the process. A well-planned career development program encourages students to identify personal aptitudes and interests, explore career options through multiple methods, and make informed postsecondary education and training decisions. In the K-12 system, these efforts begin early, intensify in the middle school years, and become even more focused during high school. Postsecondary partners utilize an aligned career development framework for their adult learners.

Based on this definition, career development would become a rich part of the school's culture and become embedded into the DNA of the school. So how do we see more schools with this career development culture? I believe that, not only do the adults in the school need to implement the action steps we share in Chapter 7, they also need to fundamentally expand their underlying conception of career development. That is the purpose of this chapter.

In section 1, I provide a historical perspective on how much America's workforce and job market have changed and continue to change. We must rethink our fundamental beliefs about career development–from a "One and Done" approach to choosing a career, to adopting the "Career Navigation Mindset" that will be applied over a worker's entire career life.

Next, in section 2, we review the key concepts for "Finding the Right Fit," particularly the valuable Holland Code model that helps users learn about themselves and then explore careers that are identified with the same model.

In section 3, we explore the four-stage career development education model and the grade-band competencies and activities that a school district can implement to play out the model.

Finally, in section 4, I share some ideas about ways to bring another group of individual volunteers into the Career Development mix, as a way to supplement and extend the work of School Counselors.

Section 1. The Career Navigation Mindset

Have career choices ever been simple? Perhaps in some cases when a trade or family business was handed down, or a father insisted that the son went on to become a lawyer or a doctor, the career choice was simple, though perhaps not easy to accept. For women, career choices were historically limited to being a mother and homemaker, a teacher, or a nurse, or working in an administrative role in a business setting. But in a reading of historical biographies of prominent Americans over the centuries, even when times were "simpler," many successful people and their children were deeply challenged in finding a meaningful career and making a successful transition to adulthood. This youth to adult transition has always been fraught with difficulty.

> *We must rethink our fundamental beliefs about Career Development – from a "one and done" approach to choosing a career, to adopting the "Career Navigation Mindset" that will be applied over a worker's entire career life.*

But in today's modern, globally connected and rapidly evolving economy, with the ups and downs of business cycles and waves of "creative destruction"[2] where occupations, companies, and whole industries rise and fall quickly, the transition is more complicated than ever before.

Some people enjoy adventure, challenge, and change when it comes to finding and selecting a career, but many human beings crave certainty. They would like career development to be a "One and Done" activity. If possible, many individuals would like to take a test, identify a preferred career, get training for that career, and stick with that job or career field for a long time.

Short Era of Certainty

Prior to the industrial revolution, the pace of change in careers was very slow. Most of the U.S. workforce was engaged in farming and other stable careers existed in the trades and professions like ministry, law, and medicine. Then with the industrial revolution, masses of individuals were dislocated from agriculture and moved to towns and cities, where they were employed in factory settings or were engaged in transporting goods. A small management class was needed to design products, engineer the manufacturing process, supervise the work, and manage the finances of corporations. New technologies continued to create new occupations and make other occupations obsolete.

Following the physical and economic devastation of Europe and Asia during World Wars I and II, the U.S. emerged in the Mid-20th century with a world dominance in manufacturing, technology innovation, agriculture, finance, and transportation. For a relatively short time from the 1940s through 1970s, lifetime employment with one company was seen as the ideal, even as the norm. This period of time was an anomaly, largely the result of huge corporations that emerged during and in the aftermath of the wars and the resulting US global economic hegemony.

Because of theses factors, today's American worker has no guarantees. Thus, he needs to adopt a completely different mindset about his career than the previous era industrial-corporate-government mindset. Americans need to regain a greater sense of responsibility for their careers with what I call the "Career Navigation Mindset."

During this era, American workers and American big business struck a bargain. If the corporation would provide lifetime employment and long-term generous retirement benefits, the worker would offer corporate loyalty and hard work for decades. Americans were lulled into an entitlement mentality that they would also have a guaranteed job. This promise of career-long work became embedded into American culture.

This cultural expectation was rocked when Germany and Japan re-emerged as economic world powers and broke the U.S. monopoly on the international economy. In the 1970s and 1980s, the implicit social compact of lifetime employment and retirement pensions evaporated quickly, and workers had to adapt. A huge upsurge in entrepreneurialism actually occurred following the mass lay-offs of the 1970s and 1980s, as experienced mid-career managers and technologists were set loose to innovate and create new structures and companies, particularly within the high-tech space of Microsoft, Apple, Cisco, and Adobe, to name a few. A brewing revolution of entrepreneurship and a new "start-up" culture was developing in California, in what came to be known as Silicon Valley.

During the late 1980s and early 1990s, the next phase of economic globalization took hold, marvelously explained by Thomas Friedman in his 2005 book, "The World is Flat."[3] The world grew smaller and more connected, and the pace of change accelerated with the "three ITs"–International Trade, Information Technology, and Inexpensive Transportation. These trends have helped create a world market for goods and services and an accelerating flow of work to create these goods and services–to wherever and whomever can provide them in the way that creates the best perceived value to the customer–factoring in speed of delivery, the highest possible quality, and the lowest feasible cost.

The Career Navigation Mindset

Because of these factors, today's American workers have no guarantees. Thus, they need to adopt a completely different mindset about careers than the previous era's industrial-corporate-government mindset. Americans need to regain a greater sense of responsibility for their careers with what I call the "Career Navigation Mindset." The Career Navigation Mindset says, "My career is a vessel at sea, and it is my personal responsibility to navigate my career to the destination I choose, based on factors that I deem important. If I leave my career navigation to the whims of someone else, most likely they will steer my career in a way that only makes sense to their interests, not the interests of me and my family."

One of the most personally limiting mindsets is that "there is one occupation and career pathway for me, and once I am on that path, I am set for life." This mindset is hard to break because humans crave certainty. I recently read of an enthusiastic backer of a newly minted Pathway Program. She said, "Once they finish this program and go out into the world of work, with these skills, they're good for life." It would be nice if this sentiment was true, but it isn't.

The Challenge for Educators Charged with Career Development

Developing a Career Navigation Mindset among youths is a bit of a contradiction to the experience of the educator working in a typical public school setting. The large majority of teachers are government employees, and while they do move between schools and among school systems, their predominant experience is of working in education for several decades, retiring, and then receiving a retirement pension for the remainder of life. New teacher evaluation systems have shaken the boat somewhat and made it a little easier to remove ineffective teachers, but tenure protections are still strong. If a teacher chooses to, and works at a reasonable level of performance, he or she can expect a long, secure career in education.

In contrast, the experience for most citizens is very different. Today, about 20 percent of U.S. workers are covered by a pension, which pays out a percentage of their pre-retirement income (called a defined benefit pension); the percentage of workers covered by a defined benefit pensions was 38 percent in 1980.

Not only are fewer individuals working for large corporations that offer traditional benefits and pensions, a large percentage of U.S. workers are working as solo consultants or freelancers, and some work in micro-enterprises, which are small businesses that employ just a handful of people.

These freelance and micro-enterprise arrangements have been made vastly more effective through personal computing and the plethora of internet solutions and apps that allow for virtual offices to operate on an anywhere and anytime basis. In 2001, author Daniel Pink estimated that approximately 30 percent of the U.S. workforce was working in these small, very flexible work environments, either by choice or necessity.[4]

This world of freelancing and micro-enterprise is wholly different from what the typical educator encounters. To help students develop a Career Navigation Mindset, educators need to work hard to understand the perspectives and dynamics facing others in the more freewheeling world of the non-governmental sector. Educators at levels of K-12 education and postsecondary education need to more clearly envision the kind of person they are trying to develop, one who has the mindset of a freelancer and a career entrepreneur.

Preparation for a Career and Continuous Adaptation

Given all these factors, a Career Navigation Mindset is essential for today's youths and adults. All youths and adults need to understand that having just one clearly marked pathway to career and personal success is unlikely. They can't make one decision at age 18 and think that's the end of the matter. Rather, they need to actively navigate their career throughout their working life.

We also want them to remember that, while it is imperative that they prepare for their career today as we know it, it will definitely change due to internal and external forces: competition, new business models, and new technologies. They will need to be adaptive learners throughout their lives.

Students should also consider the very real possibility they will need to make another career decision at some point. Perhaps their career field will be hit hard by outsourcing or disruptive technologies, so the economy can't sustain the same number of paid professionals that the industry current employs. Perhaps, through personal experience and emerging career interests, they will see new opportunities in a related field or in a completely different field.

Even "retirement" will be different. Instead of coming to a hard stop and making an immediate transition to non-working status, their experience will more likely be a process of gradually phasing-out of the workforce. This too, will be an exercise in career navigation.

Change is inevitable. What is not inevitable is how we react to change–will we embrace it or avoid it until it comes crashing down on us? We want people to know that flexibility and adaptability and responsibility for oneself and one's career path are essential characteristics that lead to success.

Decision Paralysis and the Need for a Career Development Sequence

In their fascinating book, "Switch," authors Chip and Dan Heath recount an interesting study on consumer choice in which there were two scenarios for shoppers. In one scenario, individuals in a gourmet food store were presented with a sampling of six different types of jams and jellies; another group of shoppers was offered a much more extensive array of 24 varieties of jams and jellies. On first blush, we would expect that the wider offering of options was good for the shopper. Yes, there was more customer interest when the 24 jams were displayed, but the researchers discovered that shoppers were actually 10 times more likely to buy a jar of jam when they had six options as opposed to 24 options.[5]

Why? This is what researchers have coined as "decision paralysis," the phenomenon that makes choosing so difficult that the individual defers making a choice altogether. When the decision becomes too complicated, the decision is put for another day, another place.

In the U.S., we appropriately applaud the idea that "you can be whatever you want to be," and encourage students to think far and wide about their career choices. The danger here is the onset of decision paralysis.

The decision paralysis factor has implications for how educators and other adults working with students approach the issue of career development. In the U.S., we appropriately applaud the idea that "you can be whatever you want to be," and encourage students to think far and wide about their career choices. The danger here is the onset of decision paralysis.

When we think about the decision paralysis phenomenon, the simple delineation of "college" or "not college" is a fairly simple choice. While a vast array of career options seems nebulous and daunting, a well-meaning student can think, "I'll just go to college and then figure it out when I get there." The big problem, however, is that colleges do not have a great track record of promoting thoughtful career decision making or of helping students match up their career aspirations with an appropriate college major.

While there is no nationally authoritative data, some studies estimate that about 50 percent of college students change their major at some point, and at some schools, there are even larger numbers of students who change their majors.[6] In a related study of 4,900 recent college graduates, researchers discovered that on entering the job market, *more than half of recent graduates wish they had chosen a different major or school.* Further, the McKinsey study indicates that about a third of recent graduates feel unprepared, that they don't have the right skills for the job market.[7]

So, given that career development is not guaranteed at the collegiate level and many youth do not attend any form of postsecondary education, the mandatory high school education remains the one societal opportunity to touch every American youth. Thus, public schools need to fully embrace the work of career development.

In a study of 4,900 recent college graduates, McKinsey discovered that on entering the job market, more than half of recent graduates wish they had chosen a different major or school. Further, about a third of recent graduates feel unprepared, that they don't have the right skills for the job market.

Educators should think about how to structure the continuum of career awareness, career exploration, career application/immersion and career management/entrepreneurship in a way that is developmentally sound. We should present students with a limited number of broad choices and then progressively encourage them to make more focused decisions, eliminating options that aren't a good fit, and focusing their attention to a smaller band of choices as they get older. Through a layered decision process, they are less likely to experience decision paralysis.

Section 2: Finding the Right Career Fit

The Impact of Fit on Well-Being

Earnings do matter. But money by itself does not create a sense of well-being with a career. Career development programs help youth realize that true happiness and fulfillment come when individuals are fitted for the work that they find. Gallup researchers Tom Rath and Jim Harter note that, when Gallup asks working adults the question, "Do you like what you do each day?" only 20 percent of people offer a strong "yes" in their response. This poor job fit is a problem for individuals and for the businesses where they are employed. In their book "Well Being," Rath and Harter identify five components of personal well-being: Career, Social, Financial, Physical and Community.[8]

In observing the impact of career well-being, they summarize,

People usually underestimate the influence of their career on their overall wellbeing. But *Career Wellbeing is arguably the most essential of the five elements* [emphasis added]. If you don't have the opportunity to regularly do something you enjoy – even if it's more of a passion or interest than something you get paid to do – the odds of your having high wellbeing in other areas diminish rapidly. People with high Career Wellbeing are more than twice as likely to be thriving in their lives overall.[9]

When not experiencing career well-being, people are at risk. The analysis of Gallup research cited by Rath and Harter associates a stressful workplace with the over production of the stress-related hormone Cortisol, which can induce long term, chronic health problems. Findings from research conducted in Sweden showed that individuals with an "incompetent" boss had a 24 percent increased risk of heart attack, and the risk went up even further if they worked for that boss more than four years. Further, they discovered that, when individuals used their strengths doing something they enjoyed every day, they were able to consistently work a full forty or so hours each week, but people who "do not get to use their strengths get burned out after just 20 hours of work per week."[10]

The danger of having a poor career fit raises serious implications for a person's well-being. Assuming the individual can earn a basic level of income to meet personal and family needs, the level of career well-being is going to have a much bigger impact on his or her day-to-day life than a slight bump in earnings can provide.

A strong career development experience will focus first on finding a good career fit, and secondly on making sure that career choice offers a reasonable level of income that can support lifestyle needs and wants.

The next section, dealing with the Holland Code system, hones in on tools to help students find a good career fit.

The Holland Code Personality and Job-Match System

R-I-A-S-E-C Traits

Beginning with his initial research findings in 1959 and refining his work over the next 30 years, Dr. John Holland developed a theory that people and work environments can be loosely classified into six different groups. Each of the letters above corresponds to one of the six groups.

◊ R: Realistic (Doers)

◊ I: Investigative (Thinkers)

◊ A: Artistic (Creators)

◊ S: Social (Helpers)

◊ E: Enterprising (Persuaders)

◊ C: Conventional (Organizers)[11]

While there are many useful types of personality assessments, such as Clifton Strength Finders, The DISC, and Myers-Briggs, what is so useful about the Holland Code system is that it not only has an individual component, but hundreds of occupations have also been analyzed and aligned with the model, and are displayed through the U.S. Department of Labor's O-NET system.[12] This allows a matching of personality and temperament to jobs, an extremely valuable component of career search.

Each individual may have some interests in and similarities to several of the six groups, but is usually attracted primarily to two or three of the areas. These two or three letters are his or her "Holland Code." For example, with a code of "RES" he or she would most resemble the Realistic type, and also have some affinity to the Enterprising type and the Social type. The other three types, in this case IAC, that are not in the person's code are the types that the individual resembles least of all. Most people, and most jobs, are best represented by some combination of two or three of the Holland interest areas. Not surprisingly, most people are satisfied with their career when there is a good fit between their personality and their work environment.[13]

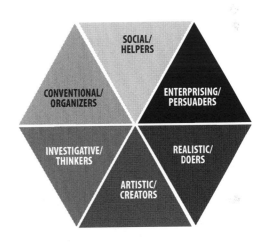

Note: The Holland Code Assessment is available for free use through the U.S. Department of Labor's O-NET Interest Profiler.[14]

In the following few pages, we share information about each of the six career personalities of the Holland Code system, based upon a summary produced by the University of Missouri's MU Career Center.[15] Further, we indicate the percentage of U.S. jobs that fall within this primary area, according to research conducted by Mary-Catherine McClain and Robert C. Reardon, Robert C. Reardon.[16]

R - Realistic *(Doers)*

People who have athletic ability, who prefer to work with objects, machines, tools, plants, or animals, or who prefer to be outdoors.

Realistic Attributes

Practical, straightforward/frank, mechanically inclined, stable, concrete, reserved, self-controlled, independent, ambitious, systematic

Percentage of Realistic-Dominant jobs in U.S. Economy, 2010: 27 percent[17]

Sampling of Realistic-Dominant Careers

Air Conditioning Mechanic (RIE), Aircraft Mechanic (RIE), Automotive Engineer (RIE), Bus driver (RES), Construction Worker (REC), Corrections Officer (RES), Dental Assistant (REI), Electrician (REI), Exercise Careers (RES), Farm Manager (RES), Fiber Optics Technician (RSE) , Firefighter (RES), Fish Hatchery Manager (RES), Floral Designer (RAE), Furnace Installer (RES), Groundskeeper (RCE), Industrial Supervisor (REI), Instrument Repair (RIE), Laboratory Technician (RIE), Line Installer (RSE), Machinist (RIE), Maintenance Repairer (RES), Mechanical Engineer (RIS), Oceanographer (RIE), Optician (REI), Painter (RES), Petroleum Engineer (RIE), Plumber (REI), Practical Nurse (RSE), Quality Control Manager (RSE), Structural Steelworker (REI), Tool and Die Maker (RIE), Truck Driver (RSE), Welder (RES)

I - Investigative *(Thinkers)*

People who like to observe, learn, investigate, analyze, evaluate, or solve problems.

Investigative Attributes

Inquisitive, analytical, scientific, observant/precise, scholarly, cautious, intellectually self-confident, independent, logical/complex, curious

Percentage of Investigative-Dominant jobs in U.S. Economy, 2010: 10 percent[18]

Sampling of Investigative-Dominant Careers

Actuary (ISE), Anesthesiologist (IRS), Biochemist (IRS), Chemical Engineer (IRE), Computer Systems Analyst (IER), Electrical Engineer (IRE), Horticulturist (IRS), Mathematician (IER), Medical Technologist (ISA),

Nurse Practitioner (ISA), Pharmacist (IES), Physician, General Practice (ISE), Research Analyst (IRC), Statistician (IRE), Surgeon (IRA), Technical Writer (IRS), Veterinarian (IRS)

A - Artistic *(Creators)*

People who have artistic, innovating, or intuitional abilities and like to work in unstructured situations using their imagination and creativity.

Artistic Attributes

Creative, imaginative, innovative, unconventional, emotional, independent, expressive, original, introspective, impulsive, sensitive, courageous, complicated, idealistic, nonconforming

Percentage of Artistic-Dominant jobs in U.S. Economy, 2010: 2 percent[19]

Sampling of Artistic-Dominant Careers

Actor (AES), Advertising Art Director (AES), Architect (AIR), Art Teacher (ASE), Drama Coach (ASE), English Teacher (ASE), Entertainer/Performer (AES), Intelligence Research Specialist (AEI), Journalist/Reporter (ASE), Landscape Architect (AIR), Museum Curator (AES), Music Teacher (ASI) , Photographer (AES)

S - Social (Helpers)

People who like to work with people to enlighten, inform, help, train, or cure them, or are skilled with words.

Social Attributes

Friendly, helpful, idealistic, insightful, outgoing, understanding, cooperative, generous, responsible, forgiving, patient, empathic, kind, persuasive

Percentage of Social-Dominant jobs in U.S. Economy, 2010: 24 percent[20]

Sampling of Social-Dominant Careers

Air Traffic Controller (SER), Athletic Trainer (SRE), College Professor (SEI), Counseling Psychologist (SIA), Cosmetologist (SEA), Dental Hygienist (SAI), Dietician (SIE), Elementary School Teacher (SEC), Executive House Keeper (SCE), High School Teacher (SAE), Historian (SEI), Home Economics Teacher (SAE), Homemaker (S), Hospital Administrator (SER), Insurance Claims Examiner (SIE), Minister/Priest/Rabbi (SAI), Nurse/Midwife (SIR), Occupational Therapist (SRE), Personnel Recruiter (SEC), Physical Therapist (SIE), Police Officer (SER), Real Estate Appraiser (SCE), Registered Nurse (SIA), School Counselor (SAE), Social Worker (SEA), Speech Pathologist (SAI)

E - Enterprising *(Persuaders)*

People who like to work with people, influencing, persuading, leading or managing for organizational goals or economic gain.

Enterprising Attributes

Self-confident, assertive, sociable, persuasive, enthusiastic, energetic, adventurous, popular, impulsive, ambitious, inquisitive, agreeable, talkative, extroverted, spontaneous, optimistic

Percentage of Enterprising-Dominant jobs in U.S. Economy, 2010: 20 percent[21]

Sampling of Enterprising-Dominant Careers

Advertising Sales Rep. (ESR), Barber/Hairdresser (ESR), Benefits Manager (ESA), Cook/Chef (ESR), Dental Assistant (E), Educational Administrator (ESA), Emergency Medical Technician (ESI), Flight Attendant (ESA), Food Service Manager (ESI), Health Care Executive (ECR), Insurance Manager (ESC), Journalist (EAS), Lawyer/Attorney (ESA), Real Estate Agent (ESR), Retail Store Manager (ESR), Sales Manager (ESA), Social Service Director (ESA), Stockbroker (ESI)

C - Conventional (organizers)

People who like to work with data, have clerical or numerical ability, carry out tasks in detail, or follow through on others' instructions.

Conventional Attributes

Well-organized, accurate, numerically inclined, methodical, conscientious, efficient, conforming, orderly, practical, thrifty, systematic, structured, polite, ambitious, obedient, persistent

Percentage of Conventional-Dominant jobs in U.S. Economy, 2010: 17 percent[22]

Sampling of Conventional-Dominant Careers

Abstractor (CSI), Accountant (CSE), Administrative Assistant (ESC), Catalog Librarian (CSE), Court Reporter (CSE), Financial Analyst (CSI), Insurance Adjuster (CSE), Kindergarten Teacher (CSE), Library Assistant (CSE), Medical Records Technician (CSE), Tax Consultant (CES)

Number and Percentage of Persons Employed in Six Kinds of Work, 1960-2010		
Census Year (Detailed Occupations)		
Kind of Work	1960	1990	2010
R (realistic)	35,029 55%	42,711 37%	31,868 27%
I (investigative)	1,986 3%	6,738 6%	11,457 10%
A (artistic)	756 1%	1,552 1%	2,027 2%
S (social)	5,611 9%	14,983 13%	29.563 24%
E (enterprising)	11,106 17%	29,668 26%	23,991 20%
C (conventional)	9,569 15%	20,086 17%	20,878 17%
Total	64,057	115,738	119,784

Note: Employment numbers are in millions rounded to the nearest thousands.
Source: The U.S. Workforce from 1960 to 2010: a RIASEC View. Mary-Catherine McLain and Robert C. Reardon, *The Professional Counselor*, 2015, NBCC Inc. and Affiliates.

Section 3. Creating a Career Development System

In this section, we explain the four components of a Career Development System, and then provide a suggested list of types of activities to help implement your system. [23]

Four Stages of Career Development Education

Career Development Education (CDE) encompasses four stages that help students move from the abstract to the experiential:

◊ Career Awareness

◊ Career Exploration

◊ Career Application/Immersion

◊ Career Management and Entrepreneurship

Career Awareness

Career development begins with career awareness. Through career awareness experiences, children, teens, and adults learn about the types of businesses and organizations that exist in the local, regional and national economy, about the occupations of the people who work in those businesses and organizations, about the educational steps needed to prepare for desired careers, and about the ways that people shape their career paths. They learn about trends in the labor market and jobs that are in demand in a range of occupations and industries.

Career awareness experiences begin in elementary school and continue through high school. They happen in the classroom, on field trips, after school, or in summer enrichment programs. They may be hands-on experiences or they may consist of reading or writing activities. Students begin to formulate career aspirations during the awareness phase.

As students progress in their learning and/or maturity, a deeper approach to career awareness should begin. Students should start to have more deliberate, structured college and career awareness experiences in middle school and continuing through high school. Many high schools offer students a range of career awareness opportunities:

◊ Career interest inventories/assessments

◊ Job market information on websites and in publications

◊ Career speakers

◊ Career day or career fair

◊ Career-related camps, after-school or summertime

Career Exploration

As students begin to identify their interests, they can learn more about specific career options through career development activities:

◊ Career exploration workshops or classes

◊ Opportunities for students to do "job shadows" in areas of interest

◊ Opportunities for informational interviews with local professionals

◊ Career-related research projects

◊ A variety of other classroom and community projects that support career development

In quality CDE, career development is complemented by a process of reflection, supported by influential adults such as guidance counselors, advisors, classroom teachers, workplace supervisors, parents, etc. Many schools use a formal college and career planning process (also referred to as a college and career plan, an education and career plan, or an individual learning plan), using print-based or electronic systems for students to track their experiences, define next steps, and continually reflect on and refine their short-term and long-term goals.

Career Application/Immersion
Through career application and immersion experiences, students participate directly in career-related activities. Career application/immersion experiences include the following:

◊ In-depth work in a career-related class

◊ Career-related clubs and after-school activities

◊ Internships or cooperative education placements

◊ Capstone projects focused on areas of interest

◊ Entrepreneurial projects

◊ School-based businesses

◊ School-based volunteer work

◊ Community-based volunteer work

◊ After-school and summer jobs

◊ Any other experience in which students are learning through active participation in a career-related role

These hands-on career application/immersion experiences are complemented by formal instruction, including classes, workshops, or one-on-one coaching. Again, reflection is a key component, with students having opportunities to reflect on what they are learning; to evaluate the skills they are gaining; and to continually re-visit, refine, and reflect on short-term and long-term goals. Quality career application/immersion experiences also incorporate assessment of skills gained, through an industry-recognized or valid educational assessment.

Career Management and Entrepreneurship
Career management is the process of securing career-related employment, keeping that job, and performing the necessary requirements to progress in a career. Career management preparation involves training in resume preparation, writing cover letters, conducting an effective phone interview, conducting a face-to-face and a virtual (video over internet) interview, and following up on the interview process. Career management also entails negotiating for salary and other employment terms and learning how to identify opportunities for enhanced responsibilities, job promotion within a firm, and advancement opportunities with other firms in the same field. Further, career management entails engaging advisors and mentors,

identifying lateral moves within an industry or to similar jobs in a different industry, and determining when and how external education and training can document existing skills or gain new knowledge and skills to advance to higher levels of responsibility and earnings.

Entrepreneurship is the process of organizing, managing, and assuming the risks of a business or enterprise. While a few individuals start a new enterprise at a young age with little prior work experience, most adults start new companies after first gaining a level of work-experience and expertise working for others and then venturing out on their own as a solo entrepreneur or in partnership with one or two other individuals.

Entrepreneurship education helps students understand the characteristics of an entrepreneur and the process of developing a business plan. This gives students the skills to create the job they want and to learn to think like an entrepreneur.

Entrepreneurship education provides the student with the concepts and skills to recognize opportunities that others have overlooked and of having the insight, self-esteem, and knowledge to act where others have hesitated. It includes instruction in recognizing opportunity, marshaling resources in the face of risk, and initiating a business venture. It also includes instruction in business management processes such as business planning, capital development, marketing, and cash flow analysis.

SEE APPENDIX 3 FOR A GLOSSARY DESCRIBING A RANGE OF CAREER DEVELOPMENT ACTIVITIES

Career Development Competencies and Activities for the K-12 System

CAREER AWARENESS (GRADES K-5)[24]

Grades K-2 Student Competencies

❏ Discuss different kinds of work.
❏ Know about goal setting and decision-making.
❏ Know what it means to be a good worker.

Grades K-2 Activities

❏ Parents and other volunteers visit the classroom for "Career Talks."
❏ Students review materials aimed at young children to help them identify basic jobs.
❏ Students participate in community field trips that include discussion of jobs.

Grades 3-5 Student Competencies

❏ Recognize that individuals have unique interests, and describe the impact of individual interests and abilities on career choices.
❏ Connect personal interests, abilities, and academic strengths to personal career options.
❏ Describe the key attributes of a person who is Career and Life Ready (as defined by the district or state).
❏ Recognize the state's key industries (e.g., manufacturing, tourism, food production, health care) and jobs in those industries.
❏ Discuss "Career Clusters" (i.e., the national or state model that organizes careers into "clusters").
❏ Identify "Pathways" (i.e., groupings of similar or related occupations within a Career Cluster).
❏ Identify how change affects the perception of and access to traditional and nontraditional careers.
❏ Explain how money is used and the value of good money management.
❏ Develop and use a personal schedule for home and school responsibilities.
❏ Define entrepreneurship and successful entrepreneurial traits.
❏ Understand the basic concepts found in career decision-making models.

Grades 3-5 Activities

☐ Parents and other volunteers visit to classroom for "Career Talks." Teachers help the guest speakers show how their business fits into the Career Clusters model.

☐ Guest speakers who are entrepreneurs visit the school to talk about starting and operating a business.

☐ Teachers create a written portfolio tool (print or electronic) that allows students to document personal development of Career and Life Readiness attributes.

☐ Teachers create classroom and community-based activities to focus on aspects of the Career and Life Readiness Framework (or a similar state/district framework.)

☐ Teachers integrate at least one career theme each year into "specials" – music, arts, and physical education.

☐ Students review career-related materials.

☐ Students compose and compare a business letter and a personal letter.

☐ Students make oral presentations to adults to strengthen public presentation skills and confidence.

☐ At media center visits, teachers show students where the career materials are located.

☐ At least one time each year, students select non-fiction reading that has career-related or entrepreneurial themes, and teachers incorporate the career theme into classroom discussions and writing assignments.

☐ 5th Grade students visit a college or university for a tour, learning about majors, careers and general campus life.

☐ The school or a partner community-based organization runs a "STEM Career Day" where students learn about a variety of careers that utilize STEM concepts.

CAREER EXPLORATION (GRADES 6-8)

Grades 6-7 Student Competencies

☐ Identify the steps of the career decision-making process:
- ☐ Who am I?
- ☐ Where am I going?
- ☐ How am I going to get there?

☐ Understand how career inventory and assessments can contribute to career decision-making.

☐ Identify at least four jobs within a Career Pathway that require different levels of education (on-the-job training, short-term certification, associate degree, and bachelor's degree).

☐ Identify and explore sources of career information, both written and web-based.

☐ Continue to develop Career and Life Readiness Skills.

Grades 6-7 Activities

☐ Students use informal career inventories to identify possible occupations.

☐ Students use assessment tools to explore their skills.

☐ Students begin career exploration activities, including identification of learning opportunities in the community.

☐ Students are introduced to the Career Pathways in each career cluster.

☐ Students take a career related assessment.

☐ Students explore careers through designated classes in Grades, 6, 7, & 8 (some states require Family Consumer Science and/or Technical Education in middle school).

☐ Teachers incorporate career understanding into core academic and other elective classes.

☐ Teachers conduct an annual research project in either English or Social Studies about a career or an industry sector.

☐ Students take a career personality assessment (e.g., Holland Codes) and discover careers based on the Holland codes.

☐ Several volunteers from different industries and careers conduct "speed-networking," with a small group of students.

☐ Students use the "fishbowl questions" technique to post multiple questions to business volunteers.

☐ Students are given a Career & Life Skills Portfolio with goals for High School Readiness. Students begin to monitor and record their own development and progress.

Grade 8 Student Competencies

- ☐ Identify one to three Pathways for career exploration, based on assessment, exploration and investigation.
- ☐ Understand the transition from middle school to high school and how expectations and the experience between the two are different.
- ☐ Understand the meaning of grade point averages and how grades and course selection may impact the ability to pursue postsecondary education.
- ☐ Be prepared to decide on high school opportunities to enroll in Pathway Programs.
- ☐ Know the general concepts of how early college credit options work, either through dual enrollment, an articulated course, or test-based college-level courses like Advanced Placement (AP) or International Baccalaureate (IB).

Grade 8 Activities

- ☐ Every student meets with parents, counselors, and teacher-advisors to develop an Education and Career Plan to include both academic and career pathway course planning.
- ☐ Students continue to track personal development of Career and Life Readiness Skills.
- ☐ Students may participate in work-based learning activities like service learning, job shadowing, and mentoring.
- ☐ Students visit specialty schools and CTE programs in the region to which they might enroll.
- ☐ Students participate in a "Real Life" simulation activity like Junior Achievement's "BizTown."
- ☐ Students choose a career pathway for high school exploration and may choose to enroll in a Pathway Program that starts during 9th grade.
- ☐ Students participate in an 8th Grade scheduling event (held at night to encourage parent participation) and learn about high school opportunities.
- ☐ Students participate in an "8th Grade Transitions Night" visit (with parents) to high school. A school-day visit is also held for students with a low-level of parent engagement.
- ☐ Students participate in a regional- or community-wide "Future Fair" (blended career and college fair) or a Career Fair. Student prepare for the fair and complete post-fair classroom activities.

CAREER APPLICATION/IMMERSION
(Grades 9-Postsecondary)

Grades 9-12 Competencies

☐ Analyze career options based on personal interests, abilities, aptitudes, achievement, and goals.

☐ Evaluate school-based opportunities for career awareness/preparation.

☐ Make ambitious choices for career preparation that take into account personal work values, educational aptitude and achievement, and financing options.

☐ Analyze and choose among career preparation opportunities that include a range of post-secondary options.

☐ Develop personal attitudes and work habits that support school success, postsecondary education and training success, and future career retention and advancement.

☐ Apply financial literacy knowledge and skills to personal money management and decisions about financing postsecondary education.

☐ Analyze how entrepreneurship relates to personal character traits, and if appropriate, begin developing an entrepreneurial concept.

☐ Understand the role of job-search skills and a professional job network as part of career development.

Grade 9 Student Activities

☐ Students review and update their Education and Career Plan annually with counselor/advisor and parent.

☐ Students participate in a "freshman seminar" course or activity to facilitate a successful transition into high school.

☐ Students begin to explore financial aid opportunities through a variety of print and web-based resources.

☐ Students participate in related Career Technical Student Organizations and other organized activities.

☐ Teachers in all courses emphasize the importance of professional skills for work-life success, such as timeliness, individual follow-through, and responsible team-work.

☐ Students will continue developing awareness of early college credit options, including dual enrollment courses, AP, and IB (International Baccalaureate).

Grades 10-11 Activities

☐ Students begin making decisions about pursuing early college credit options, reviewing dual enrollment courses as well as including AP and IB.

☐ Students review and update their Education and Career Plan, with particular attention to postsecondary goals and meeting graduation requirements.

☐ Students participate in college tours, including four-year college, two-year college, and technical training options.

☐ Students learn about apprenticeship programs available in the region and participate in tours of such programs.

☐ Students take appropriate postsecondary admissions and placement assessments, such as PSAT, SAT, ACT, Asset, etc.

☐ Students continue to choose academic and elective courses related to a selected Career Pathway and take appropriate end-of-pathway assessments or industry-based certifications related to their pathway.

Grades 12 Activities

☐ Students complete state and district graduation course requirements.

☐ Students may participate in work-based learning activities such as job shadowing, internships, and apprenticeships that contribute to a career-focused capstone project.

☐ Students take appropriate postsecondary admissions and placement assessments.

☐ Students and parents participate in a FAFSA/student financial aid activity to help them prepare to apply for financial aid.

☐ Students complete any remaining courses for the selected career pathway and take appropriate end of pathway assessments and/or industry-based certification assessments.

☐ Students begin the transition process to post-high school life by applying for admission into postsecondary education, the military, apprenticeship, or employment.

Post-Secondary Activities

☐ Students may continue to pursue a Pathway Program at the postsecondary level (through short-term certification, two-year college, four-year college, military, or apprenticeship).

☐ Some students may choose a field of study that is different from what they pursued during high school, having determined that the area of focus during high school was not the best long-term fit for them. Given the high cost of postsecondary education, discovering a poor career fit during high school and choosing a better fit is a good outcome.

☐ During postsecondary education and training, students should participate in more advanced and long-term internships and cooperative learning experiences. For well-performing students, many of these learning experiences yield job offers upon graduation.

CAREER MANAGEMENT (Grade 12 and Beyond)

Career Management Competencies (Search, Retention, Advancement, Entrepreneurship)

Competencies, Career Search

☐ Apply research skills in searching for a job.

☐ Develop job hunting documents such as a cover letter and resume.

☐ Apply effective speaking and listening skills used in a job interview.

☐ Model the "professional" skills required to hold a job – punctuality, courtesy, personal initiative, follow-up, professionalism – in the process of searching and interviewing for a job.

Competencies, Career Retention and Advancement

☐ Develop personal attitudes and work habits that support career retention and advancement.

☐ Develop and practice team member skills, such as active listening, conflict resolution, and time management.

☐ Develop a personal budget based on a personal career choice.

☐ Consider and develop strategies for career retention and advancement based on the job availability in different fields.

☐ Evaluate the need for ongoing learning (aka "lifelong learning"), both formal and informal, to support career retention and advancement.

☐ Identify and evaluate the quality and economic value of programs offered by postsecondary education and training institutions, in both on-site and online learning platforms, to access additional learning to promote career advancement.

Competencies, Entrepreneurship

☐ Analyze how entrepreneurial skills relate to personal career goals, business opportunities, and personal character traits.

☐ Develop a business plan for an entrepreneurial concept of personal interest.

☐ Research and identify available support resources such as community-based organization, financial institutions, small business administration services, and venture capital.

Career Management Activities
❏ Students create a resume and begin networking the market for possible job opportunities.
❏ Program participants or graduates obtain rewarding entry-level employment within their chosen pathway.
❏ Program participants or graduates continue to refine career choices throughout their lifetime of learning.
❏ Program participants or graduates enroll in entrepreneurship courses offered by postsecondary education providers, community-based organizations, or economic development organizations.

Section 4. Engaging New Partners

Engaging New Partners in Career Development

Almost 15 million students are enrolled in U.S. high schools today,[25] and the average counselor to student ratio across all schools is 457-1.[26] This average masks the fact that some schools, the better resourced schools, have many more counselors than do poorly resourced schools, and the schools with higher poverty are where the need for all levels of guidance and counseling is the highest. In many schools, career development will continue to be under-resourced and counselors on staff will struggle to keep up with the caseload.

The large student-to-counselor ratio (457-1) amplifies the dramatic need to not isolate career development in the school counseling office, but to inculcate all aspects of career development into the DNA of the entire K-12 school system.

First, this large student-to-counselor ratio amplifies the dramatic need to not isolate career development in the school counseling office, but to inculcate all aspects of career development into the DNA of the entire K-12 school system, so that every adult has a clearly identified role in contributing to these experiences for youths. It also hearkens for the need to involve business and community partners to model positive career management and have positive interactions with youth who need to build their understanding of the workplace and how to navigate their own career path.

This dynamic also argues for the need to engage more qualified, knowledgeable adults to move into the career development sphere and to reconsider how we utilize "lay persons." To consider the role of the trained lay person, let's look at the world of psychiatry in a seriously under-resourced nation–India. Vikram Patel, a physiatrist at the London School of Hygiene and Tropical Medicine is developing a radical new approach for mental health delivery–training ordinary people to be counselors.[27]

Gaining access to quality mental health services is a challenge, even in a highly developed country like the United States. Now, consider how much difficult this challenge is in a developing country like India, with its 1.1 billion people and high levels of poverty. It would be a fool's errand to try to replicate the mental health delivery system of a developed country like the US in India.

Dr. Patel, through an innovative approach training lay persons in the town of Goa, India, discovered that young women could learn basic psychotherapy skills and go on to help people with depression as least as well as local clinics would have. His findings were validated through a rigorous research study. Now he is advising the Indian government on how to incorporate these lay counselors into the country's national health system.

Patel explained the approach. "We're training them to do very specific tasks. It's a bit like training a community midwife: You're not training her to be an obstetrician; you're training her to deliver a baby safely and to know when to refer the mother to a doctor. The training can be as short as two days or it can be two months, but the classes are the least important part. There's a much longer period of supervised learning that happens through direct contact with patients. You don't have much theory. You go directly to the skills you need to actually help people recover. "

The reason why this approach is appealing and intriguing is this–there will definitely never be enough school counselors, trained and deployed, to provide the kind of in-depth, personalized counseling our high school students need. Nor is technology-search alone the answer either. Thinking about one's future is a very human experience. Students need to be advised by people they can see and connect with, parents, teachers, counselors, and other caring adults.

So, can this idea of trained lay-counselors, working with clear guidance and resources, and in contact with a school-based career development program, be workable? Perhaps. There are some barriers to work through. Employer and community-volunteers often, when recruited, are frustrated because they don't know exactly how to help, and historically schools aren't well-versed in how to deploy volunteers in this type of career-mentoring role. But, if experienced and caring professionals were equipped with resources and realistic-time-based training, taking on a career-mentoring role could be a powerful fit.

There is an appropriate debate as to the level of knowledge and abilities an individual should have to appropriately facilitate career development for a youth or adult. The National Career Development Association has developed 12 core competencies that are developed in the 120 hours of training for the NCDA Career Development Facilitator.[28] This training can be offered in a face-to-face format, a hybrid of face-to-face and e-learning, or in a mostly e-learning version, and it qualifies the completer to test for the Global Career Development Facilitator credential. But this training is really aimed at the full-time educator or career professional.

The Kuder company has also developed a short-course – Career Advisor Training (CAT) - for adults who want to work in a more supportive career development role. The "essentials" of CAT are offered in a 10-hour online self-paced format, and the "advanced" version of CAT is offered in a 30-hour format with an instructor. These programs are offered as focused training for individuals who are already working as guidance professionals but can be taken by anyone interested.[29] Other models of short-term training may exist that can be even more well-targeted for the interests and capabilities of a lay-volunteer.

Next Steps-Career Development

As we have explored in this chapter, creating an impactful and scalable approach to career development is essential if we want to equip our youths with the Career Navigation mind-set and skills they will need for Career and Life Success. There are excellent electronic tools and examples of good career development curriculum widely available. What's often missing, however, is the leadership needed to move a school team through a significant change process in which they embrace the role that career development must play on a school wide and district wide basis. This change won't happen overnight, but it will result in positive school culture and set of practices that will more effectively prepare American students for the dynamic economy and world of work they will face in the very near future.

* * *

In the next chapter we return to the theme of leadership. Without excellent leadership, the development of Pathway Programs and/or Pathway Systems will falter. Thus, the next chapter is essential. In it we address building the capacity of the individual school or community leader, and we address proven strategies for leading the change process.

Souderton Area High School Pathway 360°

Quick Look

Since its implementation in 2011, the administrators and staff of Souderton Area High School[30] in eastern Pennsylvania have worked consistently to develop what is now known as the Pathway 360° Program. Designed to connect today's learning to tomorrow's careers, the program equips students to make informed decisions about their immediate postsecondary plans and their future through career exploration, Pathway Programs, and work-based learning mentorships.[31]

Program Details

Career Exploration and Pathways

Souderton Area High School's Pathway 360° Program begins in grade eight and nine with a required course, Career Exploration. During grade eight, students begin developing a four-year plan on which their selection of ninth grade courses is based. Students explore and choose a Pathway that will guide the selection of courses in grades ten through twelve. Pathway choices include Arts and Humanities, Business and Communications, Health and Human Services, and industry and Engineering.

The Graduation Project and Mentorship

Freshman year students also begin building a portfolio for the graduation project presentation and choose a Pathway option that will guide high school course selection. Sophomore students continue building their portfolio, may begin to investigate and engage in a job shadow experience, and are encouraged to research possible mentorships. During junior year, students take elective classes relevant to their chosen Pathway and are strongly encouraged to complete a mentorship after school, during school breaks, or in the summer. Students are responsible for recording observations, activities, and reflections in an online journal throughout the mentorship; this work becomes an important component in the graduation project. Those who complete the mentorship requirements earn one half of a credit toward high school graduation.

The Mentorship Program is intended to provide students with relevant and authentic workplace experiences related to their career interests. The Mentorship is a work-based learning component of at least 20 hours that involves job shadowing and/or mentorship experiences, engaged with over 200 business partners. The majority of experiences take place offsite; the school also offers several onsite opportunities. The school's principal, Dr. Sam Varano, created a full-time mentorship and transition coordinator position and filled it with a reassigned teacher; responsibilities include developing procedures and communications, networking with regional businesses, meeting with students, and overseeing program details.

Although graduation projects have had a long history at the high school, the class of 2015 was the first to include their mentorship experiences as part of the graduation project, sharing reflections and ways in which the experience related to postsecondary goals. Judged by a faculty panel, each presentation was six minutes with an additional six minutes provided to address judges' questions. Those who completed a mentorship and job shadow were eligible to earn either a Pathway or a Scholars Diploma.

Pathway Coordinators

Each Pathway is led by a Pathway Coordinator, an appointed teacher whose responsibilities include identifying course sequences, organizing experiences for students, and providing guidance to individual students regarding pathways, careers, and the graduation project. The school operates on a block schedule, and the fifth block, scheduled twice weekly, serves several functions including opportunities for students to participate in career-related presentations or to meet with their Pathway Coordinator.

Teacher Externships

To support career exploration and problem-based learning, teachers are given a special professional learning opportunity every two years to engage in a one-day externship, visiting a local business of their choice to make connections between curriculum and workplace applications.

Pathways Manager Software

Seeing a need to organize all aspects of the Pathway 360° Program in a user-friendly and relevant way for students, staff, and parents, teacher Michael Olenick has developed Pathway Manager, an online computer application that was piloted in 2013-2014 and fully implemented the following school year with additional features.

Results

The class of 2015 was the first cohort of students to participate in the Pathway 360° Program for four full years. The following results have been achieved to date:

» In 2015, 76 percent of seniors[32] completed a 20-hour unpaid mentorship in a field of their choice.

» In 2015, 98 percent of students passed the graduation project, 65 percent were distinguished, making them eligible for a Pathway or Scholars Diploma.

» Since 2010, enrollment in science, technology, engineering, and math (STEM) courses increased 159 percent.

» Since 2006, enrollment in AP courses increased 355 percent.

» Approximately 200 local and regional business members are involved in the Pathway 360° Program acting as job shadow and/or mentorship hosts, serving on pathway advisory teams, and volunteering for career-related activities in the school.

» Staff reports an increase in student engagement. Students report increased clarity and understanding of postsecondary college and career goals.

» In 2014, U.S. News & World Report ranked Souderton Area High School 18th in the state of Pennsylvania and third in Montgomery County.

#

Geometry in Construction

Quick Look

The Geometry in Construction Program, first launched in Loveland High School in Loveland, Colorado, offers a fully integrated program that presents geometry in the context of a construction program. [33]

Program Details

In the 2006 school year, Loveland High School launched its Construction/ Geometry Program under the guidance of veteran geometry teacher Tom Moore and construction teacher Scott Burke. According to Loveland High School, "the original idea for the class stemmed from the large local demand for skilled workers in all aspects of the construction/building industry" (Loveland High School, 2007). While business and industry leaders needed competent employees with solid math skills, Loveland High School needed a way to improve the math skills of students. Meeting both needs, the Geometry in Construction Program benefits Loveland High School, business and industry, and most importantly, the students.

The program was designed as a three-hour block with 40 freshmen and sophomores, in which students take a rigorous high school geometry course with one teacher and apply what they learn in a construction course with another teacher. Over the course of the school year, the 40 students in the Construction/Geometry Program build a portable house to provide affordable housing in the area.

To begin the program design process, Moore and Burke essentially "ripped apart" the geometry book and rearranged the content to coincide with the sequence of constructing a house. They say the last quarter of the year contains specialized geometry content that doesn't closely match with the construction process. However, by that time, students are well grounded in geometry concepts and are able to handle the more abstract learning without direct context on the work-site. At the same time, the construction project is focused on the intense work of getting the house finished, not on learning new construction skills and concepts.

When the new program was first launched, it was organized into two sections: 20 students in the geometry classroom during the first block and

20 students out on the construction site during the first block. When the bell rang, the two groups would switch places. Even though the teachers had reorganized the curriculum, to the students the program still felt like two separate courses. Six weeks into the program, the teachers decided to combine the two groups into one and do everything together. Because they were moving together from the classroom to the construction site and were able to see their teachers working as a team, the students made stronger connections to the unity of the course. They began to view construction as an applied side of geometry rather than as two separate courses.

Business and industry gets involved in the program by sending guest speakers from fields such as engineering, architecture, surveying, real estate, marketing, construction management, construction trades, and heavy equipment operations. Employer partners also allow the class to take field trips to their sites, so students can see firsthand the stages of home construction.

Results

The integrated program began producing results very quickly. In Colorado, the CSAP, a standardized assessment, is given to sophomore students. On the geometry and measurement section of that assessment, all of the Construction/Geometry Program students who took the CSAP outperformed every geometry cohort of students in their school district, and every one of them had a rating of advanced or proficient.

#

Chapter Nine

Leading Through Change

As I said in chapter 1, leadership is the essential ingredient for taking action to address the Visible Challenges and Root Causes. That sounds cliché but it's true. The type of leadership that really matters here is the local kind; this is true regardless of whether or not good leadership is exercised in our state capitals or in Washington, DC. We can advocate for positive policies at the state and national levels, but we cannot wait to start exerting leadership.

The good news is that the people who run our schools, businesses, and social, religious and cultural institutions have an amazing wealth of creativity, energy, and goodwill. We have a deep tradition of local people rolling up their sleeves, taking responsibility, and getting to work.

The only way forward is for local leaders to emerge and make change happen.

So, does your community have the right leaders? And are leaders born, or can they be developed?

And, can you be one of these leaders?

Clearly, some people are more wired for leadership than others; still, I believe there is some latent leadership that can emerge depending on the need and the support provided. Leadership is not a simple YES or NO answer.

Whatever your degree of innate leadership talent, you can more fully develop it, perhaps temper it and sand off the rough edges, and follow proven leadership principles to be successful in leading change. While intentionally working to develop your leadership capacity will be a long journey, it will also be a worthwhile and fulfilling one.

During this chapter, I will unpack the leadership principles that have helped me the most and that will come into play as you

---

Web-Based Resources

Visit **www.powerandpromiseofpathways.com** for an annotated list of helpful leadership resources.

lead the change process. These concepts will help you lead both within your organization and with outreach to multiple organizations through your Pathways Partnership. I will be introducing several models that represent how change happens and how change is communicated, and then I will present an integrated leadership action plan that you can use for your Pathways work.

Section 1. Defining Leadership

How should we define leadership? Let's begin by considering a definition of leadership attributed to the esteemed management theorist, Peter Drucker:

> *Leadership is the lifting of people's vision to a higher sight, the raising of their performance to a higher standard, the building of their personality beyond its normal limitations.*
> – Peter Drucker

The lifting of people's vision. In Drucker's definition, he says that leadership is first about lifting people's vision to a higher sight. A leader's perspective is a healthy dose of "good is not good enough." A good leader is always pushing people to a higher vision for what the future can be. For example, the framers of the U.S. Constitution began the document with the statement, "We, the people, in order to form a more perfect union." They were focusing the nation on the idea that, with a better form of government, we could progress from a good union to a "more perfect union." They were raising the bar, raising the vision of how a loose coalition of 13 autonomous states could truly begin to live and act as a unified nation and how that nation would be better equipped to protect the rights and liberties of individuals.

Often, people get stuck in their ways and they become comfortable with "good enough." My life experience tells me that a significant percentage of people will not seek positive change unless the pain they face on a day-to-day basis becomes almost unbearable. This is short-term, reactive way to live.

By contrast, a good leader is always looking over the horizon, anticipating dangers that will one day drive the need for change. Anticipating the need for change, he or she imagines and then paints the picture for others of a more positive vision for what the future can be and how that vision will ultimately benefit the individual and the group as a whole.

The raising of their performance to a higher standard. In order to reach that higher vision of the future, people need to perform at a higher level. The leader must help identify what that higher level of performance will be, how it will be measured, and how people will know if they've achieved that higher standard. A good leader is not afraid of accountability.

The building of their personality beyond its normal limitations. The leader knows that people are the key to successful change and that to perform to a higher standard, they will need to develop deeper character and greater capacity. The leader helps identify what character and capacity will be needed and then clarifies the specific activities and resources to help people reach and perform to that higher standard. The true leader doesn't leave people hanging, simply demanding better performance without also investing in and strengthening the capacity of people to perform to a higher level. The leader fully embraces the notion of a "growth mindset," believing that people are capable of getting better.

> *The true leader doesn't leave people hanging, simply demanding better performance without also investing in and strengthening the capacity of people to perform to a higher level.*

This is the essence of leading:

◊   Creating a Positive Vision

◊   Setting Performance Expectations

◊   Investing in People

Is Leadership Simply a Position?

True leadership is not just a position; it is disposition. Disposition is defined as "a person's inherent qualities of mind and character." Leadership is an orientation to looking forward, anticipating a positive future and also being cognizant of threats to that positive future. We all know individuals who have been given the mantle of leadership but are not embodying true leadership. Some of these individuals manage their current environment but are not really looking ahead to the future. They are complying with mandates and external expectations but not anticipating a better future. They are not asking the question, "Is this truly the best we can do?"

Further, even if they have a grand vision for the future, they may not be fleshing out that vision into expectations of actual performance, so the goals for the future remain murky, and everyone under their leadership is left to try to define successful performance on their own. Further, those who are not fulfilling the role of leadership may demand action and excellence but not assess the capability of their followers to actually carry out their expectations.

Rather than investing in their people, they are quick to find fault and to appoint blame. Since they don't have a growth mindset, they can easily explain why positive change isn't happening, blaming it on workers who "can't cut it."

While the designated leader may be dropping the ball and engaging in blame, other individuals within the organization actually may be providing more true leadership that the person given the title of "leader." These individuals may be doing their best to articulate a vision, define what that vision entails, and then invest in the capacity of others to carry out the vision.

So a key maxim to remember is this: Leadership is not a Position. It's a Disposition. Wherever you stand in an organizational structure, leadership is a disposition for honestly assessing the present, looking forward, anticipating challenges, engaging others, and taking courageous action.

Section 2. Applying Models of Leadership

I. Emotional Intelligence

The next component of leadership I will talk about is something called "emotional intelligence." Harvard professor Daniel Goldman spearheaded the work on emotional intelligence. Goleman identified five components:[1]

Higher levels of responsibility and impact also require higher levels of emotional intelligence.

◊ Self-Awareness

◊ Self-Regulation

◊ Motivation

◊ Empathy

◊ Social Skills

Emotional intelligence is a set of competencies and attributes that a leader needs to develop and continually work to strengthen. Higher levels of responsibility and impact require higher levels of emotional intelligence. Some people have a greater innate sense of emotional intelligence than others, and high levels of emotional intelligence may be difficult for some people to achieve, but emotional intelligence can be developed through focused practice.

Self-Awareness. The first element of emotional intelligence is self-awareness. This means that you have developed the capacity to recognize and understand your own moods, emotions, and drives.

I can speak from personal experience that, for me, self-awareness is not necessarily an innate strength, but it can be developed. As a young man entering into adult life, I was unaware of my own "emotional baggage" that I brought with me from childhood into my marriage and my work life. Through trial and error, I had to learn the art of self-examination, so I could understand my motivations and drives in a nonjudgmental but a brutally honest way. Along the way, I engaged expertise from wise authors and trusted advisors and friends; these external inputs and sounding boards helped me gain a clearer understanding of my internal life. This personal growth allowed me to experience closer relationships and also enjoy my work more deeply.

As a person grows in his or her self-awareness, certain hallmarks begin to emerge. One is self-confidence, having a positive sense of one's individual strength, but also an awareness of personal challenges and emotional "triggers." The traits of self-awareness and self-acceptance demonstrate themselves through a self-deprecating sense of humor. Self-awareness can be very endearing and helps others feel safe and supported when they are in contact with you. Self-awareness is the foundational requisite of emotional intelligence. Without self-awareness, effective leadership of others is impossible.

Self-Regulation. A key characteristic of self-regulation is the ability to control and redirect disruptive impulses and moods. By having a better understanding of self-regulation, a person is able to conduct an internal dialogue about what is the root of different emotions and impulses and moods. This helps the person to be more objective in the way he or she deals with other people, without overreacting to their actions or outbursts, and to deal with normal organizational friction that might happen during a change initiative.

The propensity to suspend judgment is not a character flaw; it a very valuable skill, because it allows the leader to gain the maximum amount of input and to identify a true "win-win" solution.

A second characteristic of self-regulation is the propensity to suspend judgment. In our modern polarized political environment, political ideologues want simplistic answers to every problem, and politicians are castigated if they change any policy positions over time. Politicians are expected to stick to the party line and not think independently in a way that could give any credence to the perspectives and positions of the opposing party. Even our media have become segmented and often tilt to the predispositions of their audience's political persuasions and world-views. In today's society, you really don't have to listen to views and opinions that might challenge your pre-determined opinions.

This is harmful to our nation and contributes to the political paralysis in Washington, DC. Narrow-minded thinking is counter-productive to true leadership. The propensity to suspend judgment is not a character flaw, rather it is a very valuable skill, because it allows the leader to gain the maximum amount of input and to identify a true "win-win" solution instead of casting everything into a win-lose frame. There may be multiple individuals who have different perspectives on an event, a problem, or a challenge. For the leader to really engender trust and the best possible solutions, he or she needs to gather multiple sources of information in order to make a better decision in the end and to explain that decision in the face of opposition.

When leaders have a strong sense of self-regulation, others will perceive them as being trustworthy and having integrity. They will do what they say, and they are working to align their actions with their values.

Finally, those who are strong in the skill of self-regulation will have a comfort with ambiguity. They won't feel the need to make an immediate decision or cast everything as black or white options. They will have the patience to gather the necessary amount of information to make a good decision. Leaders with self-regulation are also seen as open to change. They are committed to getting the best possible results, even if it means a change in strategy. This openness to change is critical to reaching goals because as the military truism goes, "the plan of battle only lasts for the first five minutes of the battle." Setting clear goals, and maintaining flexibility in the application of strategies and tactics, is the true key to success.

Internal Motivation. The next component of emotional intelligence is internal motivation. With strong internal motivation, individuals have an inner passion to work for reasons other than external factors alone, such as money or status. If motivation is only focused on some sort of external payoff, and everyone else is also working only for that type of gain, then personal agendas will become predominate and block the capacity for true collaboration. Emotionally intelligent individuals find a deeper motivation to do the right things for the right reasons. This inner motivation is what creates the internal engine to pursue goals with energy and persistence. Those individuals have developed a maturity so that they are motivated by the bigger picture, to bring greater value to others, and believe that good things will return to them in that process. This requires individuals to have a "wealth" mindset instead of a "scarcity" mindset, believing that there is enough to go around for everyone, thus it makes sense for us to work together for a common good.

Leaders with strong internal motivation will be able to stick with their goals because their motivation is not shallow or fragile and depending on variable external factors. Those with internal motivation have a strong drive to achieve results and to make a positive difference. Persons with internal motivation cultivate optimism, believing that things will work out well in the long run, even when they're facing immediate failures or setbacks. They will have a strong commitment to the cause and to the people who are necessary to help fulfill that cause.

Empathy. Empathy is a characteristic of being able to understand the emotional makeup of other people and to treat people appropriately according to their emotional reactions. Having empathy with another person is impossible without first creating the personal foundation of self-awareness, self-regulation, and proper internal motivation. The empathetic person understands that mistakes are inevitable. Empathy allows an understanding that others might be reacting based on their own drives, emotions, and motivations, perhaps ones that are unrecognized. Empathy helps a person better understand the emotions and challenges that somebody else might be facing.

Empathetic individuals are more successful in building and retaining talent. They don't categorize others as either "good" or "bad," or "smart" or "stupid." By contrast, the empathetic leader recognizes that people are complicated, but they can change and grow for the better. Therefore, the person with empathy will have more interest in maximizing the strengths and potential of individuals.

Empathy also allows leaders to develop a greater sense of cross-cultural sensitivity. In America's highly diverse society, cross-cultural understanding and respect is more important than ever. Empathetic leaders will demonstrate an ethic of service to clients as well as to others within the organization. While they strive for excellence and achievement, their driving motivation is not to win or defeat others but to serve and empower others.

Social skills. A leader with strong social skills can manage relationships, build networks, find common ground, and build rapport. Managing relationships is the key for leading people; this hold true for relationships with individuals and relationships among organizations. Since every organization has its perspective and priorities (or "interests") that it must fulfill, a leader with social skills will recognize those institutional priorities and needs. The leader with social skills will find things that connect people and bring them together. She will identify shared values that can transcend institutional interests. Appealing to shared values can help smooth over the inevitable friction between organizations and individuals.

The hallmark of leaders with strong social skills is that they will be very effective in leading change. They will be persuasive—not persuasive by speaking louder and longer—but by exerting influence because people will recognize their interests are being respected and looked after. These leaders will take the time to answer honest, difficult questions and concerns.

The Power of Emotional Intelligence

Emotional intelligence is the key to self-leadership, growing and developing one's own life into a healthy state and sense of abundance. Emotional intelligence is the key to building and leading teams and bringing people together around common goals and interests.

All leaders needs to undertake a serious self-examination of their current level of emotional intelligence, knowing that their emotional intelligence will have a direct bearing on whether or not they can successfully bring people together to accomplish meaningful change.

2. Level 5 Leadership

In his book "Good to Great," Jim Collins describes high level leadership for those companies that made the leap from "good" to "great." Collins explained that for a long time during the research phase of the work, he resisted the notion that leadership was an integral part of helping a good company make the transformation to becoming a great organization. He felt that "leadership" was too murky of a concept, and that for a researcher, it was an easy escape route from having to explain something very important. He wanted to identify the actions and processes that helped organizations make the leap, and resisted attributing the change to the personality of one person. But he said the preponderance of evidence forced him to reconsider his bias. Based on the research, there really was something happening in the realm of leadership that was indispensable.[2]

> *"A Level 5 leader is an individual who blends personal humility and intense professional will."*
>
> Jim Collins, author,
> *Good to Great*

So, through much thought and analysis, Collins and his team identified the traits of a "Level 5 Leader." Here is how he describes the five levels of leadership:[3]

◊ Level 1 is a highly capable individual, someone who can make productive contributions through their talent, knowledge, skills, and good work habits. Level 1 is self-leadership.

◊ Level 2 is a contributing team member, someone who can contribute their individual capabilities to the achievement of the group's objectives and who can work effectively with others in a group setting. Level 2 is being a great team member.

◊ Level 3 is a competent manager, someone who can organize people and resources toward the effective and efficient pursuit of predetermined objectives. Level 3 managers are needed at all levels within an effective organization.

◊ Level 4 is an effective leader who catalyzes commitment to vigorous pursuit of a clear and compelling vision, stimulating higher performance standards. Level 4 leaders lead all successful organizations. Reaching Level 4 is, in itself, an accomplishment and should be honored.

◊ The Level 5 leader is rare. That is why, in Collins' research, so few organizations make the transition from being simply a good organization to a great one and then sustain excellent performance over a long period of time. Few organizations have a Level 5 leader.

According to Collins, a Level 5 leader is "an individual who blends personal humility and intense professional will."[4] Collins profiles a number of individuals who fit this description. Surprisingly, they don't fit the typical stereotype of the "charismatic leader," someone who has a dynamic force of personality who becomes a hero or a media darling. The research shows that, while a company with a charismatic leader might have a season of visible or heroic success, when that leader departs the scene, the company loses its footing. It cannot sustain high performance without the driving and dynamic personality at the helm.

Contrasting to the stereotype of the charismatic leader, Level 5 leaders are often quite unprepossessing in their personal style. Some are very quiet people. They possess personal humility and sincerely attribute success to "being lucky" or just having a great team of people around them. They do not allow themselves to become the focus of attention. Still, humility and a quiet style should not be perceived as weakness. These individuals have a very strong commitment, described as an "iron will," to the success of the organization and fulfilling the purpose of the organization. Level 5 leaders have a deep level of what he describes as "professional will."

This description of a Level 5 leader circles us back to the definition of emotional intelligence and the trait of internal motivation. To exert transformational leadership, internal motivation is focused on achieving the goals and expectations of the organization. Motivation provides the persistence and drive for excellence needed for success.

As you consider Level 5 leadership as a personal challenge, ask yourself the following questions:

◊ What are my deepest motivations?

◊ Is this about me or about the mission?

◊ What is my level of personal humility and intense professional will?

Section 3. The Process of Leading Change

The next resource that we're going to talk about is organizational transformation, explained by Harvard Business School professor John Kotter in his important book, "Leading Change."[5] Kotter's work focuses on leaders who take their company through a major organizational change. Sometimes these efforts are successful and yield to long-term successful results. But sometimes, these change initiatives fall short.

Kotter talks about eight common mistakes that people make in the change process:[6]

◊ Error 1: Not Establishing a Great Enough Sense of Urgency

◊ Error 2: Not Creating a Powerful Enough Guiding Coalition

◊ Error 3: Lacking a Vision

◊ Error 4: Under-communicating the Vision by a Factor of Ten

◊ Error 5: Not Removing Obstacles to the New Vision

◊ Error 6: Not Systematically Planning for, and Creating, Short-Term Wins

◊ Error 7: Declaring Victory Too Soon

◊ Error 8: Not Anchoring Changes in the Culture

After pointing out what doesn't work, he then identifies the eight steps for successfully leading major change. Not surprisingly, the action steps are the mirror image of the eight common errors. Many of these steps should sound familiar to the reader of this book, because they are echoed throughout, particularly in the Pathways System design and implementation process, explained in Chapter 7.

I. Create Urgency

The first step is to establish a sense of urgency that is driving the need for change. Kotter explains that often change efforts fail because the sense of urgency is not clear enough. People have become satisfied at the current level of outcomes. They need something very specific that will serve as the call to action for the change. These driving factors may be slightly different in each location, depending on the circumstances of the school, community, and region. The urgency needs to be posed in human terms: how is the current situation or coming threat impacting or going to impact real people–youth, adult workers, families, and individuals trying to start and grow businesses? People need to accept that the urgency is real, that it's not contrived or manufactured.

As we explored in Chapter 2, there are visible challenges and there are related root causes. Visible, external challenges are more likely to be seen in the community–low-skilled workers, under-employed workers, employer difficulty filling skilled positions, and working-age adults pulling out of the workforce. The associated root causes might be partly related to educational deficiencies–lack of career understanding and goals, rigorous academic requirements that don't clearly relate to a student's personal objectives, or classes that are not engaging curiosity and problem solving.

Finally, in communicating the urgency, lead with a description of the most universal and visible challenges–the issues that challenge all families, workers, and businesses in your community. Once you have established the broad challenge or threat, then you can point to the system deficiencies that contribute to the big challenges.

Make sure to keep the urgency statement as simple as possible and avoid educational jargon (like project-based learning, experiential learning, metacognitive strategies, etc.) that the average citizen won't understand. The diagnosis should be sophisticated, but communication should be simple and straightforward.

2. Create a Powerful Coalition

The next step is to create a powerful guiding coalition. Real change will not happen if just one person, even a person with authority, is calling for it. If people are not included in the change process, many of them will resist the change, and will adopt a "this too shall pass" mindset, doing as little as possible and holding out until the change fad has passed by. A powerful coalition makes sure that a wide variety of stakeholders are represented, helping shape the change and also driving it deeper into their respective organizations. Having the right organizations involved in the coalition is important, but even more so is making sure the right individuals from those organizations are involved. You need individuals with a high enough level of stature, with some needed expertise, and who engender respect within the community that they represent.

Remember that the guiding coalition will likely grow and evolve over time as new organizations become connected to the change process and some others fall by the wayside. If the guiding coalition needs to be large to represent the key stakeholders in a large region, consider creating an executive committee to make operational decisions and other working groups to give each member an active role.

3. Create a Vision for Change and Key Strategies

The next step is to develop a vision and supporting strategies. Working with a group of individuals from the guiding coalition, the leader and her colleagues need to articulate as clearly as possible a vision, that is, a statement of what the future will look like. This is a description of a "preferred future state," in which things will be significantly better than they are now, albeit not perfect. Many stakeholders already have some sort of vision for the future they carry around in their heads, but it is probably not written down. Unfortunately, many others have never seriously asked what they want the future to be, and instead they muddle through the present and complain about it, assuming that they are incapable of affecting true change.

Putting a vision into written form forces a greater degree of clarity, so it can become a shared vision. Putting the vision in writing also exposes the different assumptions, values, and priorities that stakeholders hold. When the vision is unwritten, stakeholders can actually hold very different visions even though they use similar terminologies in their conversations. They may not even realize they are working toward differing visions for the future. Getting the vision in writing is important.

In addition to being clear, the vision statement needs to be ambitious and realistic. One of the downfalls of the No Child Left Behind Act from 2001 was its well-intended goal that 100 percent of children would be academically proficient by 2014. This goal was set while academic standards were a moving target, and then the country experienced ongoing wars and a far-reaching recession. Even in the most utopian of times, 100 percent academic proficiency would not have been reachable. Not only was the goal out of reach, there were negative consequences associated with missing the targets. The overreach of the law's aspirations undermined its credibility on multiple levels.

To complement your new vision, the coalition also should identify key strategies related to the vision. In strategic planning parlance, strategy is a general objective for reaching toward a goal that supports the long-term vision.

◊ VISION –The preferred future state (not perfection but reflecting real progress over a certain amount of time).

◊ GOALS – The specific and measurable achievements that indicate the degree to which the vision has been realized.

◊ STRATEGY – A general category of related actions and projects that the stakeholders can work on in order to reach the specific, measurable goals.

◊ PROJECTS/ACTION STEPS – The time-bound, person-assigned activities and projects that must be carried out to fulfill the strategy.

To be honest, many observers have questioned the value of extensive long-range written plans, since circumstances on the ground often change quickly. Still, without some sort of clearly written vision and supporting strategies, sustained progress is highly unlikely.

Most organizations under-communicate by a factor of ten – meaning they should communicate ten times more than they do! They need to communicate the urgency, the vision, the strategies, as well as the short-term wins and the long-range progress.

Vision statements are relatively easy to write; identifying specific strategies is more demanding because it grounds the vision in reality. People need to see that your vision statement is connected to real strategies, projects, and action steps. The written strategies allow people to see that yours is a realistic change-oriented effort, not just an exercise in wishful thinking. Of course, some flexibility in the development and the fine-tuning of that vision and the strategies is useful, so people feel included. You want them to feel that the change process is something being done BY them, not TO them.

4. Communicate the Vision and Strategy

Communication that is extensive, multi-layered, targeted to multiple stakeholders, and consistent and ongoing is the "secret sauce" for change. Kotter observes that communication is the factor in which most organizations fall far short. He calculates that organizations under-communicate by a factor of ten – meaning they should communicate ten times more than they do! They need to communicate the urgency, the vision, and the strategies, as well as the short-term wins and the long-range progress.

Chapter 10 of this book is devoted to "Branding" and "Communicating" about your Pathways System Initiative. Branding and communicating (both internally and externally) is not always a sweet spot for education systems; thus, the branding and marketing expertise that employer partners from the private sector have developed will be an invaluable resource to the Pathways System Initiative.

5. Remove Obstacles

Inside an organization, policy and personnel barriers tend to block the desired change. The leader must take action when necessary to clear these blockages. Sometimes this requires policy changes; sometimes it requires management structure changes or replacing personnel. If the leader does not take the action necessary at these particular points, then the entire change process is put at risk, because people down the ranks will start to believe that this is not a serious effort but just a charade announced for public relations purposes. Empowering real action by removing obstacles is a major leadership challenge.

6. Create Short-Term Wins

Kotter suggests that within about 18 months of any change process, clear, visible wins need to be experienced by the organization. These wins need to be measurable and visible. So as a Pathway System is developing direction, you need to identify the kind of impact it will have on student behaviors, student attendance, and employer engagement, all of which will happen more quickly on the front end of the reform, and which can be measured and reported.

Within about 18 months of any change process, clear, visible wins need to be experienced by the organization.

7. Build on the Change

The next step in the process is to consolidate gains and produce more change. Kotter notes that after there have been some visible changes and some visible wins, there is a human tendency to back off and take a breather. But this is a time in which the original naysayers may reemerge; instead of directly opposing the continuation of the effort, they may simply say, "let's claim victory and everyone can go home." If you follow their advice, and the change effort hasn't gone deep enough yet, then things will start to revert back to their original state. To fight the tendency to ease up too much, after the initial phase of change, the leader brings the team back together, celebrates the changes that have already happened, but then identifies the remaining gap between the vision (preferred future state) and the current reality. By focusing once again on the need, the leader can re-engage the change effort to take it to the next phase of the process.

8. Anchor Change in the Organizational Culture

Kotter's observation is that culture is a set of implicit beliefs and expectations and understandings; culture is almost invisible to the people who are inside the culture. You don't really understand the assumptions of your own culture until you come into contact with another culture. That's when you realize that some of your basic beliefs about what is right and acceptable are not necessarily 100 percent accurate. For example, friends of mine who traveled to China to adopt a child soon discovered that some of the locals would get physically very close to them in public settings and stare at them. These locals didn't think what they were doing was inappropriate, but in U.S. culture, the staring would have been viewed as rude or intrusive.

The Pathways System will require and create a new culture; but be aware, these cultural shifts will not happen quickly. Little by little, people's beliefs and expectations begin to change. Over time, a new culture emerges.

The Pathways System will require and create a new culture. For example, in a mature Pathways System, all forms of postsecondary education and training and all types of careers that bring value to the world (even so-called "dirty jobs") will be given respect. Teachers will realize that developing career and life readiness among youth is just as much part of their responsibility as teaching content. Teachers across several disciplines will believe that cross-curricular collaboration is normal, even professionally rewarding. Parents will believe that career development is an asset to their child, not a threat that might divert them from a preferred postsecondary outcome. Employers will regularly partner with the schools and colleges, believing this work is part of their responsibility to the community, as well as a win-win relationship for developing a pipeline of talent.

These cultural shifts will not happen quickly. First, all the other components of the change model need to be followed, and as the Pathways System begins to yield positive results and gain momentum, little by little, people's beliefs and expectations begin to change. Over time, a new culture emerges.

Section 4. Leadership Quick-Start

Other valuable leadership resources and tools are on our annotated resources list on the website, but the topics covered in this chapter provide a good start:

◊ Grow in your emotional intelligence.

◊ Aspire to Level V leadership that is fiercely determined and deeply humble.

◊ Commit to follow the Eight Steps of Leading Change.

Here are some simple next steps to take:

❑ Download the Leadership resource inventory. Start reading leadership articles and books on a regular basis.

❑ From your studies, create your own personal Leadership "cheat sheet" to help you remember and focus on the leadership principles that are most important to you.

❑ Convene a Leadership Discussion Group with a few friends and colleagues. Share leadership insights and challenges. Set and report on individual leadership goals with the group.

❑ Engage in a focused time of personal growth goal setting and reflection on at least a quarterly basis.

The next chapter takes you directly into Step 4 of the Leading Change Framework: Communicate the Change Vision. From my observation, learning to think and work strategically with communications will revolutionize your work in implementing a Pathways System.

Communicating the Power and Promise of Pathways

> This chapter was written by Pam Daly, President of DK Brand Strategy, based on her extensive experience working with the commercial sector and education sector on brand management.

In this chapter, you will learn the fundamentals of brand strategy and how to define the benefits of your Pathways Program. You will also learn how to build a marketing and communications plan that assures your key audiences understand and support the programs.

Why Should You Care About Brand Strategy?

One of the most overlooked components of building and maintaining an effective Pathway Program is the importance of Brand Strategy. Large or small, school districts are typically shorthanded in the Communications Office, where staff must focus on crisis management and the herculean task of simply disseminating the information, key dates, events, etc. that come with operating a school district. Brand Strategy is not typically top of mind.

You cannot engage students, parents, business partners and the community in your Pathways System Initiative unless they understand the benefit it provides to them - each one of them, individually.

Families are faced with an ever-growing list of choices when it comes to attending school. Combine this with the busy lives of working parents, transient populations, and language barriers, parents and students can struggle to have a clear understanding of the benefits of a specific school or district initiative like Pathway Programs. In the same way, employers and business organizations are extremely busy, focused building and sustaining their success, reaching their own customers and serving the needs of member businesses. In order to assure your stakeholders (families, students, and employers) readily have the information they need to make good decisions, having a consistent and effectively communicated message regarding the benefits of your Pathway Program is imperative.

Clear and compelling communication of the benefits of Pathway Programs is vital to their continued success. You cannot engage students, parents, business partners, and the community in your Pathways System Initiative unless they understand the benefit it provides to them—each one of them, individually.

To sum up the importance of Brand Strategy, consider this statement:

Engagement leads to understanding and support. Understanding and support contributes to your program's ability to sustain and grow over time.

Dr. Jay Steele, the former Chief Academic Officer of Metro Nashville Public School, affirms the importance of branding. He says, "Having a common vocabulary is important when communicating a brand. A clear and consistent message helps build a strong brand for all students, parents, and the community."[1]

Brand Strategy

A strong brand is more than a logo. Your brand is the unique, compelling combination of functional and emotional elements that benefit your stakeholders. Your brand affects customer loyalty, your competitive advantage, and the ability to sustain and grow your programs.

Brand Strategy is a holistic process. The responsibility for your brand is not just the responsibility of the marketing and communications department but also the responsibility of the entire organization, from the front office staff in your school to your district superintendent to other key members of your Pathways Partnership.

Your brand is the unique, compelling combination of functional and emotional elements that benefit your stakeholders.

Steve Casa, former Executive Director of the National Career Academy

Coalition, also states the critical role that branding and communications plays, "In my twenty-five years of career academy practice, there's never been a more important time to communicate the importance of high quality career academies. With so many choices for parents and students, clearly communicating the benefits of Pathway Programs should be an imperative for all career-connected programs."[2]

Using the information contained in this chapter as a guide, you will be able to build a strong Brand Strategy for your program and identify value propositions that deliver functional and emotional benefits that resonate with your constituents.

The Value Proposition

A value proposition is simply the unique and compelling benefit you or your product or service provides to an individual stakeholder. For example, a value proposition for a Business Partner engaged in your CTE program might be developing a workforce. A value proposition for a parent might be having a child who is college and career ready.

Once you have your Brand Strategy established, you have the tools to build marketing and communication plans that are both effective in communicating your Pathway Program benefits as well as efficient and that don't cost a lot of money.

Distinguish Between "Brand" vs. "Branding"

There is a big difference between "Brand" and "Branding."

One clear explanation is from Lisa Stewart, a branding expert:

> *Brand is the sum of the perceptions that are held about you, your company or your products. This includes perceptions held by both external and internal audiences and stakeholders. A brand is a person's emotional response -a gut feeling about an organization, a product, or a service. In essence, your customers own your brand; you do not. You don't have direct control of the perceptions held by customers.*[3]

While the "brand" is the perception of your "product" (the Pathway System) over which you do not have direct control, "Branding" is something you do control. Branding is the universe of activities you undertake that affects those perceptions. In order to effectively build a positive brand perception, you must engage in both internal and external activities, which are aligned to deliver a consistent impression of who you are.

Branding is not about stamping a logo on everything, but guiding and managing relationships with your customers. Realize that you only have partial control of perceptions with your branding activities.

While the "brand" is the perception of your "product" (the Pathway Program and Pathway System) over which you do not have direct control, "Branding" is something you do control.

Before you can build your marketing and communications plan, you have to be able to identify what the current perception of your brand (Pathway Program) is from your constituent's point of view.

Then, you must establish both the functional and emotional benefits that are most important to them and that your program can deliver. The functional and emotional benefits become your Brand Promise; this is the compass you will use to establish the right path for effective and efficient marketing and communication plans. If you follow the steps outlined below and use the examples shared here, you will be able to accomplish this goal.

Step 1. Create a Brand Team

The very first thing you should consider is who is going to help you with your Brand Strategy? It is very important to establish a team that will commit to following through with the process. This team will be your brand team. The role of this team is to provide input, support and guidance throughout the process and to help build consensus both internally and externally. This team should be cross-functional, consisting of both internal and external constituents. Try and hold the total number of Brand Team members to 15 or fewer people, or it can become difficult to manage.

The role of the Brand Team is to provide input, support and guidance throughout the process and to help build consensus both internally and externally.

Brand Team Members
◊ Pathway Program Administrators
◊ Teachers
◊ Principals

◊ Parents

◊ Students

◊ Business Partners

◊ Non-Profit Partners

◊ District Administration

◊ Postsecondary Partners

"District Leadership would do well to understand the strategic benefits of clear messaging and a strong brand. Communicating a single vision builds confidence from within. It helps clarify what you stand for and, in turn, helps you communicate your position to your audience in a way that resonates."

– Connie Majka, Director, Learning & Innovation, Philadelphia Academies Inc.

Step 2. Identify Current Perceptions through a SWOT Analysis

The next step in the Brand Strategy process is to determine what your constituents (parents, students, business partners, teachers, community leaders, non-profit partners etc.) think and feel about your Pathway Program.

If you do only one thing, conduct a SWOT analysis. SWOT stands for Strengths-Opportunities-Weaknesses-Threats. By conducting a SWOT analysis, you will establish an accurate perception of your Pathway Program. It is easy to conduct a SWOT analysis. You can use a survey provider like Survey Monkey to send a survey to a list of constituents, or you can simply email the SWOT Questions from your own email account (although this will mean respondents cannot answer anonymously). Make sure you send out your survey to a broad range of your constituents. You will likely discover what you think you know about how these people view your programs can be quite different!

Once you complete your SWOT Survey, sort your answers into Strengths-Weaknesses-Opportunities and Threats and make a note of how many times the same answer is given. List responses from the most important to the least important perceptions.

Here is an example of a SWOT Survey Questionnaire:

1. What does the Pathway Program do really well?

2. What unique resources does the Pathway Program have vs. what other schools offer?

3. What do you believe are the overall benefits that the Pathway Program provides to students?

4. What could the Pathway Program do better?

5. Where does the Pathway Program have fewer resources than other schools?

6. From your perspective, what are some of the weaknesses of the Pathway Program?

7. Are there any market trends that Pathway Program could take advantage of?

8. Are there any opportunities to grow that you feel the Pathway Program should explore? This could be an expansion of current programs and services or the addition of new programs.

9. What trends might harm the future of the Pathway Program

10. What do you consider as the "competition" for the Pathway Program brand?

11. If you were asked, "What is the Pathway Program?", how would you respond?

12. Do you have any additional comments about your feeling regarding the Pathway Program and its offerings?

Sample Cover Letter

Make sure you send a cover letter that explains why you are conducting the survey. Here is an example of a simple cover letter:

WE NEED YOUR HELP!

We are undergoing a process to review and refresh (or to establish) the Brand of the Pathway Program and to establish a protocol for ongoing brand management. We want to position the Pathway Program for growth. In order to do this successfully, we need your honest opinion about the Pathway Program, as it exists today.

This simple SWOT Survey will help us gain an understanding of the current perception of the Pathway Program. SWOT stands for Strengths, Weaknesses, Opportunities, and Threats facing an organization or a program. We will use your input as the first step in our Strategic Branding Process.

Your answers are completely confidential and will only be used for internal analysis.

If you have any questions or need any assistance, feel free to contact (name of survey administrator and phone number).

THIS SURVEY SHOULD BE COMPLETED NO LATER THAN (DEADLINE DATE)

Thank you so much for your help!"

Results of a SWOT Survey

Here is an example of a SWOT Survey result for an Arts School conducted recently. How would you use the results to assure that you are providing real benefit to your constituents?

STRENGTHS	WEAKNESSES
☐ Accepting/Diverse Environment 31	☐ Faculty 25
☐ Arts Education 17	☐ Rigor/Academics 15
☐ Academic/Arts Balance 14	☐ Awareness/Marketing/ Communication 13
☐ Faculty Commitment/Passion 11	☐ Communication 11
☐ Safe Environment 10	☐ Funding 10
☐ Community Partnerships 9	☐ Facility 7
☐ College Prep Experience 7	☐ Resources 5
OPPORTUNITIES	**THREATS**
☐ New Programs 22	☐ Lack of New Programs 20
☐ Marketing 10	☐ Decreased Enrollment 16
☐ More Externships 4	☐ Magnet Schools 15
☐ New Facility 4	☐ Funding Cuts 10
☐ Community Partnerships 3	☐ Lack of Community Support 10
☐ Use of Outside Professionals to Teach 3	

Step 3. Define Your Constituents

The next step in developing your Brand Strategy is to define the constituents for your Pathway Program. Constituents are sometimes referred to as Stakeholders. Constituents are people who interact with your brand and have an opinion about your brand. Customers are stakeholders who actually buy or use the services you provide.

It's pretty obvious that parents and students are important constituents for you to consider, but there are many more. What about your own district or school staff? What about employers who partner to provide job shadows, guest lectures, and internship experiences?

Do they understand the benefits of your Pathway Programs? Can they articulate these benefits in a consistent and compelling manner?

When one large metropolitan school district decided to go "wall-to-wall" with a Career Academy structure in all their high schools, they found that the people on the front line, those who tended to be the first point of contact for their academy brand, did not understand why the schools where restructuring. Many of the staff had never been included in any training regarding the changes taking place as it related to Career Academies. How could they explain the benefits of these programs and services to students and parents if they did not know themselves? To address this communication issue, focus groups were conducted with front office staff, resulting in the development of communication tool kits. These kits were distributed to all front line employees, giving them the information they needed to help communicate the benefits of the Career Academy reform happening in their schools.

Do your constituents understand the benefits of your Pathway Programs? Can they articulate these benefits in a consistent and compelling manner?

What about your school's office staff, your school board, local politicians, and the media? Are they important constituents for you to consider?

> "District Leadership would do well to understand the strategic benefits of clear messaging and a strong brand. Communicating a single vision builds confidence from within. It helps clarify what you stand for and, in turn, helps you communicate your position to your audience in a way that resonates."
>
> – Connie Majka, Director, Learning & Innovation, Philadelphia Academies Inc.

The Constituent Matrix

Use your Brand Team to help you prepare of list of constituents for your Pathway Program and then rank them in order of importance. Once you have identified and ranked the importance of your constituents, prepare a Constituent Matrix that considers their value proposition and also lists what you want each of them to think and feel about your Pathway Program. Consider what you would like them to DO as it relates to interacting with your Pathway Program.

Here is an example of a Constituent Matrix (sometimes called a "Message Matrix"):

Constituent Matrix/Message Matrix

Constituent	Value Proposition	Feel/Believe	Business Purpose
Teachers & Counselors Academy/Non Academy Prospective Teachers	Student success a reflection on them Ownership Allowance for true counseling activities (time) Engaged student/ Focused student/ Team teaching approach/Teacher accountability/ Small group relationship building	Valued Empowered Appreciated Belong to important team Making a difference Successful Focused	Better education workforce Retention Higher grad rates/ low dropout Reduce load on community services to care for uneducated
Parent Prospective Parents Private School Parents	Successful kids Student preparedness More opportunities for life/Child has informed choices, focused Choice of program All students have a place here Safe Financial Benefits	This is the best education you can get Kids are safe and cared about Private school culture I am doing the right/best thing for my kid School and teachers are accessible/students have competitive advantage	Word of mouth Maintaining or increasing enrollment Funding Engaged parents Academic achievement Educated community

Step 4. Develop Your Brand Promise

Now you are ready for the most important part of the process, developing the Brand Promise. A Brand Promise is an internal statement of external purpose. It is written from your student's (or key audience's) point of view and is based on the most important functional and emotional benefits of a Pathway Program to them. This statement will serve as the compass for your brand, and everything associated with your Pathways Brand should be consistent with the Brand Promise.

Your brand promise is written from your student's (or key audience's) point of view and is based on the most important functional and emotional benefits of a Pathway Program to them.

Your Brand Promise is not a tag line and will not be used in any external marketing materials. It is the statement that all your internal staff understands as the promise they are making to their students.

Brand Promises can be really long or super short. Here are the brand promise statements of a few Brands you might be familiar with:

McDonalds
◊ An inexpensive, familiar, and consistent meal delivered quickly in a clean environment.

◊

Google
◊ Provide access to the world's information in one click.

Volvo
◊ Safety

Writing Out the Brand Promise
So how do you go about writing a brand promise? Follow these steps and you will be successful:

◊ Bring the Brand Team together for a 3-hour Brand Promise meeting

◊ Review what a Brand Promise is and show some examples

◊ Break the Brand Team up into three or four groups

◊ Have each group spend a half hour preparing a list of functional and emotional benefits of the Pathway Program(s) from the student's point of view

◊ Bring the group back together and spend a half hour coming to consensus on the top five functional and five emotional benefits. Try to keep these to five each, or you will end up with a very long and less specific Brand Promise!

◊ With one list of functional and emotional benefits, halve the teams.

◊ Spend another half hour writing a brand promise that uses all of the words on the list or the *meaning* of the words.

To make sure you have used all the functional and emotional words or the meaning of the words, plot out the Brand Promise using a chart, provided at our website, http://www.powerandpromiseofpathways.com.

So, here are the final functional and emotional benefits that a Brand Team in a large urban school district agreed upon for the Academy Pathway Programs in their district:

Functional	**Emotional**
◊ Working team	◊ Community/Belonging/ Family/Trust/Relationships
◊ Extra Curricular Activity	
◊ Real World Relevant Learning	◊ Public Recognition
	◊ High Expectations
◊ Safety	◊ Pride
◊ Structure	◊ Commitment
◊ Professional Opportunities/ Exposure	◊ Unique Individual Expression
◊ Leadership	◊ Student Voice

And here is the resulting Brand Promise:

"Academies are a safe and trusting environment. I love belonging to a supportive community with lots of in school activities and outside opportunities. Learning is relevant to the real world and I am challenged to meet high expectations. My voice is heard. I can express my uniqueness. It's family."

Do you think that this is a good Brand Promise that is reflective of the functional and emotional attributes of the Brand? Can you hear the student voice in this promise?

Step 5. Create the Architecture for your Brand

You may or may not need to consider developing Architecture (logo and style guide) for your Pathway Program. If you already have a logo for your program, just make sure it is reflective of the Brand Promise.

If you need to develop a logo, perhaps your Communications Department can help? Or, perhaps you have a business partner that is in the design business who will be willing to come to your aid?

Remember that "word of mouth" (people to people communications) is one of the most effective ways to communicate a message, and it doesn't cost a thing.

Districts can also use a local design firm or freelancers (maybe even excelling students in your graphic design programs) to develop the architecture on their behalf. Good design is a skill and you should let the experts help you! Make sure that you prepare a Creative Brief for your designers so they have all the information they need to develop a strong log (also called a "mark") for your Pathway Program.

Step 6. Create Your Communications Plan

A successful formula for the development of the communications plan might look like this:

STRATEGY + PLAN + IMPLEMENTATION = SUCCESS

Another way of thinking about this is to consider the following five questions in sequence. It might be helpful for your Brand Team to ask the following questions before and during your planning process:

1. What is our goal? (Use the Brand Promise as a guide!)

2. Who are we trying to reach, and what do we want them to think feel and then do? (Use your Constituent List!)

3. How do we define our message? (Brand Promise again!)

4. How do we best deliver our message? (Use

Web-Based Resources

Visit **www.powerandpromiseofpathways.com** to see links to examples of a Creative Brief and to download templates of the Communications Worksheet and the Communications Calendar newsletters, social media, and brand ambassadors.)

5. How do we complete this sentence? We will know we are successful in this effort when _____.

Also, consider these questions whenever your strategy will involve individual schools marketing their Pathway Programs:

◊ How can your school best reach parents before they make a decision on what school their children will attend?

◊ Are you considering educating the staff and students in your feeder elementary and middle schools?

◊ Will your communication strategy entail developing community-wide communication plans that will be funded by the district or included into their current plans?

Remember that "word of mouth" (people to people communications) is one of the most effective ways to communicate a message, and it doesn't cost a thing.

Step 7. Conduct a Communications Audit

Make sure you conduct a Communications Audit. This is simply a list of all of the things you or your district are currently doing to communicate information about your Pathway Programs. Some of these tactics you will want to maintain, others you may not, but it is important to have a clear understanding of who is communicating what. You might be surprised to find out that there are many different people communicating many different messages.

Step 8. Develop a Process Protocol

In order to begin establishing a consistent message, there must be a process established so that there is centralized control over the messaging. In a vacuum, people will fill in the blanks. So, make sure that you do not have a vacuum that requires teachers to individually produce materials.

You need a clear strategy and plan for communicating the benefits of your Pathway Programs for each constituent.

There should be a strategy and plan for communicating the benefits of your Pathway Programs for each constituent. This strategy should be clearly communicated to your staff so that they know what to expect. It is also critical to provide them with the basic materials they need to answer questions about your Pathway Programs from parents, students, business partners, and the community at large.

Consider who will be responsible for developing the plan and then implementing the plan. Ask the Brand Team to help establish a protocol for marketing and communication efforts that clearly identifies who will be responsible for what. Make sure your district leadership has accepted this protocol and stands behind it.

The Communications Worksheet

Now, using your list of constituents, in order of importance, begin thinking about how best to reach them with your Pathway message. Consider what your constituents do throughout their day, where they go, what they do for fun. How do they currently receive information about your school or district?

You can use a simple form (available at our website, http://www. powerandpromisesofpathways.com, to help you organize your plan. Prepare one of these sheets for each constituent group you are addressing.

The Communication Calendar

Once you have a worksheet for each stakeholder you are addressing completed, you must think about when you will begin and end your tactical plan. Using a simple Excel spreadsheet (available on our website), you can prepare a calendar for the Brand Team to review and approve.

Step 9. Identify Your Brand Ambassadors

Brand Ambassadors can be one of the most effective ways to market your Pathway Programs. Who would be strong Brand Ambassadors for your program? They can be business partners, teachers, students, and influential/active parents. What role would you like them to play in your communication strategy?

Student Ambassadors can conduct school tours and help individual schools plan events and meetings. How will you train your Ambassadors and supply them with the resources they need to be effective?

Step 10. Write the Elevator Speech and Create Related Materials

The Elevator Speech

Imagine you are in an elevator. Two people get on and notice you are wearing a Pathway Program pin. "What's is that?" they ask. You have 15 seconds between floors to explain.

It is important to make sure that you develop this short descriptor of your program and its benefits. Make sure it is simple and easy to remember. This is also a great project for Brand Team input. Once you have created an effective elevator speech, consider putting the statement on the back of your staff's business cards. This is an easy, inexpensive way to assure all of your internal stakeholders are armed with a clear and consistent message.

Collateral Material

Producing printed materials can be expensive, so think about what single item would be most beneficial to prepare. Many districts choose to produce folders with inserts for their Pathway Programs that contain common information and language but allow for individual school or programs to add information. Printed materials can become obsolete quickly as programs change and grow. Make sure you consider this before investing in this tactic.

> *Once you have created an effective elevator speech, consider putting the statement on the back of your staff's business cards.*

Electronic/Web Based Tactics

Easier to update and manage, the use of electronic tactics can be effective and efficient. It goes without saying that a basic website is important, but also consider newsletters and email as effective tactics to reach constituents. Do you have strong business partner engagement? Perhaps an electronic *Annual Report* featuring business partner involvement in your Pathway Programs might be an impressive way to feature current partners and help engage new partners. Myriad resources exist on-line that provide free templates for newsletters and direct mail. Don't be afraid to do a Google search for these resources and use them!

Step 11. Measure Success

How do you measure the success of your Communications Plan? As you prepare the Communication Plan Worksheet, list specific outcomes for each of your tactics. Make sure you follow-up and measure whenever one of your tactics was successful. Was your expected outcome to increase the number of business partners? Did it work? Did you hold an open house? How many families attended? Whenever possible, define outcomes that are measurable. "Increasing awareness" of your program is not a measurable goal unless you can measure growth within each audience over a specific period of time.

What happens if you find that a tactic did not work as well as you hoped? Stop. Move on. You won't know if your plan is successful unless you measure and analyze the results. Measure frequently so that you don't continue to support a tactic that isn't successful; determine what is working, and continue to support the tactics that are successful!

You won't know if your communication plan is successful unless you measure and analyze the results.

Words of Encouragement

Building awareness of and understanding of your Pathway Program is an important and critical goal that assures internal and external support and ultimately supports program sustainability. By implementing the tools and information provided here, you can build a Communications Plan based on sound Brand Strategy and assure that your constituents understand the functional and emotional benefits of your program. Building a communications plan should be a fun and engaging process that reaps meaningful rewards.

For more information on Branding and Communications for education and other initiatives, contact Pam Daly at <u>pdaly@dkbrand.com</u>.

Chapter Eleven

Policy Agenda for Pathways Systems

Adopting the Pathways System approach means moving from a one-size-fits-all approach for the high school to a new model, one that offers each student the option of multiple pathways to college and careers, supported by the components of the Pathways System Framework™.

To fully develop effective Pathways Systems, local efforts work best when buttressed by a rational suite of state policies, funding initiatives, and incentives.

Local leaders carry out the design and implementation of a Pathways System. But these local efforts can either be helped or hindered by state policies and funding structures. To fully develop effective Pathways Systems, local efforts work best when buttressed by a rational suite of state policies, funding initiatives, and incentives.

In this chapter, we review what has been happening at the state level in recent years related to Pathways-related policies, what a coherent suite of policies and initiatives should include, and why each state should start by conducting a policy audit.

Section 1. Emerging State Policies and Initiatives

State policymakers have become increasingly aware of the need for better programs and policies that facilitate smooth transitions to career success for youths and young adults; with this awakening, state legislatures and agencies are developing new initiatives and updating policies at an accelerating rate.

Over a three-year period beginning in 2013, approximately 300 new funding initiatives, programs, and policies were enacted across almost every state and the District of Columbia. The National Association of State Directors for Career Technical Education Consortium (now known as Advance CTE) and the Association for Career Technical Education (ACTE) have conducted an extensive review and explanation of these CTE-related policies. The full reports for 2013, 2014 and 2015 can be accessed through the Advance CTE and ACTE websites.[1]

Following are examples of some of these policies and initiatives:

Apprenticeship

Maryland, 2015. The legislature approved the Apprenticeship Maryland Pilot Program, a two-year apprenticeship pilot that would allow high school juniors and seniors to obtain a license or certification in high-skilled, high-growth manufacturing and STEM sectors. Grants to local school systems would provide for one year of classroom instruction and 450 hours of paid work-based training under the supervision of an eligible employer.[2]

Career Development

Arkansas, 2013, 2014. The Arkansas legislature authorized the "College and Career Coaches Program" (CCCP), which was first created in 2009 to help middle school and high school students prepare for postsecondary education and career opportunities beyond high school. "Coaches" would assist school counselors and school staff by providing resources for college and career development, hosting parent meetings, and helping students create individualized plans. In 2014, the legislature expanded the program so it could reach all middle and high schools.[3]

Texas 2015. New legislation required independent school districts to help students in seventh or eighth grade create personal graduation plans and also to instruct students about college-readiness expectations and career choices.[4]

Integrated Skills/Adult Education

Colorado, 2013. The legislature created a pilot program, similar to Washington State's I-BEST program, to develop integrated basic education and skills training. The bill also allowed for new certificate programs that could be accessed and completed by unemployed and underemployed adults in less than 12 months.[5]

Career Readiness Performance Indicators

Colorado 2015. Legislation added a new performance indicator to the state's K-12 accountability system, so that school districts must account for the percentage of students who enrolled in a postsecondary CTE program, community college or four-year university. Each postsecondary outcome would be weighted equally on behalf of the student's high school.[6]

Career Pathways Diploma Recognition

Louisiana, 2014. Legislation called for creation of a new career diploma, earned through a career major program and of equal status with a standard diploma. Among other provisions, the new legislation aligned with Jump

Start, a state initiative to enhance CTE programs through the use of work-based learning and industry-recognized credentials.[7]

North Carolina, 2013. The North Carolina State Board of Education approved a set of endorsements for high school graduation by which students had four options for a high school diploma – the Career Endorsement, one of two College Endorsements and/or the Academic Scholars Endorsement.[8]

Career Pathway Program Start-up Funding

New York, 2013. New York allocated $28 million (from a variety of funding sources, including Perkins) to expand the Pathways in Technology Early College High School (P-TECH) program. Each of the 16 new P-TECH partnerships featured a three-way alliance that included a local public school district or consortium of districts, a local business or group of businesses, and one or more state two- and/or four-year public institutions of higher education.[9]

Oregon, 2013. The legislature passed a bill to provide $7.5 million for the CTE Revitalization Grant Program, which provided grants to CTE programs across the state. The bill also established new criteria for the program and prioritized funding for programs that represented a diversity of students and strong partnerships between business and education.[10]

California, 2014. The state legislature formally established the Career Pathways Trust Grant and provided an additional $250 million for the competitive grant program for the development of Career Pathways Programs. The two-year total for the program was $500 million.[11]

Delaware, 2014. Delaware created the Accelerated Career Path opportunity. This two-year comprehensive program in manufacturing technologies allowed high school juniors and seniors to pursue national manufacturing certifications and college credit.[12]

South Dakota, 2015. The state legislature approved $1 million in one-time funding to assist the technical institutes in building capacity in their high-demand workforce programs. Funds could be used for equipment, adding new sections to programs, and hiring additional instructors. The increased funding also provided for high school juniors and seniors to access dual credit courses at technical institute programs at a significantly reduced cost.[13]

Indiana, 2015. The state budget allocated $24 million to the Department of Workforce Development to fund the CTE Innovation and Advancement program.[14]

CTE Program Quality

Ohio, 2013. The State Board of Education approved an Ohio Career-Technical Education Report Card—an official accountability resource that exceeded federal Perkins requirements. The report card focused on technical skill achievement, graduation, post-program outcomes, and preparation for success. The new indicators were integrated into the state's school accountability system so that grades were assigned to schools based on their performance.[15]

Virginia, 2015. New legislation was passed that required CTE programs to be aligned to state or national program certification and accreditation standards when such standards were available.[16]

Community College Access

Oregon 2015. The Oregon Promise was established by the legislature. This program provided no-cost Oregon community college scholarships for resident students who had earned a high school diploma or GED, had fewer than 90 credit hours at the institution, and maintained at least part-time status and a 2.5 GPA.[17]

Minnesota 2015. The state budget for higher education provided $8.5 million for a pilot program that offered free tuition to approximately 1,600 students studying in high-demand fields at the state's technical colleges.[18]

Tennessee, 2013. Tennessee's governor launched the Drive to 55 program, an initiative to have 55 percent of Tennesseans obtain an associate degree or higher by 2025.

Early College Programming

Georgia, 2015. The legislature enacted a bill to streamline the state's existing dual-enrollment initiatives and funding sources into one program, Move On When Ready. The consolidated initiative provided for high school students in grades nine through 12 to enroll in postsecondary institutions on a full- or part-time basis, taking courses at both their high school and the postsecondary institution concurrently. The legislation also recognized Career, Technical, and Agricultural Education (CTAE) courses and electives as eligible for dual enrollment and provided for no fees and books to be charged to participating students.[19]

Pathways System Partnerships

Indiana 2015. The Center of Excellence and Leadership of Learning (CELL) at the University of Indianapolis, in partnership with the state agencies for workforce development, education, and higher education, launched the Indiana Pathways Innovation Network (IN-PIN). The Network hosted regional pathways summits for K-12, postsecondary, adult education, and workforce partners; documented emerging practices across the state; and hosted study visits for participants. IN-PIN was facilitated jointly by CELL and the National Center for College and Career Transitions.[20]

Nebraska. 2015. Nebraska's governor launched the Nebraska Developing Youth Talent Initiative to connect young Nebraskans to careers in the manufacturing and technology sectors. The program provided career development and workplace learning for students in grades seven and eight, delivered by partnerships between business and public schools.[21]

New Jersey 2015. New Jersey's legislature approved $3 million for a County Vocational School District Partnership Grant Program. This initiative helped county vocational school districts to create CTE programs utilizing existing facilities in partnership with business, other school districts, and community colleges.[22]

Pennsylvania, 2013-2016. Pennsylvania Department of Education launched the Pennsylvania Pathways Innovation Network (PA-PIN) to pilot test Pathways System development among regional career technology centers and partner school districts, with the cooperation of other regional employer, workforce, and postsecondary education partners. In 2015, the network was expanded to include a wide variety of organizational partners to share and disseminate promising practices across the Commonwealth. The PA-PIN conducted regional workshops, maintained an active web-based resource library, supported study tours among network members, and provided customized coaching to members beginning to implement pathway systems. PA-PIN was facilitated by the National Center for College and Career Transitions.[23]

Tennessee, 2013. Several key state agencies – education, economic and community development, labor and workforce development, and higher education, launched a number of Pathways Tennessee regional partnerships. These initiatives brought together industry and education stakeholders to develop grade 7-16 Pathways for students to enter industries that had been identified as giving the region a strategic economic advantage, such as health science and advanced manufacturing.[24]

Tennessee, 2015. New legislation directed the Tennessee STEM Innovation Network (TSIN) to establish STEM innovation hubs, which were regional partnerships of school districts, postsecondary institutions, STEM businesses, and community-based organizations. In addition, the TSIN would provide middle schools with a STEM career awareness curriculum that could be used in multiple classroom settings.[25]

Work-based Learning/Simulated Workplace

West Virginia, 2015. West Virginia's Simulated Workplace program began as a pilot in 2013. The program converted the CTE classroom into a simulated workplace environment, with the class operating essentially as a for-profit company. In 2015, the State Board of Education voted to add the 12 Simulated Workplace protocols to state policy so that the Simulated Workplace protocols would be embedded in all CTE programs.[26]

Section 2. The Pathways State Policy Framework

Essential Policy Elements for Pathways System Success

The following policy elements are aligned to the six components of the Pathways System Framework™: Career and Life Readiness, Career Development, Pathway Programs, Employer Engagement, Dynamic Teaching and Learning, and Cross-Sector Partnerships.

Career and Life Readiness
Career and Life Readiness Expectations

◊ The State convenes focus groups of employers, educators, workforce development professionals, and economic development representatives to review a draft set of Career and Life Readiness standards for review and input.

◊ The State has an operational definition that defines Career and Life Readiness, with a balanced focus on academic knowledge and skills, personal attributes that contribute to success in the workplace and college (work ethic, problem solving, collaboration, time management), career development and career navigation, and citizenship.

◊ The definition of Career and Life Readiness is written broadly enough to cover a variety of applications, including readiness for postsecondary education, skilled employment, and productive citizenship.

◊ The State encourages the use of assessments (both written and applied) that measure student employability or professional skills.

◊ The State also develops a template for a student portfolio of Career and Life Readiness skills to encourage student awareness, personal ownership, and goal setting.

Career Development
Career Development Standards

◊ The State has developed and distributed a set of K-12 career development standards (utilizing the four stages of Career Development explained in Chapter 9) and requires local districts to align curriculum and instruction with the standards.

Career and Education Plan

◊ The state requires a locally developed Career and Education Plan to guide every student's course selection through high school and into postsecondary education. The Career and Education Plan requires career development objectives to be factored into the postsecondary education decision-making process.

Career Development and College Planning Platform

◊ The State sponsors a career development electronic platform that allows students and parents to conduct self-discovery and career exploration toward the goal of developing a Career and Education Plan to guide decisions about postsecondary education.

◊ The career development electronic platforms help students become aware of at least the following:

　◊ the overall supply and demand of particular occupations, including the projected number of openings;

　◊ the projected range of earnings within the occupations;

　◊ the length of education and training that is required and that most employers ask for in hiring; and

　◊ availability of affordable higher education opportunities in the region.

Materials and Resources for Career Development and Postsecondary Planning

◊ The State has developed and/or distributes electronic and print materials about career opportunities; these materials present a continuum of postsecondary options, including apprenticeship, certifications, two-year college, and four-year college.

◊ State-developed communications materials encourage students to aim high and to pursue the best personal career fit, without presenting the bachelor's degree as inherently superior over other forms of postsecondary education.

Professional Support for Career Development

◊ The State makes funding available for schools to train and/or hire Career Development Professionals as members of or as supplements to the school counseling team. These Career Development Professionals need to hold a career development certification of some sort but do not need to be fully certified school counselors.

Awareness of Workforce Trends and Needs

- The State supports efforts for professional development in which counselors and teachers learn about today's workforce, with a focus on careers that are growing and shrinking, and relate to a variety of postsecondary education and training options.

Pathway Programs

Pathway Innovation Funding and Technical Assistance

◊ The State supports development of an in-state network of schools, career technology centers, colleges, employer organizations, workforce development organizations, and other related organizations that are working to adopt a Pathways System approach. The state supports efforts to convene member on a regular basis, document and share promising practices, and assist collaboration among partners at the local and state levels.

◊ The State makes funding available for innovative programs and for delivery of Pathway Programs and STEM education Pathways that are aligned to careers that are high-skilled, in-demand, and well compensated.

Dual and Concurrent Enrollment

◊ State policy requires consistent treatment of dual/concurrent enrollment by all colleges and school districts across the state.

◊ The state offers funding and guidance that incentivizes schools, districts, and colleges to offer dual/concurrent enrollment at no cost or low cost to the student.

◊ The state's data system measures and reports on the percentage of students who obtain dual/concurrent credits and the average number of credits per participating student.

Section 3. Policy Audit

As I have worked with at the federal education department and with a couple dozen state education agencies over the years, I have observed that legislation, state agency policy directives, and other initiatives are usually generated in a fairly random manner, one-by-one and in response to a felt need or a pressing issue that catches the attention of a policy-maker. Over time, they layer upon one another, so that policies that were individually well-intended are not well-aligned with other policies, and in some cases, they actually work against the purposes of other policies.

This mix of state policy needs to be coherent and streamlined to the greatest degree possible. A good place to start is with a policy audit, which is a thorough review and analysis of what the policies and programs are and whether or not they are moving toward the same objectives.

To conduct the policy audit, convene a stakeholder team to conduct a thorough review of state laws, regulatory guidance, and state agency initiatives and organize them into a single inventory. You can use the six Pathways System components from this book or a similar framework to organize the inventory.

> *A good place to start is with a policy audit, which is a thorough review and analysis of what the policies and programs are, and whether or not they are moving toward the same objectives.*

When conducting the policy audit, make sure to review legislative language and policy guidance, but also conduct extensive interviews with individuals working in the relevant state agencies. These individuals will have a better sense of how the policies and initiatives play out and how they are implemented. Also talk to local program administrators to understand the degree to which they have an accurate understanding of policies and whether they actually follow the policies. This will provide a good gauge of what the "in-force" policy environment is versus what is "on the books."

You should not limit the policy audit to only K-12 education and workforce agencies. Talk to the state's economic development and higher education bureaus, and engage key staff members from the relevant legislative committees in the statehouse. Also, pay attention to the teacher credentialing and external accreditation agencies, which exert strong influence over K-12 and postsecondary education.

Once the audit is complete, convene a larger working group to look for overlaps, contradictions, and gaps. Prioritize the policies that will exert the most leverage in moving toward a Pathways-oriented approach. Also identify the "low hanging fruit," the policies that can be modified the most rapidly with existing agency authority, versus the ones that will require board or legislative action or inclusion in a forthcoming budget.

Finally, share the policy inventory with local education, employer, and workforce leaders to ensure that the policy inventory is as clear and concise as possible. The policy inventory should provide value at the state level and also to local administrators. An additional benefit to engage local leaders is that, since state agency personnel are sometimes constrained by where they sit in the state hierarchy, local leaders may be better positioned to advocate with agency heads or with legislators on policies that require legislative action.

The Role of the Local Leader in State Policy

Pathways Systems are locally developed and locally led. But good state policy and funding initiatives makes a huge difference in how quickly a local Pathways System Initiative can move forward. I strongly implore you to engage with leaders and policymakers at your state capitol, not just with legislators and staff but also getting to know which state agency personnel makes things happen. Encourage them to initiate a state policy audit, and subsequently, create a state policy agenda based on what has been recommended in this chapter.

I strongly implore you to engage with leaders and policymakers at your state capitol, not just with legislators and staff but also getting to know which state agency personnel make things happen.

* * *

The next and final chapter, *Advancing the Pathways Movement*, provides a glimpse into the future. What will America's communities, schools, and workforce look like as we implement the Pathways System approach? How long will this community-by-community transformation process take? Who will be actors that make it happen? And what will the role of local leaders be in making the Power and Promise of Pathways not just a hope, but a reality?

Chapter Twelve

Advancing the Pathways Movement

When I co-founded the National Center for College and Career Transitions (NC3T) with Brett Pawlowski, we spent some serious mental energy trying to find a vision statement that captured our hearts and minds. Finally, we came up with this statement. -- "Every teen with a dream and a plan; every community with a capable, ready workforce." We have since modified the statement to read, "Every LEARNER with a dream and a plan…" so that our vision would include adults as well as youth.

It is a dual vision statement. It focuses on the individual, and it also focuses on the community. We want to encourage individual growth, aspiration, and achievement, but this also needs to be linked to community prosperity and making our neighborhoods good places in which to live, to work, to worship, and recreate. This is a compelling vision statement for us – the individual and the community.

This kind of big change, for "every learner" and "every community," requires a movement of like-minded leaders who take ownership and responsibility on a community-by-community basis.

I suspect you share something like this vision, maybe worded differently, but still including a focus on the individual and the community.

This big vision is a pursuit that no one organization can accomplish alone. This kind of compelling change, for "every learner" and "every community," requires a movement of like-minded leaders who take ownership and responsibility on a community-by-community basis.

In this chapter, we are going to go beyond generalities and get specific about how to spread the Pathways Movement. Together, we will explore WHO needs to be recruited to lead the effort, WHAT specific actions are necessary to get started, and WHY—the big ideas to keep us grounded and focused. We're going to discuss the following:

◊ The spread of ideas and innovations

◊ The danger zones

◊ The simple action steps anyone can take to get started

◊ The Influentials

◊ The six pathway commitments

Section 1. How Ideas and Innovations Spread

The Law of the Few

In his book "The Tipping Point," Malcolm Gladwell talks about several factors ("laws") that govern the spread of ideas. One of these is called "The Law of the Few," in which he states that it doesn't take many people to spread an idea as long as they're the right people. Gladwell describes how a particular trend went viral "once one of these exceptional people found out about the trend, and through social connections and energy and enthusiasm and personality spread the word." He further notes that these people aren't all alike, noting that they can exhibit one of three personality traits.[1]

First, there is the "Connector." The Connector is the person who knows hundreds (even thousands) of different people from a wide variety of social networks; further, the Connector delights in helping build new connections between these networks by introducing a person in one network to a person in a different network, thus creating a new connection among two previously separated networks. Now, through these connections, there is a new relational path for ideas to travel.[2]

This concept of a Connector was also explained by sociologist Mark Granovetter as "the power of weak ties" or "weak connections." In job hunting, he explained that most of the time, we find job opportunities not through our close friends and family members, but by weak connections or acquaintances, someone we know who knows someone else. By connecting with that acquaintance, a whole new set of connections opens up to the job seeker.[3]

Secondly, Gladwell identified the "Maven." Maven is a Yiddish word meaning "someone who accumulates knowledge." Not only is a Maven obsessively knowledgeable about a field of inquiry; he or she delights in sharing that knowledge with other people.[4]

I can think of two very influential people in my professional career who were Mavens and took the time to share with me golden nuggets of information about educational innovations and Pathways-related trends. One of the two was a story-teller, who regaled me with tales of what was happening with a number of school districts and business partners. The other Maven always carried copies of a thought-provoking article or essay that he would pass along to me. Mavens are not show-off know-it-alls, rather they are sincerely trying to be helpful. As such, many people are receptive to their information and then pass it along to others as well.

Finally, there are the Salesmen. These are people who have an enthusiasm and power of personality that is infectious. Something about them makes them influential with other people. They enjoy rallying others to a cause and building momentum for a project or movement.[5]

So, as you begin to organize the work on your local Pathways initiative, make a list of the all the people you currently know are interested and see if you can categorize them in one of these three categories: Connector, Maven, and Salesman. Not everyone on your list needs to exhibit these strong character traits, but try to make sure you have at least a couple of each. Then ask yourself, "how can we deploy our Connectors, Mavens, and Salesmen" within our Pathways initiative so we maximize their strengths and impact?

Innovation Diffusion

In his authoritative work "Diffusion of Innovations," Everett M. Rogers describes the wealth of research that has emerged about why and how innovations (both technology and ideas) spread through an industry or society. He also explains why, in some cases despite very intentional actions to spread an innovation, widespread adoptions sometimes fail.[6]

One very helpful concept to consider is the "Stages in the Innovation-Decision Process." When individuals are faced with a new innovation – a technology or new way of doing things – they go through a predictable process of decision-making, even though the process itself may be below the cognitive surface, even on a subconscious level. First, they make some initial inquiries, perhaps choose to learn more, and at some point, they make a decision "yay" or "nay" about adopting the innovation.

Rogers summarizes the stages as follows:[7]

> **I. Knowledge Stage** (Knowledge occurs when an individual is exposed to an innovation's existence and gains an understanding of how it functions.)
>
> ◊ Recall of information

◊ Comprehension of messages

◊ Knowledge or skill for effective adoption of the innovation

II. Persuasion Stage (Persuasion occurs when an individual forms a favorable or an unfavorable attitude towards the innovation.)

◊ Liking the innovation

◊ Discussion of the new behavior with others

◊ Acceptance of the message about the innovation

◊ Formation of a positive image of the message and the innovation

◊ Support for the innovative behavior from the system

III. Decision Stage (Decision takes place when an individual engages in activities that lead to a choice to adopt or reject the innovation.)

◊ Intention to seek additional information about the innovation

◊ Intention to try the innovation

IV. Implementation Stage (Implementation occurs when an individual puts a new idea into use.)

◊ Acquisition of additional information about the innovation

◊ Use of the innovation on a regular basis

◊ Continued use of the innovation

V. Confirmation Stage (Confirmation takes place when an individual seeks reinforcement of an innovation-decision already made, but he or she may reverse this previous decision if exposed to conflicting messages about the innovation.)

◊ Recognition of the benefits of using the innovation

◊ Integration of the innovation into one's ongoing routine

◊ Promotion of the innovation to others

Temperaments and Timing in the Innovation Adoption Cycle

One of the best-known aspects of diffusion research is the "innovation adoption curve." Through this model, originally tested with farmers adopting hybrid corn strains, we see there are five types of people with five types of attitudes toward innovation.[8]

Innovators: Venturesome.

A very small percentage (about 2.5 percent) of individuals are true "innovators," always looking for something new and better. They are strongly oriented to the future and have little emotional attachment to the past. Innovators often have some sort of social prestige or economic power, so they don't mind taking the risk of trying out a new technology or idea, even if it doesn't pan out. But because of their high rate of innovation adoption (essentially, they try everything), they aren't viewed by others as a good judge of what innovations are or are not worthwhile.

Early Adopters: Respect

About 13.5 percent of people are "early adopters." They are thoughtful, but move quickly when they see an innovation with promise. They are respected by their peers and have the highest degree of opinion leadership in most systems. Early adopters "put their stamp approval on a new idea by adopting it."

Early Majority: Deliberate

The "early majority," about 34 percent of people, deliberate for a longer period of time before making the commitment. They like to know that the new idea really is reasonably well tested and shows results. They don't waste time or effort on something that will fail or fall by the wayside.

Late Majority: Skeptical

The "late majority," another 34 percent, are the folks who generally don't want to change unless there is little option and the nagging questions and kinks have been worked out. Late adopters eventually adopt the innovation, not necessarily because they agree with the innovation's inherent value, but because they see the tide turning. In their experience, resisting the innovation may actually take too much time and effort compared to simply adopting the innovation.

Laggards: Traditional

For "Laggards," about 16 percent of the adoption population, their point of reference is the past rather than the future. Sometimes they are in a precarious economic position, so they are more cautious about adopting a new technology or fashion if it going to cost them financially. They are often isolated and interact mostly with others who also hold to tradition-bound ways of doing things. In an education context, a typical laggard might be a teacher or administrator who is very close to retirement age and doesn't want to make the effort to revamp his or her curriculum, teaching style, or leadership habits.[9]

Implications for Pathways Diffusion

Within the innovation adoption process, be aware that each constituency in the adoption cycle has a temperament and a view toward change, and your enthusiasm and fervor will not change that. You will need to respect and allow the innovation decision cycle to play out for each person.

Given their varying temperaments and approaches to an innovation, different temperaments take different lengths of the time to actually adopt the innovation:

◊ Innovators (0.40/year)

◊ Early Adopters (0.55/year)

◊ Early Majority (1.14/year)

◊ Late Majority (2.34/year)

◊ Laggards (4.65/year)[10]

These times were identified in research relating to adoption of an agricultural weed spray, so the actual times may differ for adoption of an education innovation like Pathways. However, the relative time differentials between the adoption actors will likely be similar. Notice how innovators get onboard pretty quickly, and early adopters join just a short time after the innovators. But then there is a doubling of the time for adoption for the early majority, and then another doubling of time between the early majority and the late majority. Finally, there is another doubling of time to engage the laggards.

So while the case grows deeper and more compelling, it still takes longer to engage each progressive cohort of the adoption curve. Of course, these time differentials were observed when adoption was voluntary. In education, some reforms are mandatory, implemented district-wide or even statewide. But except for standards and accountability, there is usually

Even with a mandate, the quality of implementation may suffer if each member of the adoption cohort does not engage with the evidence about the why and how for Pathways.

wide latitude. Within a school district, for example, some schools may utilize Pathways and others not at all. Even within individual schools, Pathway Programs' implementation and participation are somewhat voluntary, so the initiative doesn't really touch all students or all staff.

Top down mandates that affect all personnel will certainly accelerate and standardize the adoption process. But even with a mandate, the quality of implementation may suffer if each member of the adoption cohort does not engage with the evidence about the why and how for Pathways. They don't necessarily need to agree with the decision to move forward, but they should absolutely understand the basis for the decision.

Engaging the Influentials

In planning your adoption cycle, you should do some eyeballing of your stakeholders, both inside the education system and among non-education partners. Within each stakeholder group (students, teachers, counselors, community non-profits, employer partners), try to discern who might be the innovators, early adopters, or the early majority. The diffusion research Rogers cites tells us that we are most strongly influenced by the opinions and beliefs of our peers or people who are positioned just slightly above us in term of social influence and social rank. For example, an assistant principal or fellow teacher will have more direct influence over the thinking of a teacher than will an associate superintendent or superintendent at the school district office. So make sure you are thinking about who are innovators and early adopters within every stakeholder group and social/professional rank in your community.

Ed Keller and Jon Berry explore similar concepts through their research and book, "The Influentials."[11] Based on 30 years of Roper Reports' consumer and political survey research, they observe that most people are most strongly influenced by "word of mouth" recommendations and informal discussions about a topic. And these decisions are most influenced by the so-called "influentials," people who gather lots of information, read extensively, and are very well connected across social networks and a range of local organizations. These "influentials" make up about one out of ten people. Among the adult population, that is somewhere in excess of 25 million individuals. Relating to the other descriptions we discussed earlier, Influentials seem to a blend between the "Mavens" and "Connectors" that Gladwell talks about and would be the "Early Adopters" in the innovation diffusion model.

> *Make sure you are thinking about who are innovators and early adopters within every stakeholder group and social/professional rank in your community.*

Section 2. Danger Zones

As you engage in the work of creating a local Pathways System, I want to raise your awareness of several areas of danger. Some combination of these danger zones has caused multiple education innovations to implode, get crushed under their own weight, or die of starvation and inattention. If you can look ahead and see these danger zones, you can more easily navigate around them as you move forward.

The Danger of Dollars

The battlefields of education and workforce reform are littered with dead initiatives that were abandoned when special designated funding dried up. Too many dollars thrown at Pathways too quickly may backfire. When local systems and programs see Pathways as a "funded program" instead of a new way of thinking about education and workforce development, then the initiative rests on the shifting sands of designated state, federal, or foundation dollars. Dollars should be "just enough" to help schools and their partners get though the change process, but only enough to support the professional development, program development, and start-up that facilitates organizational and cultural change. Ongoing operations within schools, organizations, and intermediary partners must be sustained through local and state formula funding that can be sustained over the long term.

The Danger of Right-Left Politics

In the 1990s, the School-to-Work movement was derailed because left-right politics came into play. Some advocacy organizations lived and breathed by generating conspiracy-based controversy. In the case of school-to-work, some organizations determined that the aim of the initiative was to encourage young people to bypass college and go into low-skilled jobs. They were convinced this agenda was dominated by the wishes and whims of big business. Both far-right and far-left entities fed on fears of big government and big multinational business.

When local systems and program see pathways as a "funded program" instead of a new way of thinking about education and workforce development, then the initiative rests on the shifting sands of designated state, federal or foundation dollars.

In recent years, similar dynamics emerged when the Common Core reform movement became strongly associated with a Democratic U.S. Department of Education, deep-pocketed national foundations, overly aggressive testing regimens, and teacher-evaluation systems that were seen as harsh towards teachers.

To succeed long-term, Pathways must be a locally-led, community-driven effort aimed at bettering the lives of individuals and strengthening communities. Federal dollars and national foundation dollars can have a role to play, but the work must be locally led so it can engender the trust of local partners.

The Danger of Top-Down

The death knell of any education movement is when it becomes perceived as a top down, U.S. Department of Education initiative. Federal and state policies and funding relating to Pathways should be restrained. They should offer modest funding to support the change process and carefully link accountability for results with local flexibility for how Pathways efforts are designed and implemented. Equity and opportunity for under-served individuals should be non-negotiable, but federal and state policy should recognize and account for the huge differences between large urban systems, large county-based suburban education systems, and small townships- and rural-based education systems.

The Danger of Win-Lose Thinking

Particularly in regions where small education districts butt up against one another, many dynamics can create competition among school districts for prestige, recognition, and the ability to attract well-to-do families and new home construction. Similarly, the emergence of charter schools creates a sense of competition between charters and traditional school systems and among charter schools. With shifting school age populations, school districts and colleges are in a heated competition to get "butts in the seats." To some degree, this cannot be avoided. This dynamic creates an incentive for each district to get its own employer partners and its signature programs in place and not make room to share resources or work collaboratively. To counter these forces of district-to-district competition, businesses, governmental entities, and other organizations with a regional focus must take the lead in promoting and rewarding collaboration over competition. Otherwise, Pathways will remain an isolated approach, implemented by either the innovators or those who are desperate to try anything.

The Danger of All-Or-Nothing and Know-It-All Thinking

A zealot is an individual with strong vision and passion for change but perhaps with a lack of judgment about how to create deep and lasting change. Sometimes idealism can morph into zealotry, and that zealotry can communicate that there is only one right way to accomplish a goal, or only one way to find a means to an end. This is why leaders in the Pathways movement must be grounded with strong emotional intelligence; they should be Level 5 leaders with a strong passion for results but also a high degree of personal humility. Passion and intensity should not be the only criteria considered before an individual assumes a leadership role in a local Pathways initiative. He or she must a willingness to push for fast results, but be cool-headed and recognize that some change takes time.

Don't misunderstand my message here. When social justice has been violated and individuals have been subjugated to inferior education and blocked opportunity, righteous anger and demand for change is appropriate. But this must be tempered with positivity and flexibility with how we achieve change.

To counter the forces of district-to-district competition, businesses, governmental entities, and other organizations with a regional focus must take the lead in promoting and rewarding collaboration over competition.

The Danger of Do-gooder-ism

Change must be led by the people who will benefit from the change instead of by do-gooders who come into a community and try to "fix" problems too quickly. The better approach is to take the time to engage local leaders, assist them in identifying critical needs, and learn about and test out strategies for making improvements. This "capacity-building" philosophy is the heart of how NC3T prefers to engage with its clients. This awareness has also been growing within international relief circles, such as those led by faith-based organizations, and is well expressed in the book "When Helping Hurts" by Steve Corbett and Brian Fikkert. Their book strongly encourages moving away from the idea of "doing for" and moving to the model of "doing with" and "responding to." These more beneficial models of participation include Cooperation, Co-Learning, and Community Initiated.[12]

The Danger of Second Generation Drift

A long-term danger comes when first generation innovators of the Pathways work begin to move on, either through reassignments, retirement, or other personal or career changes. Little by little, a new generation of educators and community advocates will take the reins. If these new leaders were not given the opportunity to wrestle with the data and findings and argumentation, both pro and con, then their understanding and commitment to the Pathways work will be weak. If the initiative hits some hard times, such as a major fiscal challenge or an important industry partner shutting its doors, they may be inclined to jettison the effort rather than make adjustments and improvements to keep the Pathways System Initiative going.

The Danger of Throwing the Baby Out

The Pathways System Framework™ is intended to bring coherence and alignment among the work of schools, colleges, and workforce systems.

Implementing the framework does require a hard-eyed look at all current activities to determine whether they should be continued, modified, or abandoned. But good judgment requires us to keep what is positive and valuable, such as having appropriate testing, holding teachers to high standards, and encouraging students to stretch to higher levels of postsecondary education. Just because some aspects of the education accountability movement or the college-access movement may have overreached, they should be refocused and improved, not abandoned.

The Danger of Complacency

The biggest challenge facing many schools is complacency brought on by a short-term focus on seemingly positive results. Schools that have strong attendance, high graduation rates, and large numbers of students enrolling in college may not realize that many of their students are being under-served. Even in affluent communities, a significant percentage of students go on to college but don't enter college with good sense of career direction or career decision-making skills. Further, a large percentage of students who start college do not finish at all, and many others finish only after an expensive journey of trial and error.

Every high school should strongly consider sharing its high school graduate data with the National Student Clearinghouse.

Every high school should strongly consider sharing its high school graduate data with the National Student Clearinghouse. This would allow a school leadership team to see, with a high degree of accuracy, what actually happens to school graduates over the course of the next six to eight years after high school. Even for affluent community high schools that enjoy a high graduation rate and a high college going rate, the long-term students' results can be startling and unsettling. But this is the real data needed to break through complacency to action.

The Danger of Defeatism

Some communities are struggling with serious long-term problems like multi-generational poverty, lack of decent jobs in the community, endemic violence, and substance abuse. Leaders in these situations may feel that the lift is just too big to start to implementing a Pathways System. This would be a serious mistake, because the elements of the Pathways System Framework™ can begin to restore hope and aspiration among youths and young adults. Leaders must take responsibility, seek and accept help when they can get it, and begin to move forward in any way they can.

Section 3. Who are the Influentials?

With such a geographically and demographically diverse country as the U.S., how will the Pathways model spread? Let's think about how many employers, schools, and communities will be involved in going to scale with the Pathways movement.

Population. The U.S. population in 2016 is over 324 million.[13] Recent data indicates there are about 50.1 million students attending public elementary and secondary schools, of which about 14.9 million are enrolled in grades 9 through 12. In fall 2015, about 4.1 million students enrolled in 9th grade.[14]

Employers. Thinking about business, in 2010 there were 27.9 million small businesses (more than 75% of these were solo businesses) and just 18,500 firms with 500 employees or more.[15] Importantly, these companies are members of chambers of commerce and industry sector coalitions. In the U.S., there are about 13,000 chambers of commerce that are registered but only about 3,000 chambers of commerce that actually employ at least one full-time staff person. Thousands of others are established as strictly volunteer entities.[16] Several thousand trade and industry coalitions also exist, operating both nationally and at state and regional levels.

As "Pathway Influentials" begin to understand and move forward with the pathways message, they will engage their peers with these ideas. So, when we step back, the actual number of individuals that we need to reach and influence is much more manageable.

The Public K-12 system. The U.S. has about 13,500 public school districts, operating nearly 98,500 public schools. Among these public schools are 6,100 charter schools. Each of these public school districts and most charter schools have a governing board. The National Schools Board Association, a national organization that represents individual school board members, has over 90,000 members.[17]

Secondary (Middle and High) Schools. Among these 98,500 public schools in the U.S., there are many variations and sizes of public secondary schools, including about 16,000 middle school/junior high schools and a little over 20,000 high schools or combined middle school/high schools.[18]

Career Technical Education Schools. Approximately 1,400 regional career technical education schools exist in the U.S., which provide specialized technical education programs to high school students. Some schools also provide education and training to adult students.[19]

Postsecondary Education. Community colleges are often among the most active partners in a local Pathways initiative. Out of a total of 1,108 community colleges, 982 are public, 90 are independent, and 36 are tribal. Many of these colleges, of course, have more than one campus, but there doesn't appear to be a firm count as to the number of campuses. These colleges enroll about 12.3 million students for credit and noncredit classes, and this represents about 45 percent of all U.S. undergraduates.[20] In addition, over 4,700 public universities, private universities, and private colleges offer bachelor's and graduate degrees.[21] A universe of for-profit trade schools and for-profit postsecondary education providers also exists.[22]

Local Government. In terms of local governance, the U.S. Census Bureau counts 39,044 general purpose local governments, which include over 19,492 municipal governments, 16,519 township governments, and 3,033 county governments.[23]

Local Workforce Development Boards. Workforce Development Boards are local governing councils that manage the implementation of federally funded workforce programs. The U.S. has about 550 local workforce development boards, representing about 12,000 business members who sit on the boards. About 3,000 one-stop career centers are the physical sites that job-seekers can visit to access workforce development services.[24]

Education Writers. Education writers and correspondents are the staff members who work for national and local media outlets and have some affinity and understanding of education issues. The education writers' association has approximately 3,000 members.[25]

State Policy-Makers. State legislators who serve on their respective education committees and appropriation/budget committees are among the most influential state policymakers for helping drive the funding and policy changes needed. Key staff members who work for these committees strongly influence the agenda and decisions of the legislators. Further, other analysts and decision-makers work in several state agencies that govern education, workforce, and economic development as well as in the governor's office. In total, approximately 40 key influencers and decision makers in each state capitol and the District of Columbia will impact a state's Pathways policy framework. This is a total of 2,040 Individuals.

So, whew! As we consider how a Pathways movement might spread, this mix of schools, districts, colleges, businesses and policymakers might seem overwhelming. Remember, although there are over 320 million individuals in the U.S. and several million administrators and staff and elected officials governing our education and training system, we don't have to reach each and every one of them directly. We need to reach the influencers and decision-makers. We estimate that about 25 million adults are the "Influentials," the early adopters who are well connected socially, like to share information, and exert influence on what and how others think. Even just targeting the Influentials seems like an overwhelming task.

Certainly, the number of "Pathway Influentials" will be more manageable, at least for a first level of outreach and communication. I am suggesting that we target a much smaller number of individuals, a few key people in each targeted segment. I expect that, as these "Pathway Influentials" begin to understand and move forward with the Pathways message, they will engage their peers with these ideas. So, when we step back, the actual number of individuals that we need to reach and influence is much more manageable.

Here are some numbers to consider:

◊ 3,000 chambers of commerce have at least one employee. Three people targeted from each, including one staff person and two employers that are on the board. **Total: 9,000**

◊ 13,500 school districts. Three people targeted from each, including the superintendent, a director of curriculum/instruction, and director of guidance. **Total: 40,500**

◊ 13,500 school districts, each with a school board. Two people targeted from each school board. **Total: 27,000**

◊ 16,000 middle schools. Four people targeted from each middle school, including administrators, teachers and counselors. **Total: 64,000**

◊ 20,000 high schools. Four people targeted from each middle school, including administrators, teachers and counselors. **Total: 80,000**

◊ 1,400 regional career technical education schools. Two administrators targeted from each. **Total: 2,800**

◊ 1,100 community colleges. Seven targeted people from each, including three administrators, two student services representatives, and two

The near-term goal is to begin reaching the 364,000 "Pathway Influentials" in the U.S. who will then begin to share the Pathways message via word-of-mouth (and with electronic and social media) within their circle of influence, and then begin to take action.

faculty members. **Total: 7,700**

◊ 4,700 colleges and universities. Seven people targeted from each, including three administrators, two student services representatives, and two faculty members. **Total: 32,900**

◊ 40,000 local governments. Approximately 2 people targeted from each. **Total: 80,000**

◊ 550 workforce development centers. Two staff members and three business partners from each, as well as two staff members from each of the one-stop career centers. **Total: 8,750**

◊ 3,300 education writers. **Total: 3,300**

◊ 50 states and DC, State-based policymakers. The 40 key influencers and decision makers in each. **Total: 2,040**

◊ Finally, Gallup Organization President Jim Clifton estimates that, in each of America's 100 largest cities, there are 100 of what he calls "city mothers and fathers" (the key local influencers) who will have the most direct impact on whether or not America can succeed with sustainable and vibrant local job creation.[26] **Total: 10,000**

Total "Pathway Influentials"—367,990

Thus, according to these calculations, we don't have to actually reach 325 million individuals. Rather, we need to connect with and communicate with a about 368,000 individuals. That certainly is a lot of people, but just a bit more than 1 percent of the U.S. population. And fortunately, these are people who are already well-connected and active in their field of influence, so they're easier to find and communicate with.

Remember, this is not the actual number of individuals who need to buy-in to the change or actually implement the change. That will be a much bigger number. But our near-term goal is to begin reaching the 368,000 "Pathway Influentials" who will then begin to share the Pathways message via word-of-mouth (and with electronic and social media) within their circle of influence and then begin to take action. In the innovation adoption cycle, these will be the Early Adopters and some of the Early Majority.

Strategic Outreach – Your Local Opportunity

One organization can't reach each and every one of these influencers and decision-makers across the United States. But at the local level, you are well positioned to get started. You can likely identify a list of 20 to 50 people in your community who might be important "Pathway Influentials." As you make your list, you can begin systematically reaching out, building rapport, and passing along ideas about the Pathway System approach. The Pathways message inherently resonates with many people, so you should be able to engender a fledgling coalition fairly quickly. As you do, you will begin to find your Connectors, your Mavens, and your Salespeople. You will find your " Influentials."

If you are working from outside of education, make sure you engage innovative and change-oriented educators as soon as possible. The Pathways approach will not succeed if it is perceived as an "attack" on education; rather it should be something we do in partnership between the community and education. Of course, not everyone in the education system will embrace this change; still, you will need a critical mass of educators buying in and leading the change from within.

Section 4. Action Steps to Get Started Today

As we encourage each and every reader to be a *Pathway Influential* and to build a network of Influentials, I want to suggest very practical first steps you can take almost immediately. The following action steps are listed for these individuals:

◊ Employers and Community Leaders

◊ School District or College Leaders

◊ Campus-Based Leaders

◊ Parents

◊ Students

◊ Teachers

◊ Counselors

◊ State Policymakers

I. Employer and Community Leaders

◊ Conduct a web search to find out if a business-education coalition already exists in your region.

◊ Talk to the executive director of your local chamber of commerce, and see if they would be willing to explore a business-education initiative.

◊ Get in touch with your local Workforce Board (part of the public workforce system), and find out if they already have or plan to create industry-sector working groups to coordinate between workforce and education.

◊ Get in contact with a local economic development authority and/ or workforce board, and ask if they could provide a briefing to you or a group of employers about projected workforce and economic development trends in your region.

◊ Find out what kind of programs are offered at your local colleges or community colleges that relate to your industry or occupational specialty. Find out if those programs utilize business advisory boards.

◊ Find out if there are local career-related programs at local high schools or career technology centers, and find out if they engage business advisory boards.

◊ Ask to meet with a local high school principal to talk about Pathways.

◊ Arrange for a visit and tour with the director of the career technology center in your region. While touring, pay attention to whether programs there are focused on entry-level jobs only, or if they also provide training related to careers that lead to associate degrees and four-year college degrees.

2. School District or College Leaders

◊ Talk informally about Pathways and career readiness concepts with school principals, program deans, and administrative office staff to find out what people are thinking.

◊ Convene a meeting among the district director of counseling, the director of curriculum and instruction, the director of special education, and the director of career technical education, and others who may have an interest.

◊ Talk to leadership counterparts at either the college level or school district level. Talk about moving from a course-by-course approach for dual enrollment to an aligning programs-of-study between secondary and postsecondary education.

◊ Within the school district, talk about Pathways and career readiness with principals of middle schools and high schools, and asked them to explore and learn about Pathways concepts, and to offer recommendations to you.

◊ Contact your state department of education career technical education office and find out what kind of career pathway or career readiness initiatives is being implemented or being planned. Make sure to focus on efforts for all students, not just students enrolled in CTE programs.

◊   Contact your state association for school administrators.

◊   Reach out to the director of a regional education services agency to find if they know about current or future activities are happening around career exploration and Pathways.

3. Campus-Based Leaders

◊   Talk informally to teachers, faculty, counselors and other staff, and ask if they would be interested in participating in a school-based study team to learn about Pathways and what options there are for your school.

◊   Convene a study group among administrators, teachers, and counselors. Frame two or three guiding questions for the group to learn about, and then report back with findings and recommendations.

◊   Talk to other school leaders in your region to find out if there are career-pathway related activities in the works at different schools.

◊   Find out who at your state department of education is in charge of career technical education and related Pathways activities. Contact them and ask what type of state-level initiatives or activities are being implemented or considered for the future. Ask specifically about "Pathways" and "career readiness" and be clear that you are interested in approaches that touch all students, not just traditional career technical education programs.

◊   Get in touch with your state-level association for school principals or school administrators. Ask them what type of Pathways or career readiness initiatives they are working on or plan to work on.

◊   Get in touch with your local chamber of commerce executive director and ask if they are developing an education business coalition around Pathways. If nothing is happening, ask if they would consider forming a study group to explore the idea with employers and other school district leaders.

4. Parents

◊   Talk to fellow parents about Pathways, and engage in a conversation emphasizing that this is about helping students make good career and college choices, NOT pitting careers against college. Emphasize that this approach will help our children make better choices and be more likely to find successful careers, whatever level of postsecondary education they choose to pursue.

◊   For parents of middle school and high school students, begin to talk more to your students about finding a good fit for a career other than just asking what college they want to attend or saying they need to study hard so they can go to college. Remember, careers answer the "why question," and college becomes a tool instead of a destination.

◊ For parents of elementary students, ask your school about career days and career-related field trips.

◊ Think about how your employer or industry group could get involved with education. Find out if there is a business-education coalition already working in your community to help with the education-to-employer connection.

5. Students

◊ Ask your student government to advocate for more career-related activities at school, such as career days, career field trips, or a workshop to help students explore the Holland Code system for career development.

◊ Find out about career-related student activities already taking place in your school.

◊ Ask an engaged teacher to help sponsor a career-futures club among students.

◊ See if recent school alumni can come back and share about their career development experiences.

6. Teachers

◊ Form a study group of teachers in your department to explore career integration curriculum activities.

◊ Find ways to demonstrate how your academic curriculum supports skills that individuals will need in the workplace.

◊ Create a college/career life readiness study team. Review the college/career life readiness attributes and explore how different teachers can support those skills and knowledge.

◊ Talk to other teachers and find out what kind of career-related activities already happen in your classes, and create an inventory of these activities.

◊ Talk to your school counselors and find out what they do for career development with your students.

◊ Talk to your students, and asked them what kinds of activities and learning experiences are most engaging and interesting to them. Ask them for suggestions on how to make other activities more engaging and real to them.

◊ Ask the CTE teachers in your school to give the core academic teacher teams a tour of the CTE classes and explain what they cover in their programs.

◊ Find out about project-based learning professional development supports that might be available in your district or in your state. Bring these opportunities to the attention of the administrator in your building responsible for facilitating professional development.

7. Counselors

◊ Meet with fellow counselors and identify what action steps and professional development could help you enhance your career development strategies.

◊ Identify tasks and responsibilities that have been added that make it difficult for you to carry out your career development role.

◊ Seek out schools in the state or other states that are implementing Pathways, and ask for permission to conduct a study visit.

◊ Find other teachers that might want to form a Pathways Study Team to explore options for your school.

◊ Ask the CTE teachers in your school to give you a tour of their classes and explain what they cover in their programs.

8. State policymakers

◊ Review the recommended policy agenda in Chapter 11.

◊ Conduct a Policy Audit.

◊ Prioritize a policy agenda.

◊ Begin by creating a cross-agency working group of education, workforce, postsecondary education, and economic development.

◊ Support creation of an in-state Pathways innovation network for raising awareness about the Pathways System approach, identifying and connecting those who are already innovating with Pathway Programs within the state, and sharing and advancing promising practices.

Section 5. Return to the Six Pathway Commitments

As we conclude this chapter and this book, I have been trying to think very practically about how to carry out the transformative work of the Pathways System model.

For me, when I get deep into daily responsibilities and the tasks of a particular project, I can quickly lose the big picture and ultimately, my motivation to keep moving forward. While I have tried to be very practical and very action-step focused in this book, I also believe we must stay focused on our strategic vision and mission we have talked about.

If the Pathways Movement is to be locally-led and self-sustaining, we need thousands of men and women who are navigating according to the some big, shared ideas – the Six Pathway Commitments.

The Vision for a Pathways System (every learner with a dream and plan; every community with a capable, ready workforce) is like the North Star, which mariners used for navigations for thousands of years. Even if you get violently blown off track by a storm or just gently and gradually drift off course by inattention, looking up at the North Star helps you find your bearings and then gets you back on your original course.

So if the Pathways Movement is to be locally-led and self-sustaining, we need thousands of men and women who are navigating according to the some big, shared ideas, not necessarily proscriptive implementation models. Models can help simplify the planning and implementation process, but invariably, a lot of adaption and continuing innovations will be needed at the local level. But the big ideas – here described as Six Commitments - provide clarity as to the purpose and outcomes you are seeking.

Here are the Six Pathway Commitments that I suggest each Pathways System be built upon and that each Pathways System Leadership Team adopt, in some form or fashion.

We, as the adults with responsibility for our schools, our families, our places of business, and related organizations, systems and services, will help our youth and young adults make well-informed decisions about their future education and careers, and equip them so they can successfully navigate through life obstacles to achieve their aspirations for career and life success. Specifically:

◊ *We will recapture the essential purpose of education to Prepare Individuals for Success (not just teaching subjects). We will work to ensure that every learner, both youth and young adult, develops the knowledge, skills, and attitudes necessary for career and life success.*

◊ *We will ensure that every youth and young adult participates in meaningful career development to help them find a good personal fit between their skills, knowledge and passion and quality career opportunities.*

◊ *We will build a variety of engaging and relevant Pathway Programs so youth and young adults can explore their career interests and participate in secondary and postsecondary education, training, and apprenticeships that support their career aspirations.*

◊ *We will strive to make every class and school experience engaging and meaningful by utilizing dynamic teaching and learning strategies.*

◊ *We will engage a large percentage of employers and community organizations with our Pathway Programs in schools and colleges, so learners can get a meaningful understanding of the expectations of the workplace.*

◊ *We will develop strong and sustainable collaboration between key community partners, including schools, colleges, employers, community organizations, and workforce systems.*

These are the commitments that will guide your work in transforming your schools and communities. Refer to them. Act on them. Start, in some small but meaningful way, today. Thank you.

Terms Related to Careers and Career-Technical Education

Career and Technical Education (Perkins Act Definition)

A Career Technical Education (CTE) program has a specific definition provided by the Perkins Act, the federal law that governs funding for local CTE programs. States may also add additional requirements to specify what local programs may be eligible to receive the federal funds and/or state-appropriated funds. The following is the definition of CTE provided in the text of the Perkins Improvement Act of 2016. It is the federal law that provides funding and parameters for CTE programs at the state and local levels:[1]

"(5) CAREER AND TECHNICAL EDUCATION. — The term 'career and technical education' means organized educational activities that— '

'(A) offer a sequence of courses that—

"(i) provides individuals with coherent and rigorous content aligned with challenging academic standards and relevant technical knowledge and skills needed to prepare for further education and careers in current or emerging professions;

"(ii) provides technical skill proficiency, an industry-recognized credential, a certificate, or an associate degree; and

"(iii) may include prerequisite courses (other than a remedial course) that meet the requirements of this subparagraph; and '

'(B) include competency-based applied learning that contributes to the academic knowledge, higher-order reasoning and problem-solving skills, work attitudes, general employability skills, technical skills, and occupation-specific skills, and knowledge of all aspects of an industry, including entrepreneurship, of an individual.

Career Clusters

Career clusters are the model of organization and communication about careers that was developed and ratified by state directors of career and technical education in 2000. The new organizational model is an attempt to understand and organize the full breadth of careers and to aid the expansion and modernizing of career-focused programs. Prior to the career clusters model, most states and local schools used a narrower conception of CTE programs that was derived from structures that originated in the 1940s and 50s when vocational education programs mostly consisted of agriculture, automotive repair, the building trades, office support, and home economics.

The career clusters model includes the following:

◊   Agriculture, food, and natural resources

◊   Architecture and construction

◊   Arts, A/V technology, and communications

◊   Business management and administration

◊   Education and training

◊   Finance

◊   Government and public administration

◊   Health science

◊   Hospitality and tourism

◊   Human services

◊   Information technology

◊   Law, public safety, corrections, and security

◊   Manufacturing

◊   Marketing

◊   Science, technology, engineering, and mathematics (STEM)

◊   Transportation, distribution, and logistics

A full explanation of the career clusters model and the supporting Pathways can be accessed at the state CTE directors' website, http://careertech.org.

Career Fields

Some states (such as Kansas, Minnesota, Nebraska, among others) have chosen to organize their career information into six broad career fields. Each career field aggregates a number of related career clusters and the Pathways within it. Below are the six career fields used, at state discretion:

◊ Agriculture, food, and natural resources

◊ Arts, communications, and information systems

◊ Business management and administration

◊ Engineering, manufacturing, and technology

◊ Health science technology

◊ Human services

Career Pathways in the Career Clusters Framework

Within the original Career Clusters framework, 79 Career Pathways were identified. In this usage, a Career Pathway represented the organization of related occupational areas within a specific career cluster. Within each pathway, a number of discreet occupations have a shared set of technical knowledge and skills, so if the individual develops competencies within this pathway, he or she will be more likely to secure employment.

For example, within the Law, Public Safety, Corrections, and Security Pathway, there are the following Pathways:

◊ Correction Services

◊ Emergency and Fire Management Services

◊ Law Enforcement Services

◊ Legal Services

◊ Security and Protective Services

To view all of the identified Pathways, visit: https://careertech.org/career-clusters

"Career Pathway" Federal Program Definition

The first federal definition of the term "Career Pathway" was included in the Workforce Innovation and Opportunities Act (WIOA).[2] This legislation was enacted by Congress in 2014, and provides funding and guidance to state and local workforce development systems. In 2016, Congress was considering an update to the Perkins Career Technical Act of 2006. In the bills under consideration at the time, the Perkins Act would utilize the same definition of "Career Pathway" that was enacted in WIOA.

Workforce Innovation and Opportunities Act
Section 3. DEFINITIONS

"(7) CAREER PATHWAY.—The term "career pathway" means a combination of rigorous and high-quality education, training, and other services that—

(A) aligns with the skill needs of industries in the economy of the State or regional economy involved;

(B) prepares an individual to be successful in any of a full range of secondary or postsecondary education options, including apprenticeships registered under the Act of August 16, 1937 (commonly known as the "National Apprenticeship Act"; 50 Stat. 664, chapter 663; 29 U.S.C. 50 et seq.) (referred to individually in this Act as an "apprenticeship", except in section 171);

(C) includes counseling to support an individual in achieving the individual's education and career goals;

(D) includes, as appropriate, education offered concurrently with and in the same context as workforce preparation activities and training for a specific occupation or occupational cluster;

(E) organizes education, training, and other services to meet the particular needs of an individual in a manner that accelerates the educational and career advancement of the individual to the extent practicable;

(F) enables an individual to attain a secondary school diploma or its recognized equivalent, and at least 1 recognized postsecondary credential; and

(G) helps an individual enter or advance within a specific occupation or occupational cluster."

Common Career Technical Core (Advance CTE)

In 2010, the National Association of State Directors of Career Technical Education (now known as Advance CTE: State Leaders Connecting Learning to Work) convened an initiative to create an updated set of knowledge and skill statements for the Clusters/Pathways framework, something that had not been done since the original framework was created in 2000. Forty two states designated teams of teachers, employers, and employer organizations to give input and validate the standards. The participating states were not required to adopt the resulting Common Career Technical Core (CCTC), but they were encouraged to review the model standards and make changes to their state standards as appropriate. The CCTC also included an overarching set of Career Ready Practices that applied to all Pathway Programs. The Career Ready Practices included 12 statements that addressed the knowledge, skills, and dispositions that were important to becoming career ready. These statements were incorporated into NC3T's integrated definition of College, Career, and Life Readiness.

The Common Career Technical Core can be reviewed at: http://www. careertech.org/CCTC

CTE Program of Study (Perkins Act Definition)

The 2006 congressional update of the federal Perkins Act, which distributes money to local schools and colleges for the purpose of supporting career and technical education programs, includes a new definition of something called a "program of study." This term is used to emphasize the seamless connection of CTE programs between secondary and postsecondary education, as opposed to a CTE program that just resides within the provenance of a high school. Under the Perkins Act, each local school district or college has to deploy at least one program that meets the federal definition of "CTE Program of Study."

At a minimum, according to the definition put forward in the Perkins Act, Pathway Programs must do the following:

◊   incorporate and align secondary and postsecondary education elements

◊   include academic and CTE content in a coordinated, non-duplicative progression of courses

◊   offer the opportunity, where appropriate, for secondary students to acquire postsecondary credits, and

◊   lead to an industry-recognized credential or certificate at the postsecondary level, or an associate or baccalaureate degree.

U.S. DoE Rigorous Program of Study

The U.S. Department of Education's Office of Vocational and Adult Education (OVAE) went further in creating its own guidance (of what it called a "Rigorous Program of Study") and this model included 10 components.[3]

The Rigorous Program of Study Design Framework Components are the following:

◊ Legislation and Policies

◊ Partnerships

◊ Professional Development

◊ Accountability and Evaluation Systems

◊ College and Career Readiness Standards

◊ Course Sequences

◊ Credit Transfer Agreements

◊ Guidance Counseling and Academic Advisement

◊ Teaching and Learning Strategies,

◊ Technical Skills Assessments

Pathway Programs/System/Related Standards and Practices

NC3T Pathway Systems Design Specifications. See -- http://nc3t.com/white-paper/

High Schools That Work, Ten Key Practices. See -- http://www.sreb.org/sites/main/files/file-attachments/02v07_2002_hstw_brochure1.pdf

National Career Academy Coalition. National Standards of Practice. See -- http://www.ncacinc.com/nsop

Ford Next Generation Learning, Essential Practices. See - https://fordngl.com/essential-practices

Linked Learning/ConnectED California. Essential Elements of High Quality Linked Learning Pathways. See - http://www.connectedcalifornia.org/linked_learning/essential_elements

Pathways Support Organizations

Advance CTE

Advance CTE: State Leaders Connecting Learning to Work is the longest-standing national non-profit that represents State Directors and state leaders responsible for secondary, postsecondary, and adult Career Technical Education (CTE) across all 50 states and U.S. territories. Advance CTE was formerly known as the National Association of State Directors of Career Technical Education Consortium (NASDCTEc).

Advance CTE's vision is "to support an innovative CTE system that prepares individuals to succeed in education and their careers and poises the United States to flourish in a global, dynamic economy through leadership, advocacy and partnerships." Its stated mission "is to support visionary state leadership, cultivate best practices and speak with a collective voice on national policy to promote academic and technical excellence that ensures a career-ready workforce." Advance CTE has been an active proponent of Pathways as a key reform strategy. Advance CTE is a partner with the Council of Chief State School Officers and JPMorgan Chase for the New Skills for Youth initiative.

Website: www.careertech.org

Association for Career and Technical Education

The **Association for Career and Technical Education**® (ACTE) is the largest national education association dedicated to the advancement of education that prepares youth and adults for careers. Its stated mission is "to provide educational leadership in developing a competitive workforce." ACTE promotes career and technical education in all its forms at both secondary and postsecondary levels, including Pathway Programs and Career Academies.

Website: www.acteonline.org

Alignment Nashville

The **Alignment Nashville** organization brings together community partners to align and coordinate resources to help all area youth be successful. Alignment Nashville is focused on using collaborative initiatives to support students in Metro Nashville Public Schools (MNPS) in an effort to improve school performance, children's health, and the overall community. Members of the organization include MNPS administrators and a wide range of committed community partners.[4]

Alignment Nashville uses a collective impact approach to address the needs identified in the MNPS strategic plan by making resources available and aligning them across community networks of education, businesses, and families. These collaborative partnerships define a common vision and goals for supporting area youth and for enacting systemic, long-term change to address challenges. Alignment Nashville emphasizes a cradle-to-career vision for helping Nashville youth succeed in school and in careers.[5]

Alignment Teams are at the heart of how Alignment Nashville is organized. These teams, also called A-Teams, are organized around a grade level or health issue and are comprised of members from various community, school and government entities. Alignment teams develop tactical plans focused on one or more of the organization's long-term outcomes. The Alignment Team process requires that any work done by the team is planned out, includes a diverse group of stakeholders, and is evaluated before being implemented.[6] Alignment Nashville has also formed a national organization, **Alignment USA**, to promote collective impact in other cities and states.

Websites: http://portal.alignmentnashville.org. http://www.alignmentusa.org

Center for Law and Social Policy (CLASP)

CLASP is based in Washington, DC, and embraces a goal of shrinking the employment gap between disadvantaged youth while reconnecting youth to education and workforce readiness. CLASP aims to educate Congress and state and local policymakers on how policies and programs can better serve disconnected and low-income youth, as well as advocate for funding streams to create delivery programs that reconnect youth to Pathways of success.

In 2012, CLASP launched its initiative, the Alliance for Quality Career Pathways (AQCP) to focus on Career Pathways as a crucial element to helping youth, the unemployed, and other at-risk populations gain education and employability skills.[7] This initiative hopes to provide a common understanding of high-quality Career Pathway systems while helping state and local partnerships build and strengthen new and existing programs.

Policymakers, funders, and other stakeholders can use the CLASP Pathways framework to enhance investments, provide technical assistance, guide building, and scale Pathway systems. The framework will be customizable with a set of criteria, indicators, metrics, and self-assessment tools to enhance the quality of existing Pathway efforts.

Website: http://www.clasp.org/

College and Career Academy Support Network

Since 1998, the **College and Career Academy Support Network (CCASN)**, based at the University of California Berkeley, has been working to increase educational opportunities that offer each young person support and guidance, productive engagement in the world outside of school, and preparation for both college and careers. This research-based strategy has been effective for hundreds of thousands of teenagers, including low-income students of color.

CCASN offers professional development, coaching, resource materials, and technical assistance for secondary educators, schools, and districts. CCASN also conducts research to document and improve practice, and advises policy makers at all levels.

Website: http://casn.berkeley.edu

ConnectED California

During the 2000s, the James Irvine Foundation provided support to the **ConnectEd California** to develop and roll-out in several communities a Pathways-oriented reform model called "Linked Learning." The Linked Learning model emphasized four core components:

◊ Rigorous academics. Core subjects that prepare all students for college, including the a-g coursework required by California's public universities and aligned to the common core state standards.

◊ Career-based learning in the classroom. Professional skills and industry-related knowledge woven into lessons and assignments to give students context for what they're learning.

◊ Work-based learning in professional settings. A range of real-world experiences—from mentoring and job shadowing to internships—that expose students to possible career paths.

◊   Integrated student supports. Dedicated support services tailored to the needs of students, such as counseling and supplemental instruction that help ensure students are successful in school and life.[8]

ConnectEd: The California Center for College and Career is dedicated to advancing practice, policy, and research aimed at helping young people prepare for both college and career through Linked Learning. Linked Learning offers students a multiyear program of study that combines academic and technical learning organized around broad industry themes, like biomedical and health sciences; construction and building design; agriculture and renewable resources; and arts, media and entertainment. This approach prepares high school students for careers and for a full range of postsecondary options, including two- and four-year college or university, apprenticeship, and formal employment training programs.

Website: http://www.connectedcalifornia.org

Council of Chief State School Officers

The **Council of Chief State School Officers (CCSSO)** is a nonpartisan, nationwide, nonprofit organization of public officials who head departments of elementary and secondary education in the states, the District of Columbia, the Department of Defense Education Activity, and five U.S. extra-state jurisdictions. CCSSO provides leadership, advocacy, and technical assistance on major educational issues.

CCSSO's Career Readiness Initiative is rooted in the work of CCSSO's Career Readiness Task Force. The Initiative includes ongoing career readiness support to all states and targeted technical assistance to a network of states committed to being early adopters of the Task Force recommendations.

CCSSO has partnered with JPMorgan Chase & Co. on New Skills for Youth, a $75 million, five-year investment from JPMorgan Chase to increase the number of youth throughout the world who are prepared to compete for high-skill jobs. As part of this overall initiative, JPMorgan Chase dedicated $35 million of grant funding for CCSSO to lead the New Skills for Youth grant opportunity for states in partnership with Advance CTE (formerly NASDCTEc). New Skills for Youth has given every state the opportunity to apply for significant grants that will help turn their bold visions for improving career readiness in K-12 education into a reality.

Website: http://www.ccsso.org

Ford Next Generation Learning

Ford Next Generation Learning (FNGL) is an education initiative by the Ford Motor Company Fund dedicated to transforming high schools with a collaborative community approach. FNGL brings together educators, employers, and community leaders to implement their model for transforming high schools while helping a new generation of learners to graduate from high school both college- and career-ready. [9]

To achieve this, FNGL provides communities with a framework for high school redesign that aims to meet the expectations and academic rigor of college preparatory academic programs with the real-world relevance and rigor of career and technical education. Such programs come in several varieties, such as multiple career academies and other themed programs within a larger high school, single-themed small schools, or "early college high schools."

Career pathway concentrations offered through FNGL include STEM, business, media arts, and law and justice; however, most focus on STEM. There are currently 20 Ford Learning Communities found throughout Florida, California, Georgia, Kentucky, Tennessee, Missouri, Pennsylvania, and Illinois.

Website: https://fordngl.com

Global Pathways Institute

Global Pathways Institute, founded by Pathways to Prosperity author William Symonds, is committed to creating an America in which all young people are prepared to lead productive and successful lives. They believe that providing young people with high-quality multiple Pathways is the best way to help them discover and develop their potential and achieve economic independence. The GPI stated mission is to "advance a national movement to provide high-quality multiple Pathways to economic independence for all young people. We will work with the organizations, institutions, and individuals aligned with GPI to accelerate awareness and adoption of effective Pathways models, to facilitate development of innovative Pathways programs and policies, and to build support for the national movement."

Website: http://globalpathwaysinstitute.org

High Schools That Work/SREB

High Schools That Work (HSTW), managed by the Southern Region Education Board (SREB), is one of the nation's largest school improvement initiatives for high school leaders and teachers. Established in 1987, the

HSTW program is based on the belief that most students can master complex academic and technical concepts if schools create an environment that encourages students to make the effort to succeed. To enact school improvement, HSTW developed their "10 Key Practices" for changing what is expected of students, what they are taught, and how they are taught.

In conjunction with HSTW, the SREB is partnering with a consortium of states and industry leaders to develop sequences of academically rigorous, standards-based career technical education courses in high-demand, high-skill, high-wage career areas targeted to the economic needs and opportunities of each participating state. Named the **Advanced Career Initiative**, this new program aims to prepare high school students - especially high-risk students - for the highest levels of education possible by creating multiple paths to college and careers that keep academic and upper-level job options open. The Pathways are: Aerospace Engineering, Clean Energy Technology, Energy and Power, Global Logistics, Health Informatics, Informatics, Innovations in Science and Technology, and Integrated Production Technologies.[10]

Website: http://www.sreb.org/high-schools-work

National Academy Foundation

National Academy Foundation (NAF) supports the development of academies primarily in urban public school district, but also exists in many suburban and rural areas. NAF academies are best described as 'schools within schools' and serve a small community of students for two or more years. NAF currently has academies in 21 of the 25 largest school districts in the United States. There are over 650 academies in schools throughout 38 states and 190 school districts.

NAF academies are organized around one of five career themes – Finance, Hospitality and Tourism, Information Technology, Health Sciences, or Engineering – viable industries with demonstrated growth and strong potential in the years ahead. In addition to core academic courses, students take industry-specific classes related to these themes and participate in work-based learning activities to put their lessons into action.

Website: http://naf.org

National Career Academy Coalition

With a board comprised of organizations representing career academies, business, and education, the **National Career Academy Coalition (NCAC)** serves as an umbrella group, convening and advocating for career academies. Members have access to the following:

◊ A yearly, high quality national conference that draws from up 900 practitioners and stakeholders.

◊ Technical assistance on starting and maintaining high quality career academies.

◊ A variety of professional development opportunities based on the needs of the school district.

◊ Access to resources from other organizations that support and sustain career academies.

◊ An academy review or accreditation process that identifies and rewards best practices found in model career academies.

◊ National information that can keep them abreast of information valuable to career academy local implementation and sustainability.[11]

Website: http://www.ncacinc.com

National Career Pathways Network

The **National Career Pathways Network (NCPN)** is a membership organization for educators, employers, and others involved in the advancement of Career Pathways, career technical education (CTE), and related education reform initiatives. NCPN is housed at the Center for Occupational Research and Development (CORD).[12] The network previously supported professionals working in tech prep programs and was known as the National Tech Prep Network.

NCPN assists its more than 2,000 members in planning, implementing, evaluating, and improving secondary and postsecondary transition programs by facilitating the exchange of best practices among the country's leading practitioners.

Website: http://www.ncpn.info

National Center for College and Career Transitions (NC3T)

The **National Center for College and Career Transitions** (NC3T) is a mission-driven organization focusing on the development of secondary and postsecondary Pathways designed to provide learners with the academic, technical, and workplace skills needed to be career and life ready. Hans Meeder and Brett Pawlowski formed NC3T in 2012, adopting the vision statement — "every learner with a dream and a plan and every community with a capable and ready workforce." The organization embraces a vision of individual education and career success that complements and mutually reinforces the societal goal of greater economic opportunity and community prosperity.[13]

NC3T offers targeted and customized support to entities involved in this work by providing onsite and virtual coaching, technical assistance, and proven resources during all phases of a Pathways System Initiative. In addition, NC3T offers a scalable approach for entities working at a statewide level by organizing and leading Pathways Innovation Networks. NC3T supports individual district Pathways System Implementation, facilitates statewide Pathway Innovation Networks, and also provides a variety of workshops and professional development opportunities.[14]

Website: www.nc3t.com

Pathways to Prosperity Network/Jobs for the Future

In 2011, the Harvard Graduate School of Education released *Pathways to Prosperity: Meeting the Challenge of Preparing Young Americans for the 21st Century*, a report that argued the current education system was too narrowly focused on the goal of preparing all students to pursue a four-year postsecondary degree immediately after high school despite the fact other postsecondary routes to careers might suit significant numbers of students far better.

As a follow-up to the publication of the *Pathways to Prosperity* report in 2011, Jobs for the Future and Harvard University partnered in 2012 to create **Pathways to Prosperity Network**, an initiative focused on creating educational and economic opportunities for low-income youth and adults. The Network, consisting of up to 12 state members, develops Career Pathways that span grades 9 – 14, enabling students to transition smoothly through high school into higher education and onto well-paying careers in high demand sectors like IT, health care, and advanced manufacturing. [15]

Website: http://www.jff.org/initiatives/pathways-prosperity-network

Project Lead the Way

Project Lead the Way (PLTW) is one of the nation's leading providers of K-12 STEM programs. The program is offered in over 6,500 schools throughout the country and can be found in all 50 states. PLTW's activity-, project-, and problem-based curriculum and high-quality teacher professional development, combined with an engaged network of educators and corporate partners, help students develop the skills they need to be successful in post-secondary education and beyond.

PLTW offers five programs. All programs are completely developed and designed to be implemented in a designated sequence:

❏ **PLTW Launch** is offered for kindergarten through fifth grade students.

❏ **PLTW Gateway** provides engineering and biomedical science curriculum for middle school students.

❏ **PLTW Engineering** teaches high school students how to engage in open-ended problem solving, learn and apply the engineering design process, and use the same industry-leading technology and software as are used in the world's top companies.

❏ **PLTW Biomedical Science** teaches students to investigate the roles of biomedical professionals as they study the concepts of human medicine, physiology, genetics, microbiology, and public health.

❏ **PLTW Computer Science** engages high school students in computational thinking and prepares a computationally aware and capable workforce.

Website: https://www.pltw.org

Strive Together

Established in 2006 to serve the greater Cincinnati area (including northern Kentucky), the Strive Partnership focuses on improving the academic success of every student by coordinating and targeting resources across the community. Serving three school districts in the Cincinnati region (Cincinnati, Covington and Newport), the Strive Partnership was the first community in the **Strive Together Cradle to Career Network**, a national network of 63 communities in 32 states and Washington.[16]

Strive Together focuses on using a collective impact approach to improve academic success among students. By uniting leaders across education, nonprofit, community, civic, and philanthropic sectors, Strive creates a partnership that sets a common vision and goals for supporting all children "from cradle to career."[17] Specifically, it aims to transform education by achieving five goals – ensure every child:

◊   Is prepared for school

◊   Is supported outside of school

◊   Succeeds academically

◊   Completes some form of postsecondary education or training, and

◊   Enters and advances in a meaningful career.[18]

Strive Together uses three key practices to meet its goals and have a collective impact: collaborative action, use of data, and resource alignment.[19] Rather than working in silos, partners coordinate their resources and reform efforts to invest in common goals.

Website: http://www.strivetogether.org

Types of Career Awareness, Exploration and Application Activities

Career Awareness

Career Day/Career Fair: Typically a career day/career fair is a half-day or all-day event. Representatives from numerous businesses and organizations participate and present information about their organization and the careers their organization represents. Some large organizations, like a hospital for example, actually employ health care workers but also have facilities managers and workers, information technology managers, and business, finance, and marketing professionals. Students often prepare for a career day by identifying their areas of interest, deciding which companies and organizations they want to visit with, identifying questions to ask in advance, and taking notes that can be incorporated into a subsequent classroom assignment or report.

Career Interest Inventory/ Career Interest Assessments. A wide variety of instruments, from simple checklists to paper- and computer-based assessments allow students to identify occupations and career fields of interest. Some tools are free to use, and others require a school, district, or state-based subscription:

◊ State based Career Information Systems, built on the national CIS infrastructure.

◊ Kuder System. http://www.kuder.com

◊ Career Cruising. http://www.careercruising.com

◊ Naviance. http://www.naviance.com

◊ O-NET Interest Profiler (using the Holland Code system): http://www.onetcenter.org/IP.html.

◊ My Next Move: http://www.mynextmove.org

◊ Your Plan for the Future: http://www.yourplanforthefuture.org

A comprehensive set of resources can be accessed through the National Career Development Association at: http://www.ncda.org/aws/NCDA/pt/sp/resources

Career Speakers: Individuals from the community are invited to school to speak to students. Typically, the speaker provides a perspective on their personal career journey, the types of jobs that are available within his or her field, and the knowledge, skills, and education needed to enter and advance the field. Similar to a Career Day/Career Fair, students can prepare questions in advance and take on follow-up research activities in class.

Individual Academic and Career Plans (IACP). While the names of this tool range from Academic and Career Plan, Individualized Learning Plan, and College-Career Plan, depending on local or state designations, the IACP is a tool for a student to integrate career development, self-assessment, planning for coursework, and exploration and planning related to postsecondary education. Many states require a student to establish a first draft of the plan by 8th grade and to continue to revisit and refine the plan throughout all phases of career awareness, exploration, and immersion during their school experience and postsecondary education and learning as well. Web-based tools, referenced in the Career Assessment definition, allow a web-based platform for the Individualized Academic and Career Plan.

Company Tours/Career-Related Field Trips. Generally, these are half-day or full-day activities. Groups of students visit a workplace, observe work-related activities, and learn from employees about the jobs and education needed for the jobs there. Other activities can include trips to museums, science centers, career-related conferences or participation in career-specific projects.

Labor Market Information Analysis. During a class or workshop setting, learners can review labor market information, find out about the prevalence of careers, project growth or retractions, find out about salaries, and discover information about the work setting. Students often use the results of a career-interest profiler to identify a handful of careers to learn more about. Instructors create assignments so students can share their findings with fellow students and use the information learned to insert into their IACP. This type of activity can also precede a career fair, career-related field trip, or guest speaker, helping students to ask more informed questions.

School Tours and Open Houses. Students at the middle school often tour a local high school or a regional technology center/high school that offers Pathways Programs, using their career interests to select which programs to tour during the school visit. Middle and high school students also visit community college, technical colleges, and four-year colleges, learning about the types of career-related programs and majors offered at these schools.

Regional or District-Wide Pathway Expositions. In districts that have a wide offering at schools, where there is an open enrollment policy, a district-wide pathway exposition at a central location is held for students and families to attend and learn about all the Pathway offerings held across the district or region.

Career Exploration and Planning

Advisory Program. An advisory program involves course or class time designated in the school day at regular intervals, whether they be daily, weekly, bi-weekly, or monthly. A group of students is identified to meet with a designated faculty advisor during these sessions (30 minutes to one hour), and a scope and sequence of activities are developed. A well-developed advisory program addresses career development, social-emotional skills, study skills, college awareness and search, and other pertinent topics identified by the school. Success of the advisory system requires a well-structured program, professional development and support for the teacher advisors, and strong support from the school leadership, so the program is viewed as an integral component to the school's College, Career and Life Readiness mission.

Career Exploration Courses/Freshman Academy Courses. The school district, school, or college offers, either as a required course or as an elective course, a structured course that allows students to conduct focused career development and learn about job search, financial literacy, and college-search skills. These courses can be offered as semester-long or full-year courses.

Pathways Intensive School System Freshman Academy Course. A Freshman Academy Course is offered to all freshman students within a wall-to-wall Pathways school. During this course, students can spend several days or weeks visiting and observing the Pathways Programs in action and interacting with the upperclassmen who are enrolled in these programs.

A Freshman Academy Course can include the following topics:

Individualized Coaching and Career Guidance. Students meet in one-on-one sessions with a counselor or graduation coach, discussing their career interests, identifying opportunities for deeper exploration and immersion, and deciding on appropriate course selection related to the student's career interest.

Workshops. Workshops, special presentations, and classes for students can be organized around a variety of topics and skill-building exercises, such as resume writing, interviewing, job searching, networking, financial literacy and planning, and conducting self-assessment of their College, Career, and Life Readiness skills.

Experiential Learning/Contextual Learning. Experiential learning involves projects completed in class and out of school that allow students to apply academic skills to their career interests, conducting a wide range of projects.

Community Service/Service Learning. Community service and service learning give students the opportunity to address a topic of compelling local need while benefitting from the opportunity to interact with adults whose jobs pertain to the students' area of career interest. The community service experience gives students the opportunity to develop their knowledge and apply their energy to a real-world problem or issue. The Community service can be short-term, finished over a number of days, or can extend across an entire semester or school year.

Informational Interviews. Students interview a professional, either on a one-on-one or small group basis, asking about his or her career. The interview can be in-person, by phone, through on-line chat, or through on-line videoconference. Students prepare questions, take notes, and provide a report following the interview. Adult supervision of the interaction is maintained throughout the interview process.

Job Shadow Days. A job shadow is an experience, either for a few hours or more, at a workplace where a student or group of students follows and observes an employee through his or her workday. Students prepare a reflection or journal of their job shadow experience and write thank you notes to the job shadow host.

Career Application (Immersion)

Pathway Program. For a robust career application, the student participates in a Pathway Program.

Capstone Projects/Senior Projects. A capstone project is a major project, conducted over a semester or full-year, in which a student applies knowledge and skills from a number of disciplines. The project may include completing a hands-on project, writing a research paper, going deeper with career development, or developing a portfolio of project-related materials. Students often present the findings from their project to a group of adults from the community.

Career Clubs. After-school clubs and career-technology student organizations give students the chance to practice their career-related skills, meet professional in their field of interest, and connect with other students who share similar interests. Career clubs meet on a variety of schedules, from weekly to monthly, or they have special summer institutes.

Mentorship Programs. Mentorship programs connect students with adults in workplaces who serve as mentors and who introduce students to their workplaces and their industries. Mentors provide professional and personal guidance and support. Mentors can work with individual students or with groups of students interested in a career field. Mentorships take place over many weeks, a semester, or a school year. In some pathway programs, a community-based mentor may work with a group of students over more than one year, as part of the school's Advisory Program.

Internship or Mentorship. The most intensive expansive version of work-based learning is a student internship (sometimes called an educational internship or mentorship program), through which a student gains an extended and regular connection with a specific company, a workplace setting, and group of professionals, one or more of which provide supervision, coaching, and mentoring to the student intern. The internship, paid or non-paid, helps students gain work experience, build and apply their skills, and deepen their career understanding. The work-based learning experience also helps students deepen their application of career and employability skills. A well-structured educational internship program provides preparation for the learner, preparation and support for the employer-host, a job description, a list of skills to be developed and tasks to be accomplished, an evaluation of the student's performance, and an evaluation of the employer performance. Depending on criteria established by the district or state, the internship should have a minimum number of hours (20 to 40) and last over several weeks or over an entire semester or summer. Work-based learning may be paid or non-paid. Often, a school or college's comprehensive insurance policy provides liability coverage for the student in the workplace.

Acknowledgements

I would like to thank Brett Pawlowski for his support and advice in the writing of this book. Kathy Schick provided valuable organizational assistance to develop our Pathways Framework and organize initial work on this book and some of the case studies. Nichole Jackson and Michelle Hebert-Giffen provided their invaluable research assistance for many sections of this book. I would also like to thank other members of NC3T team who have helped go deep and advance our work – Kandice Dickover, Jennifer Youtz Grams, Thom Suddreth, and Cassandra Vincent.

Thank you, Pam Daly, for your enthusiastic authorship of Chapter 10 on branding and communications. Your insight and experience bring great benefit to this work.

I want to express my gratitude to Rick Delano and Cheryl Carrier, with whom I worked as a team member with Ford Next Generation Learning for my early introduction to the world of career academies. This period of work was indispensable in helping me frame and develop my understanding of Pathway Programs and how the different components of the Pathway Framework can be brought together. Your guidance and input were invaluable. I would also like to express my gratitude to Sandra Mittelsteadt, who made those initial introductions and connections for us.

There are many others I would like to thank who have generously shared with me and mentored me in my learning over the years that led to the development of this book. Among the many (and this is certainly not all) who shared with me are Patrick Ainsworth, Kelly Amy, Rob Atterbury, Patti Beltram, Thom Besaw, Kate Blosveren-Creamer, Sheila Byrd Carmichael, James (Gene) Bottoms, Betsy Brand, Jan Bray, Lee Burkett, Doug Carnine, Steve Casa, Blouke Carus, Michael Cohen, James (Bob) Couch, Willard (Bill) Daggett, Carol D'Amico, Michael DiMaggio, Jay Eagan, John Ferrandino, Michael Fitzpatrick, Matt Fleck, John Foster, Kimberly Greene, Starr Herrmann, Marc Hill, Gary Hoachlander, Vic Klatt, Kim McNulty, Ray McNulty, John Mulhavy, Timothy Ott, Hillary Pennington, Natalie Prim, Sydney Rogers, Sally Lovejoy, Susan Sclafani, Robert Schwartz, Jay Steele, Bill Symonds, Sheila Thornton, Marc Tucker, Robert Wise, and Aimee Wyatt.

Finally I would like to thank my dear wife, Lisa Spence Meeder, for her support and encouragement and for acting as a sounding board after many long days of research and writing. I was with you as you delivered our four amazing children; you were with me for the delivery of this book. You had the harder and more important job, but I still want to say - Thank you!

About the Author

Hans Meeder is co-founder and President of the National Center for College and Career Transitions (NC3T). The National Center for College and Career Transitions is a mission-driven organization with the purpose of communicating the urgency and benefit of the Pathways model and developing the capacity of local leaders to take action on a Pathways System agenda.

Mr. Meeder has an extensive and varied career in education and workforce policy and government leadership, with an emphasis on high school redesign, career and technical education, and workforce quality. Prior his work with NC3T, Meeder was Deputy Assistant Secretary for Education in the U.S. Department of Education Office of Vocational and Adult Education. Other roles have included Director of the 21st Century CTE Leadership Initiative, Senior Vice President for Workforce Development and Postsecondary Learning at the National Alliance of Business, Executive Director of the 21st Century Workforce Commission, and Education Policy and Outreach Director for the House of Representatives Committee on Education and the Workforce.

Hans lives in Columbia, Maryland, with his wife Lisa, with whom he raised and launched his four adult children. He is a graduate of the University of Maryland College Park and also holds a Master's in Business Administration from the University of Maryland's University College.

This book is intended to be the starting point, not the end point, for your work on Pathways. To continue learning and to join the conversation, visit the following website for additional resources and regular updates from the author:

www.pathwayssherpa.com

Endnotes

Chapter One

1. Toliver, Z. (2016), The Opioid Epidemic: Testing the Limits of Rural Healthcare, May 18, 2016, The Rural Monitor, Rural Health Information Hub, Retrieved from https://www.ruralhealthinfo.org/rural-monitor/opioid-epidemic/

2. Pew Research Center, (2014), Most See Inequality Growing, but Partisans Differ over Solutions
54% Favor Taxing the Wealthy to Expand Aid to Poor, January 23, 2014, Pew Research Center, U.S. Politics and Policy. Retrieved from http://www.people-press.org/2014/01/23/most-see-inequality-growing-but-partisans-differ-over-solutions/

3. Gentile, D. A. (2009). Pathological video game use among youth 8 to 18: A national study. Psychological Science, 20, 594-602. Retrieved from http://www.drdouglas.org/drdpdfs/Gentile_Pathological_VG_Use_2009e.pdf

4. a) Enrollment: NCES (2014), Fast Facts, Immediate transition to college, U.S. Department of Education, National Center for Education Statistics, Retrieved from https://nces.ed.gov/fastfacts/display.asp?id=51

   b) Completion: National Center for Higher Education Management Systems. (2016). ACS Educational Attainment by Degree-Level and Age-Group (American Community Survey). Retrieved from http://www.higheredinfo.org/dbrowser/?level=nation&mode=graph&state=0&submeasure=239

   c) Loan Debt: Institute for College Access and Success. (n.d.). Student Debt and the Class of 2014. The Project on Student Debt. October 2015, from http://ticas.org/posd/map-state-data

5. OECD (2014), Education at a Glance 2014: OECD Indicators, Table A1.1a, OECD Publishing. http://dx.doi.org/10.1787/eag-2014-en

6. Gallup Organization (2016), Real Unemployment, Omaha, Nebraska. Retrieved August 20, 2016 from http://www.gallup.com/poll/189068/bls-unemployment-seasonally-adjusted.aspx

7. a) Savings: Jeanine Skowronsk, J., America's best savers are not the wealthy, Bankrate.com, Retrieved from http://www.bankrate.com/finance/consumer-index/americas-best-savers-are-not-the-wealthy.aspx?ic_id=Top_Financial%20News%20Center_link_4

   b) Housing bubble: Holt, J., (2009) A Summary of the Primary Causes of the Housing Bubble and the Resulting Credit Crisis: A Non-Technical Paper, The Journal of Business Inquiry 2009, 8, 1, 120-129, Retrieved from https://www.uvu.edu/woodbury/docs/summaryoftheprimarycauseofthehousingbubble.pdf

8. Carnevale, A. P., Smith, N., & Strohl, J. (2010). *Job growth and education requirements through 2020* [Executive summary]. Retrieved from https://cew.georgetown.edu/wp-content/uploads/2014/11/Recovery2020.ES.Web.pdf

9. Ibid. (page 6)

10. For competing views on the reality or breadth of the skills gap, see the following articles:

    a) Dimon, J, Seltzer, M., (2014), Closing the Skills Gap, January 05, 2014, Politico. Retrieved from http://www.politico.com/magazine/story/2014/01/closing-the-skills-gap-101478#.UzgKOPldWT8.

    b) Krugman, P. (2014), Jobs and Skills and Zombies, March 30, 2014, New York Times.

Retrieved from http://www.nytimes.com/2014/03/31/opinion/krugman-jobs-and-skills-and-zombies.html?_r=0

11. Davis, A., Kimball, W., Gould, E., (2015) The Class of 2015, Despite an Improving Economy, Young Grads Still Face an Uphill Climb, May 27, 2015, Economic Policy Institute, Washington, DC. Retrieved from http://www.epi.org/publication/the-class-of-2015/

12. Brynjolfsson, Erik; McAfee, Andrew (2011-10-17). Race Against The Machine: How the Digital Revolution is Accelerating Innovation, Driving Productivity, and Irreversibly Transforming Employment and the Economy (Kindle Locations 14-15). Digital Frontier Press.

13. Ravitch, D. (2001). *Left back: A century of failed school reforms.* New York: Simon & Schuster

14. William C. Symonds, Robert B. Schwartz and Ronald Ferguson, February 2011. *Pathways to Prosperity: Meeting the Challenge of Preparing Young Americans for the 21ˢᵗ Century.* Report issued by the Pathways to Prosperity Project, Harvard Graduate School of Education. Retrieved from https://dash.harvard.edu/bitstream/handle/1/4740480/Pathways_to_Prosperity_Feb2011-1.pdf?sequence=1

15. Ibid

16. Philadelphia Academies, Inc. (nd), Our Story. Retrieved from http://www.academiesinc.org/our-story/

17. Clifton, J. (2011), The Coming Jobs War, What every leader must know about the future of job creation, Gallup Press, New York, NY

18. Rothwell, J., (2013), The Hidden STEM Economy (May 2013), The Brookings Institution, Metropolitan Policy Program, Washington, DC. Retrieved from https://www.brookings.edu/wp-content/uploads/2016/06/TheHiddenSTEMEconomy610.pdf

19. Meeder, H (2012), The STEM Leader Guide, Allview Creek Media, Columbia, MD.

Chapter Two

1. Bureau of Labor Statistics (2015), Job Openings And Labor Turnover – March 2016, U.S. Department of Labor. Retrieved at: http://www.bls.gov/news.release/pdf/jolts.pdf

2. DHI Group. (2015, July). Mean Job Vacancy Duration Rose to 28.0 Working Days in March (Report 25). Retrieved from http://dhihiringindicators.com/wp-content/uploads/2016/05/2016-05-DHI-Hiring-Indicators-FINAL.pdf

3. Career Builder (2014), "The Shocking Truth About the Skills Gap," Career Builder Retrieved at: http://www.careerbuildercommunications.com/pdf/skills-gap-2014.pdf

4. Manpower Group. (2015). U.S. talent shortage survey. Retrieved from http://www.manpowergroup.us/campaigns/talent-shortage-2015/assets/pdf/2015-Talent-Shortage-Whitepaper.pdf

5. Ibid

6. Career Builder. (2014, March 6). Companies losing money to the skills gap. Retrieved from http://www.careerbuilder.com/share/aboutus/pressreleasesdetail.aspx?sd=3/6/2014&id=pr807&ed=12/31/2014

7. Ibid

8. Manpower Group. (2015). U.S. talent shortage survey. Retrieved from http://www.manpowergroup.us/campaigns/talent-shortage-2015/assets/pdf/2015-Talent-Shortage-Whitepaper.pdf

9. Mondragón-Vélez, C. (2015, May 21). How does middle-class financial health affect entrepreneurship in America? Retrieved from https://www.americanprogress.org/issues/

economy/report/2015/05/21/109169/how-does-middle-class-financial-health-affect-entrepreneurship-in-america/

10. Fairlie, R, Morelix, A,. Reedy, E. and Russell, J. (2015), The 2015 Kauffman Index, Main Street Entrepreneurship, National Trends, December 2015, Ewing Marion Kauffman Foundation.

11. Institute for College Access and Success. (n.d.). Student Debt and the Class of 2014. The Project on Student Debt. October 2015, from http://ticas.org/posd/map-state-data

12. Remarks of Brandon Busteed, Gallup Education Director, Speaker's remarks at Close-It Summit, October 14, 2015, Washington, DC.

13. U.S. Labor Force Participation Rate: Federal Reserve Bank of St. Louis. (n.d.). Civilian labor force participation rate: 25 to 65 years. Retrieved September 18, 2016, from https://research.stlouisfed.org/fred2/series/LNU01300000

14. Lewis, K., & Burd-Sharps, S. (2015). Zeroing in on place and race: Youth disconnection in America's cities. Retrieved from http://www.measureofamerica.org/youth-disconnection-2015/

15. Ibid

16. Measure of America of the Social Research Council (2015), "Zeroing In On Race And Place Youth Disconnection In America's Cities, Methodological Note" Retrieved at: http://ssrc-static.s3.amazonaws.com/wp-content/uploads/2015/06/MOA-Zeroing-In-Method.pdf

17. Fernandes-Alcantara, A. L. (2015). Disconnected youth: A look at 16- to 24- year olds who are not working or in school (CRS 7-5700) Retrieved from https://www.fas.org/sgp/crs/misc/R40535.pdf.

18. MDRC. (2013). Building better programs for disconnected youth [Brief]. Retrieved from http://www.mdrc.org/publication/building-better-programs-disconnected-youth

19. Belfield, C. R., Levin, H. M., & Rosen, R. (2012). The economic value of opportunity youth. Retrieved from http://www.serve.gov/new-images/council/pdf/econ_value_opportunity_youth.pdf

20. IES/NCES (2015), Immediate College Enrollment Rate, Last Updated March 2015, Institute for Education Sciences, National Center for Education Statistics, U.S. Department of Education. Retrieved at: http://nces.ed.gov/programs/coe/indicator_cpa.asp

21. National Center for Higher Education Management Systems. (2016). Graduation rates. Retrieved from http://www.higheredinfo.org/dbrowser/?level=nation&mode=graph&state=0&submeasure=27

22. IES/NCES (2014), Digest of Education Statistics, Recent high school completers and their enrollment in 2-year and 4-year colleges, by sex: 1960 through 2014. Table 302.10. Retrieved at: https://nces.ed.gov/programs/digest/d14/tables/dt14_302.10.asp

23. National Center for Higher Education Management Systems. (2016). ACS Educational Attainment by Degree-Level and Age-Group (American Community Survey). Retrieved from http://www.higheredinfo.org/dbrowser/?level=nation&mode=graph&state=0&submeasure=232

24. OECD (2014), Education at a Glance 2014 OECD Indicators, Retrieved at: https://www.oecd.org/edu/Education-at-a-Glance-2014.pdf

25. OECD (2013) Outlook 2013, First Results from the Survey of Adult Skills. Retrieved at: http://www.oecd.org/site/piaac/Skills%20volume%201%20(eng)--full%20v12--eBook%20(04%2011%202013).pdf

26. Ibid

27. Goodman, M. J., Sands, A. M., Coley, R. J., & Educational Testing Service. (2015). America's skills challenge: Millennials and the future. Retrieved from http://www.ets.org/s/research/29836/

28. Ibid

29. Institute for College Access and Success. (n.d.). Student Debt and the Class of 2014. The Project on Student Debt. October 2015, from http://ticas.org/posd/map-state-data

30. Board of Governors of the Federal Reserve (2015), Report on the Economic Well-Being of U.S. Households in 2014, May 2015, Retrieved at: https://www.federalreserve.gov/econresdata/2014-report-economic-well-being-us-households-201505.pdf

31. U.S. Census Bureau (2011), More Young Adults are Living in Their Parents' Home, Census Bureau Reports, Press Release, November 3, 2011, U.S. Census Bureau. Retrieved at: https://www.census.gov/newsroom/releases/archives/families_households/cb11-183.html

32. Hurley, D., & Thorp, M. (2002). Decisions without direction: Career guidance and decisions making among American youth. Big Rapids, MI: Ferris State University.

33. YouthTruth (2015), Less than half of U.S. high school students nationwide feel prepared for college and career, YouthTruth finds, Press Release: July 30, 2015, YouthTruth, San Francisco, California. Retrieved from: http://www.youthtruthsurvey.org/wp-content/uploads/2014/12/YT-College-Career-Readiness.pdf

34. Career Builder (2014), "The Shocking Truth About the Skills Gap," Career Builder Retrieved at: http://www.careerbuildercommunications.com/pdf/skills-gap-2014.pdf

35. McKinsey for Government (2012), Education to Employment: Designing a System That Works, McKinsey, Retrieved from http://www.mckinsey.com/industries/social-sector/our-insights/education-to-employment-designing-a-system-that-works

36. ACT (2013), College Choice Report, Part 1, ACT Inc, November 2015. Retrieved from http://www.act.org/content/dam/act/unsecured/documents/CollegeChoiceRpt-2013-14-Part1.pdf

37. Baum, S., Ma, J., & Payea, K. (2013). Education pays 2013: The benefits of higher education for individuals and society. Retrieved from http://trends.collegeboard.org/education-pays

38. Ibid

39. Hart Research Associates. (2015). Falling short? College learning and career success Retrieved from http://www.aacu.org/sites/default/files/files/LEAP/2015employerstudentsurvey.pdf.

40. Ibid

41. Hanover Research. (June 2016). McGraw-Hill Education 2016 Workforce Readiness Survey. Retrieved from http://www.mheducation.com/news-media/press-releases/2016-workforce-readiness-survey.html

42. Ibid

43. Damon, W. (2008). The path to purpose: Helping our children find their calling in life. New York, NY: Free Press.

44. Yazzie-Mintz, E. (2010). Charting the path from engagement to achievement: A report on the 2009 high school survey of student engagement. Bloomington, IN: Center for Evaluation & Education Policy. Retrieved at: http://hub.mspnet.org/index.cfm/20806

45. College Board. (2015). 2015 College Board program results. Retrieved from https://www.collegeboard.org/program-results

46. ACT. (2015), The Condition of College & Career Readiness 2015. http://forms.act.org/research/policymakers/cccr15/pdf/CCCR15-NationalReadinessRpt.pdf

47. ACT. (2013). ACT national curriculum survey 2012. Retrieved from http://files.eric.ed.gov/fulltext/ED542018.pdf

48. IES/NCES (2016). Public High School Graduation Rates. Retrieved from http://nces.ed.gov/programs/coe/indicator_coi.asp

49. Alliance for Excellent Education (2015). Progress is No Accident: Why ESEA Can't

Backtrack on High School Graduation Rates. Retrieved from http://all4ed.org/wp-content/uploads/2015/11/NoAccident.pdf

50. Yazzie-Mintz, E. (2010). Charting the path from engagement to achievement: A report on the 2009 high school survey of student engagement. Bloomington, IN: Center for Evaluation & Education Policy. Retrieved at: http://hub.mspnet.org/index.cfm/20806

51. Bridgeland, J. M., DiIulio, J. J., Jr., & Morison, K. B. (2006). The silent epidemic: Perspectives of high school dropouts. Retrieved from http://www.civicenterprises.net/MediaLibrary/Docs/the_silent_epidemic.pdf

52. IES/NCES (2009), Career/Technical Education (CTE) Statistics, Table H124. Percentage of public high school graduates who earned at least 2.0 credits or at least 3.0 credits in the occupational area, by career/technical education (CTE) occupational area: 2009. Retrieved from https://nces.ed.gov/surveys/ctes/tables/h124.asp

53. National Center for Education Statistics (2014), Condition of Education, 2013 Tables and Figures, Enrollment and percentage distribution of enrollment in public elementary and secondary schools, by race/ethnicity and region: Selected years, fall 1995 through fall 2023, Table 203.50. U.S. Department of Education. Retrieved from http://nces.ed.gov/programs/digest/d13/tables/dt13_203.50.asp

    --For a discussion of the topic, see: Maxwell, L. A. (2014, August 19). U.S. school enrollment hits majority-minority milestone. Education Week. Retrieved from http://www.edweek.org/ew/articles/2014/08/20/01demographics.h34.html

54. Brian T. Prescott and Peace Bransberger. Knocking at the College Door: Projections of High School Graduates (eighth edition). Boulder, CO: Western Interstate Commission for Higher Education, 2012. Retrieved from http://www.wiche.edu/info/publications/knocking-8th/knocking-8th.pdf

55. U.S. Census Bureau (2012), Most Children Younger Than Age 1 are Minorities, Census Bureau Reports, (May 17, 2012), Retrieved from https://www.census.gov/newsroom/releases/archives/population/cb12-90.html

56. U.S. Census Bureau (2015), Projections of the Size and Composition of the U.S. Population: 2014 to 2060. Retrieved from http://www.census.gov/content/dam/Census/library/publications/2015/demo/p25-1143.pdf

    --To read more, see report from Brookings Institution. Frey, W. H. (2014, December 12). New projections point to a majority minority nation in 2044. Retrieved from http://www.brookings.edu/blogs/the-avenue/posts/2014/12/12-majority-minority-nation-2044-frey

57. U.S. Department of Education, Institute of Education Sciences, National Center for Education Statistics. (2014). A first look: 2013 mathematics and reading: National assessment of educational progress at grades 4 and 8, (NCES 2014-451). Retrieved from http://nces.ed.gov/nationsreportcard/subject/publications/main2013/pdf/2014451.pdf

58. Ibid

59. Education Trust. (2013, November 7). Statement and analysis from the Education Trust on the 2013 NAEP reading and mathematics results [Press release]. Retrieved from https://edtrust.org/press_release/statement-and-analysis-from-the-education-trust-on-the-2013-naep-reading-and-mathematics-results/

60. Ibid

61. Ibid

62. Cavanaugh, S. (2007, December 7). Poverty's effect on U.S. scores greater than for other nations. Education Week. Retrieved from http://www.edweek.org/ew/articles/2007/12/12/15pisa.h27.html

63. For more information:

Metro Nashville Public Schools: http://www.mnps.org/pages/mnps/Academics/Academies_of_Nashville

Career Academy virtual tours: https://www.youtube.com/watch?v=rVqDl5TQmzg&list=PL7nHaBiL9UHGixRoVVtdUJMXDp5zjB2dZ

Study Visit Information, Alignment Nashville: http://portal.alignmentnashville.org/

64. Metropolitan Nashville Public Schools. (2014). 2015–2015 facts. Retrieved from http://www.mnps.org/dynimg/_IXAAA_/docid/0x7AC106B6F3B9D054/2/Facts201415_web.pdf

65. Ibid

66. MNPS Department of Research, Assessment and Evaluation (2015), MNPS High School Student Performance Trends, 2015, Metro Nashville Public Schools. Retrieved from http://www.ncacinc.com/sites/default/files/media/documents/MNPS_High_School_Performance_2015.pdf

67. To learn more about upcoming study visits, see: https://academiesstudyvisit.com/

Chapter Three

1. ConnectEd: California Center for College and Career. (2008). Evidence from California partnership academies: One model of link learning pathways. Retrieved from http://www.connectedcalifornia.org/downloads/LL_Evidence_CPA%20Summary_web.pdf

2. Ibid

3. Ibid

4. National High School Center (2012), Local Spotlight: Mountain Home High School Career Academies, November 5, 2012, National High School Center at the American Institutes for Research (AIR), Washington, DC. Retrieved from http://www.ccrscenter.org/blog/local-spotlight-mountain-home-high-school-career-academies

5. ConnectEd: California Center for College and Career. (2008). Evidence from California partnership academies: One model of link learning pathways. Retrieved from http://www.connectedcalifornia.org/downloads/LL_Evidence_CPA%20Summary_web.pdf

6. Ibid

7. Chamber Education Report Card Committee (2015), 2015 Education Report Card, Nashville Area Chamber of Commerce, Nashville, TN. Retrieved from http://www.nashvillechamber.com/docs/default-source/education-reports-and-publications/2015-education-report-card.pdf?sfvrsn=2

8. Guha, N et al (2014), Taking Stock of the California Linked Learning District Initiative, 2014, SRI International. Retrieved from https://www.sri.com/sites/default/files/publications/llyr4execsumm_2014feb20.pdf

9. Kemple, J. J. (2008). Career academies: Long-term impacts on work, education, and transitions to adulthood. Retrieved from http://www.mdrc.org/publication/career-academies-long-term-impacts-work-education-and-transitions-adulthood.

10. Ibid

11. Ibid

12. Neumann, G., Olitsky, N., & Robbins, S. (2009). Job congruence, academic achievement, and earnings. Labour Economics, 16(5), 503–509.

13. Tracey, T. J. G., & Robbins, S. B. (2006). The interest-major congruence and college success relation: A longitudinal study. Journal of Vocational Behavior, 69(1), 64–89

14. Hughes, K. L., & Karp, M. H. (2004). School-based career development: A synthesis

of the literature. Retrieved from http://www.tc.columbia.edu/iee/PAPERS/ CareerDevelopment02_04.pdf

15. Trusty, J., Niles, S. G., & Carney, J.V. (2005). Education-career planning and middle school counselors. Professional School Counseling, 9(2), 136–143. This is a link to an abstract for a subscription service. Better to just cite the journal.

16. Southern Regional Education Board. (2004) "Linking Career/Technical Studies to Broader High School Reform," SREB. Retrieved from http://publications.sreb.org/2004/04V09_ ResearchBrief_CT_studies.pdf

17. Fouad, N. A. (1995). Career linking: An intervention to promote math and science career awareness. Journal of Counseling and Development, 73(5), 527–34.

18. Carnevale, A., Smith, N., Strohl, J. (2010), Help Wanted: Projections of Jobs and Education Requirements Through 2018. (June 2010). p. 106, Georgetown University Center on Education and the Workforce, Retrieved from https://cew.georgetown.edu/cew-reports/help-wanted/

19. Plank, S., DeLuca, S., Estacion, A., (2005), Dropping Out of High School and the Place of Career and Technical Education, October 2005, The National Center For Career And Technical Education. Retrieved from http://www.nrccte.org/sites/default/files/publication-files/droppingout-plank.pdf

20. Alfeld, C., et al, (2007), Looking Inside The Black Box: The Value Added By Career And Technical Student Organizations To Students High School Experience, June 2007, National Research Center for CTE. Retrieved from http://www.nrccte.org/resources/publications/looking-inside-black-box-value-added-career-and-technical-student

21. Lekes, N., et al, (2007), Career and Technical Education Pathway Programs, Academic Performance, and the Transition to College And Career, May 2007, National Research Center for CTE. Retrieved from http://www.nrccte.org/sites/default/files/publication-files/cte_pathway_programs.pdf

22. Dougherty, S., (2016), Career and Technical Education in High School: Does It Improve Student Outcomes?, June 2016, The Fordham Institute, Washington, DC. Retrieved from http://edexcellence.net/publications/career-and-technical-education-in-high-school-does-it-improve-student-outcome

23. Ibid

24. Fraser, A. (2008), Vocational Technical Education in Massachusetts, October 2008, No. 42, Pioneer Institute Public Policy Research, Boston, Massachusetts. Retrieved from www.pioneerinstitute.org

25. Ibid

26. Mann, A., Lopez, D., Stanley, J. (2010) What Is to Be Gained through Partnership, 2nd Edition, Education and Employers Taskforce, 2010, London. Retrieved from http://www.leics-ebc.org.uk/files/uploads/What_is_to_be_gained_through_partnership_v_2.pdf

27. Institute for Education Business Excellence National Support Group for Work Experience (2008), Students' Perceptions of Work Experience. Retrieved from http://www.educationandemployers.org/research/students-perceptions-of-work-experience-by-the-national-support-group-for-work-experience-report-of-impact-measures-2008/

28. KPMG (2010), Evaluation of Education Employer Partnerships. Retrieved from http://www.educationandemployers.org/wp-content/uploads/2014/06/investigation_of_school_employer_partnerships_-_final_report.pdf

29. Miller, A. (1998), Business and Community Mentoring in Schools. DfEE Research Report No. 43, University of Warwick. Retrieved from http://webarchive.nationalarchives.gov.uk/20130401151715/http://www.education.gov.uk/publications/eOrderingDownload/RB43.pdf

30. Mann, A., Lopez, D., Stanley, J. (2010) What Is to Be Gained through Partnership, 2nd

Edition, Education and Employers Taskforce, 2010, London. Retrieved from http://www. leics-ebc.org.uk/files/uploads/What_is_to_be_gained_through_partnership_v_2.pdf

31. National Dropout Prevention Center. (n.d.). 15 Effective Strategies for Dropout Prevention. Retrieved from http://dropoutprevention.org/effective-strategies/overview/

32. PRNewswire-USNewswire. (2014), National Research Study Confirms Minority and Low Socioeconomic Students Outpace Peers Into Secondary Year in College. Dec. 17, 2014. From AVID Center. Retrieved from http://www.prnewswire.com/news-releases/national-research-study-confirms-minority-and-low-socioeconomic-students-outpace-peers-into-second-year-in-college-300010933.html

33. Scrivener, S , & Weiss, M. J. (2013). More graduates: Two-year results from an evaluation of accelerated study in associate programs (ASAP) for developmental education students. Retrieved from http://www.mdrc.org/sites/default/files/More_Graduates.pdf

34. Scrivener, S. (2014). Expanding a successful reform for increasing graduation rates: The continuing story of CUNY's accelerated study in associate programs (ASAP). Presentation slide note handout, American Youth Policy Forum, Washington, DC, October 17, 2014.

35. Abdul-Alim, J. (2014). Ohio Group Wins $1 Million for Spurring College Attainment. Education Week, November 4, 2014. Retrieved from http://www.edweek.org/ew/articles/2014/11/05/11prize.h34. html?qs=Ohio+Group+Wins+$1+Million+for+Spurring+College+Attainment (print reference: (Ohio group wins $1 million prize for college attainment. Education Week. 34(11), 7.

36. Berger, A., Turk-Bicakci, L, Garet, M., Knudson, J., & Hoshen, G. (2014). Early college, continued success: Early college high school initiative impact study. Retrieved from http://www. air.org/sites/default/files/AIR_ECHSI_Impact_Study_Report-_NSC_Update_01-14-14.pdf

37. Ibid

38. Bailey, T, Jaggars, S.S., & Jenkins, D (2015). What we know about guided pathways. New York, NY: Columbia University, Teachers College, Community College Research Center. Retrieved from http://ccrc.tc.columbia.edu/media/k2/attachments/What-We-Know-Guided-Pathways.pdf

39. Bailey, T., Jaggars, S.S. & Jenkins, D. (2015), Implementing Guided Pathways at Miami Dade College: A Case Study New York, NY: Columbia University, Teachers College, Community College Research Center. Retrieved from http://ccrc.tc.columbia.edu/media/k2/attachments/Implementing-Guided-Pathways-Miami-Dade.pdf

40. Prince, M. (2004). Does active learning work? A review of the research. Journal of Engineering Education, 93(3), 223–231. Retrieved from http://www4.ncsu.edu/unity/lockers/users/f/felder/public/Papers/Prince_AL.pdf

41. Freeman, S., Eddy, S. L., McDonough, M., Smith, M. K., Okoroafor, N., Jordt, H., & Wenderoth, M. P. (2014). Active learning increases student performance in science, engineering, and mathematics. Retrieved from http://www.pnas.org/cgi/doi/10.1073/pnas.1319030111

42. Ibid

43. See "Carl Perkins Career and Technical Education Act of 2006," http://www2.ed.gov/policy/sectech/leg/perkins/index.html

44. Stone, J. R. III, Alfeld, C., & Pearson, D. (2008). Rigor and relevance: Testing a model of enhanced math learning in career and technical education. American Educational Research Journal, 45(3), 767-795.) Retrieved from http://www.nrccte.org/sites/default/files/publication-files/rigor_and_relevance.pdf

45. Authentic Literacy Applications in CTE: Helping All Students Learn http://www.nrccte.org/sites/default/files/publication-files/authentic_literacy.pdf

46. Ibid

47. Ibid

48. Bailey, Tom (2009), Rethinking Developmental Education in Community College, February 2009, Community College Research Center, Columbia University, New York, NY. Retrieved from http://ccrc.tc.columbia.edu/media/k2/attachments/rethinking-developmental-education-in-community-college-brief.pdf

49. Jenkins, D., Zeidenberg, M., Kienzl, G., (2009) Educational Outcomes of I-BEST Washington State Community and Technical College System's Integrated Basic Education and Skills Training Program: Findings from a Multivariate Analysis, May 2009, Community College Research Center, Teachers College, Columbia University, New York. Retrieved from http://ccrc.tc.columbia.edu/publications/i-best-multivariate-analysis.html

50. Washington State Board for Community and Technical Colleges. (2012). 2012 I-BEST review: Lessons being learned from traditional programs and new innovations – Next steps and issues for scaling up (Research report 12-1). Retrieved from http://www.sbctc.edu/resources/documents/colleges-staff/research-data/pre-college-research/resh_rpt_12_1_ibest_review.pdf

51. Bragg, D. D., Baker, E. D., & Puryear, M. (2010). 2010 follow-up of the Community College of Denver Fast Start program. Retrieved from http://files.eric.ed.gov/fulltext/ED521421.pdf

52. Collaborative for Academic, Social, and Emotional Learning (nd), What is Social, Emotional Learning? Retrieved from https://casel.squarespace.com/social-and-emotional-learning/

53. Collaborative for Academic, Social, and Emotional Learning. (2015). 2015 CASEL Guide: Effective social and emotional learning programs—middle and high school edition. Retrieved fromhttp://www.casel.org/middle-and-high-school-edition-casel-guide/

54. Durlak, J.A., Weissberg, R.P., Dymnicki, A.B., Taylor, R.D. & Schellinger, K.B. (2011). The Impact Of Enhancing Students' Social And Emotion Learning: A Meta-Analysis of School-Based Universal Interventions. Child Development, 82(1): 405-432. Retrieved from CASEL website. http://www.casel.org/

55. The P-Tech profile was created from several sources:

    1) Foroohar, R. (2012, April 9). These schools mean business. Time. Retrieved from http://business.time.com/2012/03/29/schools-that-mean-business/

    2) Cavanaugh, S. (2014, April 24). Industry shapes goals and tech focus at N.Y.C. school. Education Week. 32(29), S4–S6. Retrieved from http://www.edweek.org/ew/articles/2013/04/24/29ii-publicprivatepartnerships.h32.html?tkn=XLLFxXjbw%2BP%2BRQBmwEbN5coBFI1F6A4zXVyM&print=1

    3) Aspen Institute. (n.d.). Economic opportunities program: IBM P-TECH. Retrieved February 26, 2016, from http://www.aspeninstitute.org/policy-work/economic-opportunities/skills-americas-future/models-success/ibm

56. See informational website at http://www.ptech.org/

57. Aspen Institute. (n.d.). Economic opportunities program: IBM P-TECH. Retrieved February 26, 2016 from http://www.aspeninstitute.org/policy-work/economic-opportunities/skills-americas-future/models-success/ibm

Chapter Four

1. Gardner, David P., et al (1983), A Nation At Risk: The Imperative For Educational Reform. An Open Letter to the American People. A Report to the Nation and the Secretary of Education. April 1983. U.S. Department of Education, Washington, DC. Retrieved from http://eric.ed.gov/?id=ED226006

2. Green, K., and Hinkley, R. (2012), The Career Pathways Effect, Linking Education and Economic Prosperity, 2012, CORD Communications, Waco, Texas

3. Lumina Foundation (2016), A Stronger Nation. Postsecondary learning builds the talent that helps us rise, 2016, Lumina Foundation, Indianapolis, Indiana. Retrieved from https://www.luminafoundation.org/files/publications/stronger_nation/2016/A_Stronger_Nation-2016-National.pdf

4. Bailey, T, Jaggars, S.S., & Jenkins, D (2015). What we know about guided pathways. New York, NY: Columbia University, Teachers College, Community College Research Center. Retrieved from http://ccrc.tc.columbia.edu/media/k2/attachments/What-We-Know-Guided-Pathways.pdf

5. Kania, J. and Kramer, M. (2011), Collective Impact, Winter 2011, Stanford Social Innovation Review. Retrieved from http://ssir.org/articles/entry/collective_impact

6. Meeder, H. (2016), College and Career Pathways System Design Specifications, September 2016, National Center for College and Career Transitions, Columbia, MD. Retrieved from http://nc3t.com/white-paper/

7. Ibid

8. Ibid

9. U.S. Department of Education (2013) National Assessment of Career and Technical Education: Interim Report, 2013, U.S. Department of Education, Office of Planning, Evaluation and Policy Development, Policy and Program Studies Service, Washington, D.C., 2013.

10. Davidson, C. (2011), Now You See It: How The Brain Science Of Attention Will Transform The Way We Live, Work, And Learn, Viking, New York

11. Heffernan, V., (2011), Education Needs a Digital-Age Upgrade, New York Times Opinion Page. Retrieved from http://opinionator.blogs.nytimes.com/2011/08/07/education-needs-a-digital-age-upgrade/?_r=1

12. U.S. Department of Labor (1999), Futurework - Trends and Challenges for Work in the 21st Century. Washington, DC. Retrieved from https://www.dol.gov/oasam/programs/history/herman/reports/futurework/report.htm

13. CST Inspired Minds, Careers 2030. Retrieved at http://careers2030.cst.org/jobs/. Also, see. Dvorsky, G., (2014), These are the Surprising Jobs You'll be Doing by the 2030s., Retrieved from http://io9.gizmodo.com/these-are-the-surprising-jobs-youll-be-doing-by-the-203-1577363367?utm_campaign=socialflow_io9_facebook&utm_source=io9_facebook&utm_medium=socialflow

14. Volusia County Schools. (2014). Volusia County Schools: At a glance. Retrieved from http://myvolusiaschools.org/Community-Information-Services/Documents/At%20A%20Glance14-15.pdf

15. For more information visit the Career Connection website at www.career-connection.org.

16. Volusia County Schools High School Showcase: Navigate your Future, 2016-2017 retrieved at http://www.career-connection.org/pdf/Academy/booklet_16-17.pdf

17. Volusia County Schools. (2014). Volusia County Schools: At a glance. Retrieved from http://myvolusiaschools.org/Community-Information-Services/Documents/At%20A%20Glance14-15.pdf

Chapter Five

1. Covey, S. R. (2004). The 7 habits of highly effective people: Restoring the character ethic. New York: Free Press.

2. American Diploma Project. (2004). Ready or not: Creating a high school diploma that counts. Retrieved from http://www.achieve.org/ReadyorNot

3. Common Core State Standards Initiative. (About the standards development process. Retrieved from http://www.corestandards.org/about-the-standards/development-process/

4. Common Core State Standards Initiative. (2010, June 2). Introduction of the Common Core State Standards. Retrieved from http://www.corestandards.org/assets/ccssi-introduction.pdf

5. Conley, D. T. (2008). What makes a student college ready? Educational Leadership. Retrieved from http://www.ascd.org/publications/educational-leadership/oct08/vol66/num02/What-Makes-a-Student-College-Ready%C2%A2.aspx

6. Ibid

7. Ibid

8. Ibid

9. Ibid

10. Duncan, A. (2011, February 2). The new CTE: Secretary Duncan's remarks on career and technical education. Retrieved from http://www.ed.gov/news/speeches/new-cte-secretary-duncans-remarks-career-and-technical-education

11. The Secretary's Commission On Achieving Necessary Skills (1991), What Work Requires of Schools: A SCANS Report for America 2000, June 1991, U.S. Department of Labor. Retrieved from https://wdr.doleta.gov/SCANS/whatwork/whatwork.pdf

12. To learn more about the Partnership for 21st Century Learning, see http://www.p21.org/about-us/p21-framework

13. A set of national Personal Finance Education standards has been created and maintained by the Jump$tart Coalition* for Personal Financial Literacy. This set of standards explains the personal finance knowledge and skills that K-12 students should possess. Jump$tart Coalition* for Personal Financial Literacy. (2015). National standards in K–12 personal finance education (4th ed.). Retrieved from http://www.jumpstart.org/national-standards.html

14. The first three components in this framework – Applied Knowledge, Effective Relationships, Executive and Communications Skills – are adapted closely from the Employability Skills Framework (the Framework) developed as part of an initiative of the Office of Career, Technical and Adult Education (OCTAE) at the U.S. Department of Education. Retrieved from http://cte.ed.gov/employabilityskills/

15. Adapted from Conley, D. (2008). What makes a student college ready? Educational Leadership. Retrieved from http://www.ascd.org/publications/educational-leadership/oct08/vol66/num02/What-Makes-a-Student-College-Ready%C2%A2.aspx

16. Jump$tart Coalition* for Personal Financial Literacy. (2015). National standards in K–12 personal finance education (4th ed.). Retrieved from http://www.jumpstart.org/national-standards.html - See previous note on edition.

17. Greater Clark County Schools. (n.d.), Jeffersonville, Indiana. Retrieved from http://gcs.k12.in.us/work-ethic-certification/

18. To learn more about the AVID program, see http://www.avid.org

Chapter Six

1. Dayton, C. (2010). Planning guide for *career academies*. *Retrieved from* http://casn.berkeley.edu/resource_files/Planning_Guide_for_C.A.pdf

2. See Advance CTE website. http://www.careertech.org

3. National High School Center. (2012, November 15). Local spotlight: Mountain Home High School Career Academies [Blog post]. Retrieved from http://www.ccrscenter.org/products-resources/blog/local-spotlight-mountain-home-high-school-career-academies

4. Arkansas Department of Career Education. (n.d.). Bridging the gap: A community mentoring program for high school homeroom advisory groups. Retrieved February 26, 2016, from https://www.acteonline.org/uploadedFiles/Assets_and_Documents/Global/files/ Policy/Mentoring_Program_Bridging_the_Gap.pdf

5. National Career Academy Coalition. (n.d.). NCAC model academies from 2010 to present. Retrieved from http://www.ncacinc.com/nsop/model-academies

Chapter Seven

1. Note: Definitive research on the percent of college students who change their majors is difficult to locate. According to a research referenced in a study on the impact of time to degree for students changing their majors, 46% of all first-time, full-time students entering four-year institutions in 2003 switched majors at least once by 2009. Furthermore, this figure varied between 10% and 75% at the institutions included in that California study. See: Sklar, Jeffrey (2014), The Impact of Change of Major on Time to Bachelor's Degree Completion with Special Emphasis on STEM Disciplines: A Multilevel Discrete-Time Hazard Modeling Approach, Final Report, September 12, 2014, Statistics Department California Polytechnic State University. Retrieved from https://www.airweb.org/GrantsAndScholarships/ Documents/Grants2013/SklarFinalReport.pdf

2. NACAC-Hobsons (2015), Individual Learning Plans for College and Career Readiness: State Policies and School-Based Practices A National Study (October 2015), The National Association for College Admission Counseling (NACAC), Arlington, VA. Retrieved from http://www.nacacnet.org/research/research-data/nacac-research/Documents/ NACACILPReport.pdf

3. To learn more about the ASAP initiative, see: Scrivener, S, & Weiss, M. J. (2013). More graduates: Two-year results from an evaluation of accelerated study in associate programs (ASAP) for developmental education students. Retrieved from http://www.mdrc.org/sites/ default/files/More_Graduates.pdf

4. Srikameswaran, Anita (2014), 5 ways parents can help teens excel in school, November 20th, 2014, Futuricity. Retrieved from http://www.futurity.org/parents-teens-school-806392/

5. Hurley, D., & Thorp, M. (2002). *Decisions without direction: Career guidance and decisions making among American youth.* Big Rapids, MI: Ferris State University.

6. See Buck Institute for Education. http://www.bie.org/about

7. Medina, John (2008), Brain Rules: 12 Principles for Surviving and Thriving at Work, Home, and School, 2008, Pear Press, Seattle, Washington

8. Vacca, R.T., (2002), From Efficient Decoders to Strategic Readers, Reading and Writing in the Content Areas, November 2002, Educational Leadership, Volume 60, Number 3, ASCD, Arlington, VA. Retrieved from http://www.ascd.org/publications/educational-leadership/ nov02/vol60/num03/From-Efficient-Decoders-to-Strategic-Readers.aspx

9. Medina, John (2008), Brain Rules: 12 Principles for Surviving and Thriving at Work, Home, and School, 2008, Pear Press, Seattle, Washington

10. Kania, J. & Kramer, M. (2011) Collective Impact, Stanford Social Innovation Review, Winter 2011. Retrieved at: http://ssir.org/articles/entry/collective_impact

11. To learn more about these organizations, see: Alignment Nashville/Alignment USA, http:// www.alignmentusa.org/ and StriveTogether, http://strivetogether.org/

12. Kotter, J. (2007). Leading change: Why transformation efforts fail, *Harvard Business Review.* 85(1), 96–103 and Kotter, J. P., (1996), Leading Change, Harvard Business School Press, Boston, Massachusetts

13. Note: According to NCES, "institutions reported that approximately 1,277,100 high school

students took courses for college credit within a dual enrollment program and approximately 136,400 high school students took courses for college credit outside a dual enrollment program during the 12-month 2010–11 academic year." See: IES/NCES (2013), Dual Enrollment Programs and Courses for High School Students at Postsecondary Institutions: 2010–11, February 2013, U.S. Department of Education. Retrieved from http://ncov/ pubs2013/2013002.pdf

14. A Student Advisory Program is an approach where small groups of students meet on a regular basis with a teacher or other adult staff member to discuss topics such as career development, goal setting, social-emotional learning, study skills, and other topics the school deems important. The adult "advisor" role is focused on building a relational rapport with students, apart from the need to teach and assess specific content.

15. Adapted from Profile of Employer Engagement, Food and Finance High School, prepared by NC3T for the CTE Technical Assistance Center of New York, a Division of the Successful Practices Network. The original profile can be retrieved from http://www.nyctecenter.org/ spn/userMedia/36/26936/files/CASE_STUDY_FOOD__FINANCE_HS.pdf

16. http://www.careerstreeterie.org/about/what-is-career-street

17. http://www.erietogether.org/about-our-initiative

18. Career Street (nd), Resource Documents., Erie, PA. Retrieved at http://www.careerstreeterie. org/resources/resource-documents

19. Erie.together.org. As of August 4, 2016.

Chapter Eight

1. NACAC-Hobsons (2015), Individual Learning Plans for College and Career Readiness: State Policies and School-Based Practices A National Study (October 2015), The National Association for College Admission Counseling (NACAC), Arlington, VA. Retrieved from http://www.nacacnet.org/research/research-data/nacac-research/Documents/ NACACILPReport.pdf

2. "Creative destruction" is a term popularized by economist Joseph Schumpeter. To learn more about this theory, see The Concise Encyclopedia of Economics article at http://www. econlib.org/library/Enc/CreativeDestruction.html

3. Friedman, T. L. (2005). The world is flat: A brief history of the twenty-first century. New York: Farrar, Straus and Giroux.

4. Pink, D. (2001). Free agent nation: The future of working for yourself. New York, NY: Warner Books.

5. Heath, C. and Heath, D. (2010), Switch, How to change things when change is hard," page 51, Broadway Books, New York

6. Sklar, Jeffrey (2014), The Impact of Change of Major on Time to Bachelor's Degree Completion with Special Emphasis on STEM Disciplines: A Multilevel Discrete-Time Hazard Modeling Approach, Final Report, September 12, 2014, Statistics Department California Polytechnic State University. Retrieved from https://www.airweb.org/ GrantsAndScholarships/Documents/Grants2013/SklarFinalReport.pdf

7. McKinsey & Company in collaboration with Chegg, Inc, (2013), Voice of the Graduate, McKinsey. Retrieved at: http://mckinseyonsociety.com/downloads/reports/Education/ UXC001%20Voice%20of%20the%20Graduate%20v7.pdf

8. Rath, Tom & Harter, Jim (2010) Well Being, The Five Essential Elements, Gallup Press, New York, NY

9. Ibid

10. Ibid

11. Holland, John L., (1973, 1985), Making Vocational Choices, A Theory of Vocational Personalities & Work Environments, 2nd Edition, Prentice-Hall Inc., Englewood Cliffs, New Jersey.

12. See O-NET Online. Under each occupational description, the "interest" section indicates the three-letter Holland Code. http://www.onetonline.org/find/

13. Holland, John L., (1973, 1985), Making Vocational Choices, A Theory of Vocational Personalities & Work Environments, 2nd Edition, Prentice-Hall Inc., Englewood Cliffs, New Jersey.

14. See the O-Net Resource Center and the O-Net Interest Profiler™, which is adapted from the Holland Code Structure. Retrieved from http://www.onetcenter.org/IP.html

15. University of Missouri, MU Career Center, (2010), Guide to Holland Code, University of Missouri, Columbia, Missouri. Retrieved from http://www.wiu.edu/advising/docs/Holland_Code.pdf

16. McClain, Mary-Catherine, Reardon, Robert C., (2015), "The U.S. Workforce from 1960 to 2010: a RIASEC View, The Professional Counselor, Volume 5, Issue 1, Pages 1-14, NBCC, Inc. and Affiliates, Retrieved from http://tpcjournal.nbcc.org/wp-content/uploads/2015/02/Pages-1-14%20-%20McClain.pdf

17. Ibid

18. Ibid

19. Ibid

20. Ibid

21. Ibid

22. Ibid

23. This section is adapted from two sources:

    1) Making Career Clusters Work: A Guide for South Carolina District Administration, Principals, and Teachers, and Career Development Education, Activities Guide, Retrieved from https://ed.sc.gov/scdoe/assets/File/agency/ccr/Career-and-Technology-Education/documents/EducGuide.pdf,

    2) Glossary, Massachusetts Department of Education, Retrieved from http://www.doe.mass.edu/connect/cde/guideglossary.pdf

24. This framework is adapted from –

    1) Georgia Department of Education (2012), Elementary Career Cluster Activities Guidance Elementary Career Awareness Grades 1-5, December 2012, Georgia Department of Education, Atlanta, GA. Retrieved from https://www.gadoe.org/Curriculum-Instruction-and-Assessment/CTAE/Documents/Elementary-Career-Guidance-document.pdf

    2) Pennsylvania Department of Education (nd), Career Education and Work Standards Toolkit, Pennsylvania Department of Education, Harrisburg, PA Retrieved from http://www.pacareerstandards.com/

25. NCES (2015), Fast Facts, Back to School Statistics. U.S. Department of Education. Retrieved from http://nces.ed.gov/fastfacts/display.asp?id=372

26. Source: The American Counseling Association, Alexandria, VA. Retrieved from http://www.counseling.org/PublicPolicy/ACA_Ratio_Chart_2011_Overall.pdf

27. Miller, G. (2013). How to treat depression when psychiatrists are scarce. WIRED Magazine. December 3, 2013. Retrieved from http://www.wired.com/2013/12/patelqa/

28. National Career Development Association (n.d.), NCDA Career Development Facilitator Training, NCDA, Retrieved from http://www.ncda.org/aws/NCDA/pt/sp/facilitator_overview

29. Kuder, Inc. (n.d.), Kuder Career Advisor Training. Retrieved from http://www.kuder.com/ product/professional-services/kuder-career-advisor-training/

30. Souderton Area School District, located in suburban Montgomery County, Pennsylvania 25 miles north of Philadelphia, includes one high school with an approximate enrollment of 2,200 and a graduating class of 500.

31. Sam Varano, High School Principal, Community Press Conference held at Souderton Area High School on January 14, 2015

32. This percentage does not include profoundly disabled students or students attending the half-day career and technical center.

33. Adapted from Colorado Innovation Profile, Meeder Consulting Group, 2008. Prepared for Colorado Community College System. Learn more about the program at Contextual Learning Concepts. Retrieved from http://www.contextuallc.com/

Chapter Nine

1. Goleman, D. (1998), What Makes a Leader?, 1998, Harvard Business Review.

2. Collins, J. C. (2001). Good to great: Why some companies make the leap ... and others don't. New York, NY: HarperBusiness.

3. Ibid

4. Ibid, Page 21

5. Kotter, J. P., (1996), Leading Change, Harvard Business School Press, Boston, Massachusetts and Kotter, J. (2007). Leading change: Why transformation efforts fail, Harvard Business Review. 85(1), 96–103 and

6. Ibid

Chapter Ten

1. Author interview with Dr. Jay Steele, August 11, 2015

2. Author interview with Steve Casa, August 10, 2015

3. Stewart, L. (n.d.), Do you know the difference between Brand and Branding?. Retrieved from http://indiecreatives.com/2010/11/02/do-you-know-the-difference-between-brand-vs-branding/

Chapter Eleven

1. 2013 report: https://www.acteonline.org/uploadedfiles/assets_and_documents/global/files/ cte_info/acte-nasdctec_state_policy_review_2013.pdf 2014 report: https://www.acteonline. org/uploadedfiles/assets_and_documents/global/files/cte_info/acte-nasdctec_state_policy_ review_2014.pdf 2015 report: https://www.acteonline.org/uploadedFiles/Who_We_Are/ Press/2015_State-Policy-Review_FINAL%20(1).pdf

2. NASDCTE/ACTE (2016) State Policies Impacting CTE, 2015 Year in Review. National Association of State Directors of Career Technical Education Consortium, Association for Career and Technical Education.

3. NASDCTE/ACTE (2013), State Policies Impacting CTE, 2013 Year in Review. National Association of State Directors of Career Technical Education Consortium, Association for Career and Technical Education. NASDCTE/ACTE (2014), State Policies Impacting CTE, 2014 Year in Review. National Association of State Directors of Career Technical Education Consortium, Association for Career and Technical Education.

4. NASDCTE/ACTE (2016), State Policies Impacting CTE, 2015 Year in Review. National Association of State Directors of Career Technical Education, Association for Career and Technical Education.

5. NASDCTE/ACTE (2013), State Policies Impacting CTE, 2013 Year in Review. National Association of State Directors of Career Technical Education Consortium, Association for Career and Technical Education.

6. NASDCTE/ACTE (2015), State Policies Impacting CTE, 2015 Year in Review. National Association of State Directors of Career Technical Education Consortium, Association for Career and Technical Education.

7. NASDCTE/ACTE (2014), State Policies Impacting CTE, 2014 Year in Review. National Association of State Directors of Career Technical Education Consortium, Association for Career and Technical Education.

8. NASDCTE/ACTE (2013), State Policies Impacting CTE, 2013 Year in Review. National Association of State Directors of Career Technical Education Consortium, Association for Career and Technical Education.

9. Ibid

10. Ibid

11. NASDCTE/ACTE (2014), State Policies Impacting CTE, 2014 Year in Review. National Association of State Directors of Career Technical Education Consortium, Association for Career and Technical Education.

12. Ibid

13. NASDCTE/ACTE (2015), State Policies Impacting CTE, 2015 Year in Review. National Association of State Directors of Career Technical Education Consortium, Association for Career and Technical Education.

14. Ibid

15. NASDCTE/ACTE (2013), State Policies Impacting CTE, 2013 Year in Review. National Association of State Directors of Career Technical Education Consortium, Association for Career and Technical Education.

16. NASDCTE/ACTE (2015), State Policies Impacting CTE, 2015 Year in Review. National Association of State Directors of Career Technical Education, Association for Career and Technical Education.

17. Ibid

18. Ibid

19. Ibid

20. For more information on IN-PIN, visit http://nc3t.com/indiana-pin/

21. NASDCTE/ACTE (2015), State Policies Impacting CTE, 2015 Year in Review. National Association of State Directors of Career Technical Education Consortium, Association for Career and Technical Education.

22. NASDCTE/ACTE (2015), State Policies Impacting CTE, 2015 Year in Review. National Association of State Directors of Career Technical Education Consortium, Association for Career and Technical Education.

23. For more information on PA-PIN, visit http://nc3t.com/pennsylvania-pin/

24. NASDCTE/ACTE (2013), State Policies Impacting CTE, 2013 Year in Review. National Association of State Directors of Career Technical Education Consortium, Association for Career and Technical Education.

25. NASDCTE/ACTE (2015), State Policies Impacting CTE, 2015 Year in Review. National Association of State Directors of Career Technical Education Consortium, Association for

Career and Technical Education.

26. NASDCTE/ACTE (2015), State Policies Impacting CTE, 2015 Year in Review. National Association of State Directors of Career Technical Education, Association for Career and Technical Education.

Chapter Twelve

1. Gladwell, M. (2000, 2002), The Tipping Point: How Little Things Can Make a Big Difference. Boston: Little, Brown, 2000.

2. Ibid

3. Granovetter, M. (1995), Getting a Job. A Study of Contacts and Careers. Second Edition. University of Chicago Press, Chicago, IL 60637.

4. Gladwell, M. (2000, 2002), The Tipping Point: How Little Things Can Make a Big Difference. Boston: Little, Brown, 2000.

5. Ibid

6. Rogers, E. (2003), Diffusion of Innovation, Fifth Edition (2003), Free Press/Simon and Shuster,

7. Ibid (pp. 169, 199)

8. Ibid (p. 282)

9. Ibid (p. 283)

10. Ibid, (p. 215)

11. Keller, E, and Berry, J. (2003), The Influentials, 2003, Free Press, New York, NY

12. Corbett, S., Fikker, B., (2009, 2012), When Helping Hurts; How to alleviate poverty without hurting the poor and yourself. (2012, p 147). Moody Publishers, Chicago, IL

13. U.S. and World Population Clock. http://www.census.gov/popclock/

14. NCES (2015), Fast Facts, Back to School Statistics. U.S. Department of Education. Retrieved from http://nces.ed.gov/fastfacts/display.asp?id=372

15. SBA (2012), Frequently Asked Questions, Small Business Administration, Office of Advocacy, September 2012. Retrieved from www.sba.gov/advocacy

16. Association of Chamber of Commerce Executives. What is a Chamber? Retrieved from http://www.acce.org/whatisachamber/

17. National School Boards Association. http://www.nsba.org/about-us

18. NCES (2015), Digest of Education Statistics, Table 216.10 Public elementary and secondary schools, by level of school: Selected years, 1967-68 through 2013-14. U.S. Department of Education.

19. Association for Career and Technical Education (n.d.), Frequently Asked Questions, ACTE, Alexandria, VA. Retrieved from https://www.acteonline.org/general.aspx?id=2733#many_cte

20. American Association of Community Colleges (2016), Fast Facts. AACC, Washington, DC. Retrieved from http://www.aacc.nche.edu/AboutCC/Documents/AACCFactSheetsR2.pdf

21. National Center for Education Statistics (December 2013). "Table 5 Number of educational institutions, by level and control of institution: Selected years, 1980-81 through 2011-12". U.S. Department of Education. Retrieved from http://nces.ed.gov/pubs2014/2014015_1.pdf

22. Because of their high cost, aggressive marketing techniques, and sometimes very poor results for students, I would recommend caution about including most for-profit postsecondary providers in a local pathways initiative. Certainly, the decision would need to be carefully considered on a case-by-case basis.

23. U.S. Census Bureau. (2007). Government Division, Government Organization, Table 7: Subcounty General-Purpose Governments by Population-Size Group and State. Census of Government

24. National Association of Workforce Boards. http://www.nawb.org/about_us.asp

25. Education Writers Association. http://www.ewa.org/who-we-are

26. Clifton, J., (2011), The Coming Jobs War, Gallup Press, New York, NY

Appendix

1. More information about the Perkins Career Technical Education Act of 2006 can be found at: http://www2.ed.gov/policy/sectech/leg/perkins/index.html

2. To read the text of the WIAO, visit: https://www.congress.gov/113/bills/hr803/BILLS-113hr803enr.pdf. To read an overview of the WIAO from the U.S. Department of Labor, visit: https://www.doleta.gov/wioa/Overview.cfm

3. For more information about Rigorous Programs of Study, see U.S. Department of Education, Office of Career Technical and Adult Education website at http://cte.ed.gov/initiatives/octaes-programs-of-study-design-framework